American Drama
in the Age of Film

AMERICAN DRAMA IN THE AGE OF FILM

ZANDER BRIETZKE

THE UNIVERSITY OF ALABAMA PRESS

Tuscaloosa

Typeface: Granjon

∞

The paper on which this book is printed meets the minimum requirements of
American National Standard for Information Sciences-Permanence of Paper for Printed
Library Materials, ANSI Z39.48–1984.

Library of Congress Cataloging-in-Publication Data

Brietzke, Zander, 1960–
American drama in the age of film / Zander Brietzke.
p.   cm.
Includes bibliographical references (p.) and index.
ISBN-13: 978-0-8173-1571-9 (cloth : alk. paper)
ISBN-10: 0-8173-1571-3 (alk. paper)
1. American drama—20th century—History and criticism. 2. Theater—United
States—History—20th century. 3. American drama—20th century—Film and video
adaptations. 4. Motion pictures and literature—United States. 5. Theater and society—
United States. I. Title.
PS350.B75 2007
792.0973—dc22

2006102656

for Jamie and John,
original lamebrains

When a frog starves in the presence of dead, immobile flies, which would make perfectly good food, he reminds us of the blindness of a man whose mind is "made up" and therefore incapable of responding to unforeseen opportunities. Those are the wages of economy.

—Rudolf Arnheim, *Visual Thinking*

Contents

Acknowledgments   ix

Introduction: Beyond the Box   xi

1. Revaluations of Virtues   1

2. Dramatic Projections   18

3. A Vicious Cycle at Sea   35

4. There's Something about Mary   51

5. Bedroom Ballet in the Delta   64

6. Jungled Dreams   78

7. Getting the Guests   91

8. Lamebrains across Texas   103

9. Cadillacs Are for Closers   117

10. Making Oneself Big   132

11. Cancer and the Classroom   144

12. Stairway to Heaven   156

Conclusion: Revivals Versus Remakes   170

Notes   173

Works Cited   181

Index   191

Acknowledgments

The solitude of writing fosters an illusion that you're on your own with whatever little or big ideas. You know that's not exactly true, but it feels true as you slog through drafts, endlessly rewrite, refine, attempt to cut all the precious darlings that once seemed fresh and so very interesting, search for a publisher, secure a contract, then repeat the cycle. Only now, with the end truly in sight, with the opportunity to step back and appreciate the entire process, does a more accurate picture come into focus.

It is a real pleasure, at last, to thank publicly the people who supported and encouraged me to write the kind of book I wanted to write. First of all, my immediate family gave me needed time to work. That includes, of course, much time spent beyond the keyboard: attending conferences, doing legwork at the libraries, engaging in conversations and speculations, and enjoying hours of deep thoughts twirling pencils and pens. In short, Jack, Sasha, and especially Carol indulged me more than even the great Hjalmar Ekdal! Indeed, my beautiful wife has observed, not entirely falsely, that my eyes are rarely fully open.

I wrote the bulk of this book while I was vice president and then president of the Eugene O'Neill Society. The ongoing support and fellowship of that organization, peopled by many fine scholars among its ranks, have been extremely helpful. Two international conferences, in Tours, France, and Provincetown, Massachusetts, proved to be particularly stimulating and collegial gatherings.

As editor of the annual *Eugene O'Neill Review* at Suffolk University in Boston, I have worked closely with writers during the past three years to prepare their essays and articles for publication. I am grateful for their abilities to put up with my protests and intrusions and, frankly, my mistakes, as I've learned how to do this difficult yet quite rewarding job. They have made me a better writer and taught me a lot about how to accept criticism.

All the readers of this manuscript, known and anonymous, have contributed to the shape of the final product. I'm grateful to them for inspiring further rounds of judicious and radical cutting and editing. I thank Jackson R. Bryer for his insistence on clarity and keeping the big picture in mind. Brenda Murphy responded to the manuscript on its own terms, no small gift there, and deftly guided me toward my true intentions. A special debt of gratitude and friendship is due Martin Puchner, whose comments, insightful and actionable and supportive, promoted the breezy direction of the book. Readers might be relieved to find out that while my original version numbered more than 150,000 words, a solid third of that initial excess has been excised. The benefits of weight loss apply to heavy manuscripts as well as people.

The staff at The University of Alabama Press proved that I can go back home again. My work could not have been in more capable hands. The sensitivity and skill of my copy editor, Lady Vowell Smith, saved me much embarrassment and left me with no one to blame for any fault that remains. Alice Rayner helped me to select a cover photo (although she doesn't know it!). More directly, I thank the folks at the Southern Theater in Minneapolis, Artistic Director Jeff Bartlett, Marketing and Communications Director Kate Nordstrum, and Production Manager Jennifer Kult for promoting their space on the Web and putting me in contact with photographer Stephen Kmetz, who very graciously permitted me to publish his work.

Finally, while it seems as if I've been writing this book forever (my family concurs), I realize that I actually *have* been thinking about it for more than twenty years. The genesis goes back to grad school (the first time) at Alabama, long evenings and early mornings on the front porch, deep thoughts (accompanied by a twirling pen and a frequent nap), and good friends. I directed John Erlanger and Jamie Lawrence in a production of *True West* that helped to formulate in practice, then, much of what I've finally committed to words, here. It's taken a long time to distill. But, as I told them often enough on a late night, I like scotch. Cheers.

Introduction
Beyond the Box

Unlike the stage actor, the film actor cannot get over the footlights.

——Leo Braudy, "Acting: Stage vs. Screen"

Actor Franchot Tone left New York for Hollywood in the 1930s. Among all the stories of similar passage in *The Fervent Years,* Harold Clurman's chronicle of the Group Theatre, this one reads as the most biblical tale of temptation in paradise. The theater offered meaningful work, artistic growth and experimentation, communal living, and a hand-to-mouth existence. Movies, by contrast, promised much better pay, swimming pools, and an easy lifestyle. During the Group's tenure (1931–41), many of its best actors, Tone among the first, left for the West Coast in pursuit of a decent living. In theater's "Golden Age," Hollywood beckoned such trained stage talents to star in the new motion picture industry of "talkies." Success in New York actually helped to launch a career in film.

Today that migratory pattern has reversed directions. Success in the movies now downloads a ticket for the Broadway stage, but this shift is only symptomatic of a more important phenomenon. Until recently, plays were always considered as source material for movies. Even as late as the late 1960s, Susan Sontag claimed that plays could not be made from movies. Today, especially with musicals, that is simply not true. Theater now often serves merely as the brand extension of the larger and more lucrative film cartels. Even if a play is the source material for a subsequent film or television adaptation, the viewer is likely to accept the adaptation as the original and the stage play as the derived copy. Modern "smart" classrooms, a term invoked with no discernible irony, come loaded with television monitors and DVD and VCR players. It's never been easier to present visual aids, and access to classic and contemporary plays has never been more immediately attainable. Unfortunately, students often now watch a film adaptation of a play as though it were the same as a theatrical production. Why bother to see stage drama, they reason logically, if the same thing is available to see in a much more accessible format?

This book tries to answer that question by showing through numerous examples that plays and films do different things and create different experiences and that those differences that the stage offers are worth seeing. If the theater is to continue to survive as a viable art form, it must do so on formal grounds and intrinsic qualities apart from any related cultural/social status. While it could be argued, I suppose, that theater still curries favor based upon exclusivity relative to mass entertainments such as film, that sad note is not something about which to brag. The fact that you often can't see a play because it's too expensive, too far away, too much in demand, too hard to hear, and maybe even too hard to understand is a problem, an admittedly annoying one, but unfortunately one that goes beyond the pale of my abilities and expertise to solve. I have restricted this study to a formal analysis of stage drama by comparing dramatic texts to their film and television adaptations. If I can demonstrate a play's unique values, then perhaps I can redeem the physical and financial efforts required to witness it in performance.

What follows, however, attempts not to aggrandize theater at the expense of film, a dubious proposition anyway, but to cite film as a tool for better seeing stage drama. Comparisons to be made are not so much side by side as they are layered, one on top of the other. Film provides the screen, the background of common experience, against which the drama plays and through which it can be interpreted and understood. Film language is now the vocabulary for modern experience: rapid cutting from one thing and place to another, quick and numerous alterations of perspective, shifts in time, and technological and mechanical reliance rooted in photography. The theater, which offers none of that, sticks viewers in one spot before the homogenous space of the stage. Owing to such relatively impoverished conditions, theater has often been considered as a predominantly literary experience, as opposed to the primarily visual experience of film, but one of the things I try to do in the following chapters is to blur that distinction and make a case for a spectacular theater. Cinema has historically taken a lot from the theater. Theater can take back as well and adapt cinematic techniques for theatrical purposes. I'll attempt to highlight the tensions of equivalence and difference between the two forms through specific examples in order to see what drama does and can do.

The opening chapter, "Revaluations of Virtues," dismisses the significance of theater as a live event, a long-cherished belief, and defines spectacle as the most important element. Chapter 2, "Dramatic Projections," invokes a wide range of examples anecdotally to talk about the different ways that plays, players, and playwrights, combined with directors, fill theatrical space in comparison to the mechanical arts of film and television. After that, the ten plays that I discuss at length range from the beginnings of the American theater and the one-act sea plays of Eugene O'Neill to Tony Kushner's *Angels in America* at the end of the last century. In between, I've included a representative list of that span with plays by Lillian Hellman, Tennessee Williams, Arthur Miller, Edward Albee, Sam Shepard, David Mamet, August Wilson, and Margaret Edson. I've picked material that I like, definitely, but I've also chosen works both that are well known and that have television or film adaptations that are also widely available.

The advantage of a film version of a play is that it can be examined objectively, replayed again and again, and studied as a set of choices designed to solve the problem, "How to transform this play into a film?" Stage directors do something quite similar when they produce a play and ask, "How to transform a dramatic text into a theatrical event?" In the theater the answers to that question become manifest in a performance that disappears in time and space. The materiality of film and its permanent record contrasts with the ephemeral nature of theater, and the concreteness of the former invites speculation about what might or could happen on the stage. A film adaptation offers one way to solve a problem, but it also allows the critic to consider different ways a stage production might choose to handle similar problems.

My analysis of individual works begins in chapter 3 with O'Neill's plays and John Ford's *The Long Voyage Home,* a film that updates the time period and unifies O'Neill's four disparate one-acts into a single, cohesive narrative. The playwright didn't write them at one time or even conceive them as a group. Films of *The Children's Hour* and *Cat on a Hot Tin Roof* distanced themselves from their source plays for quite different reasons due to outside forces. Produced under the censorship grip of the Hays Code, they had to downplay sex, specifically homosexuality, in order to be released. Director William Wyler turned Hellman's drama into *These Three,* a heterosexual love triangle, and Richard Brooks made Williams's play into a story about love and loss between father and son. Wyler later directed another version of *The Children's Hour* with Audrey Hepburn and Shirley MacLaine, more authentic to the original play but, revealingly, less interesting as an independent film than his earlier effort. Mike Nichols directed his first film, *Who's Afraid of Virginia Woolf?,* just as the Hays Code was losing power, and his faithful rendition of Albee's text displays cinematic solutions to dramatic problems. Similar to Nichols's efforts, both television adaptations of *Death of a Salesman* that I consider follow the dramatic text closely, but they also explore the possibilities of the television medium in the methods of presentation.

Among all the screen adaptations, I give short shrift to the two made-for-TV productions of *True West.* Both simply record the theatrical play onstage with very little original directorial intervention. I argue that Shepard's play is, despite his own protestations in his stage directions, evocatively metaphoric and therefore difficult to capture within a small screen. A true film could be made of his play, but it hasn't been made yet, and I try to explain why this is so in light of the play's overt theatricality. The televised production of *The Piano Lesson,* conversely, departs from August Wilson's play by including scenes and events that are only alluded to in the dramatic text. Deviating further from the play by David Mamet, James Foley's *Glengarry Glen Ross* alters the sequence of scenes, adds a major character, and moves the action from Chicago to New York. Interestingly, just as August Wilson wrote the expansive teleplay for *The Piano Lesson,* David Mamet authored the significant changes to the screenplay of his award-winning drama. Finally, Mike Nichols's *Wit* and *Angels in America,* both produced by HBO on cable TV, largely adhere to their dramatic antecedents but use the camera to tell the story differently. Nichols, a respected veteran of both stage and screen, develops a system of equivalences as he attempts to transpose the essence of a work from one medium to another.

It would be easy to conclude that the film and television versions succeed to the extent that they deviate from the original plays. To deviate from the dramatic text would seem to mark the independence of the film, and in such a schema the television production of *The Piano Lesson* would be superior to, say, *Death of a Salesman,* and the film of *Glengarry Glen Ross* would be better than *Who's Afraid of Virginia Woolf?*

August Wilson's teleplay added many scenes to divert focus away from the domestic interior in *The Piano Lesson.* The Hallmark production established location outside the family house and presented scenes on Highway 61 in transit to Pittsburgh, on the street showing people selling watermelons or going to the movie theater, in skyscrapers downtown, at rich people's houses, even upstairs with the ghost at Doaker's house. Volker Schlondörff's *Death of a Salesman,* on the other hand, produced soon after a triumphant Broadway production with Dustin Hoffman, Kate Reid, John Malkovich, and Stephen Lang, kept Miller's text intact and, aside from one brief expressionistic and transitional scene, didn't add any elements to open up the play.

David Mamet's screenplay also added a lot to his prize-winning play by incorporating constant rainfall, a lively jazz score, a world outside the Chinese restaurant to give a context to the life of the play—including an overhead el, a doughnut shop, other houses to "sit," phone booths, cars, multiple places to gather in both the restaurant (bathroom, bar, jukebox) and the office (desks, back room, coffee machine)—rearranged scenes that don't correspond to the order in the play, and, most important of all, one character (Blake) who catalyzes the action in the film but who does not even appear and is not even mentioned in the play. Mike Nichols did not take any such liberties with the film version of Albee's play. With the exception of a single line, all the words remain the playwright's, and the dramatic action and sequence remain the same in both the stage and cinematic versions. Nichols moved the camera and characters around a bit to get them out of the living room, but, on the whole, his film follows the play closely. When he does depart from Albee's script, he does so in search of a cinematic response to a theatrical moment on the stage.

Despite the liberal approach of Wilson and Mamet to their own plays, the film versions of *The Piano Lesson* and *Glengarry Glen Ross* are no better than the respective adaptations of *Death of a Salesman* and *Who's Afraid of Virginia Woolf?* Wilson's teleplay, in fact, is not very effective on its own terms. Other than one brief shot of Berniece cleaning a glass chandelier in a rich person's house, none of the added scenes advances Wilson's drama about the need for African Americans to claim their heritage, stand up for themselves, and break free of oppression. By contrast, Schlondörff's film, while adhering to Miller's great dramatic text, uses cinematic techniques to tell the familiar story in a uniquely cinematic way. His camera looks down or peers up at Willy at such exaggerated angles that the protagonist looks very small. Schlondörff juxtaposes the colors red and brown for heightened emotional and psychological effects. The play calls for actors to step "through" the walls of the house into scenes of the past; the film version shows openings in the interior walls through which the massive apartment complexes loom in the background. This last design choice solves in part a problem regarding the need to make the apartments present at all times. Extreme close-ups in the penultimate knockdown confrontation between Biff and Willy strengthen their violent bond in a way that is not possible to see on-stage. Faithful to the dramatic text, this *Salesman* is a much more radical film venture than *The Piano Lesson*.

Likewise, *Who's Afraid of Virginia Woolf?* doesn't lack when compared to *Glengarry Glen Ross*. Nichols's film adheres to Albee's text while Mamet takes liberties with the film treatment of his own play, yet the two movies remain remarkably similar in their search for cinematic means to tell a theatrical story. Both films cast stars into dramatic roles. Both films feature outstanding musical scores that enrich the viewing experience. Both films take the action outside of a theatrical "room" in order not so much to open up the play but to convey meanings and emotions that cannot be conveyed in any other way. The torrential rain in Mamet's film makes the job of the salesmen even more difficult, but it also makes them more sympathetic to an audience. In Nichols's film, the night walk across campus as well as Martha's later staggering around in the yard heightens a sense of despair that is possible to get across only in film. The use and number of close-up shots in both films create empathy for the characters, particularly Jack Lemmon as Levene and Richard Burton and Elizabeth Taylor as George and Martha, in ways that the distant and more objective theatrical point of view cannot reach. While both films remind the viewer of the play that came first, and it is true that almost every film adaptation bears some imprint of the play, these films interpret the drama astutely and personally and exploit cinematic and tele-visual techniques to assert themselves as films in their own right.

The best plays and films exploit their respective medium: the best theater is theatrical; the best film is cinematic. By that, I simply mean that a theatrical event is suited for the theater and should be seen upon a stage. The best films are ones that achieve distinction as projected shadows upon a blank screen. "I liked the movie, but the book was better" is the sort of statement one overhears at the lo-cal cineplex as patrons head for the exit. Of course, the opposite is also frequently voiced along with all the possible comparative permutations (good, better, best). Such evaluations are unavoidable when the source material has been available to an audience prior to adaptation into a different medium, and they imply that for a given subject matter there is an ideal form in which to express it. The reason for preferring one medium over another, however, may have to do not at all with the suitability of the particular medium for the material at hand, but rather with merely the execution and exploitation of the novelistic, cinematic, or theatrical strengths of the chosen medium. Furthermore, there is simply no way to predict reliably whether an excellent novel can turn into an equally outstanding film and drama. The proof of the pudding, as Brecht said, is in the eating.

John Steinbeck's *Of Mice and Men* (1937) and *The Grapes of Wrath* (1939) provide two cases in point. The author worked with George S. Kaufman to adapt the former into a very successful stage drama that premiered during the same year in which Steinbeck published his short novel. Lewis Milestone pro-duced and directed a very good film version in 1939 starring Burgess Meredith, Lon Chaney Jr., and Betty Field, and there have been at least two subsequent film/television productions since the Milestone film. Director John Ford won the Academy Award for Best Director for his version of *The Grapes of Wrath* in 1940. Unlike the novella *Of Mice and Men* with its limited number of charac-ters and locales, emphasis upon dialogue, and action that unravels in three days, this Depression-era epic of more than six hundred pages, which follows the Joad family on its months-long journey on the road from the Dust Bowl in Oklahoma to the fertile valleys of California, through intense heat and rising floodwaters, past thousands of itinerant faces along the way, might seem to defy stage pro-duction. But fifty years later, the Steppenwolf Theatre Company of Chicago pre-sented a powerful production of the novel, adapted by Frank Galati, with a cast of thirty-five at the Cort Theatre on Broadway.

The experiences of reading Steinbeck's novels, seeing the Ford film, and at-tending a production of Galati's stage adaptation are all quite different and all potentially rewarding. I don't wish to argue that one is better or more valid than another. I do claim that the theatrical experience can offer something that can-not be found in any other artistic form, and that conviction informs every page of this book. I further believe that an appreciation of the unique properties of one artistic form can lead to a better understanding and enjoyment of other forms. While I use film in this book to make theatrical points, I hope that it will be clear, at least by the conclusion, that I view the two forms not as competitive but as complementary.

Robert Knopf's recent comparative anthology, *Theater and Film* (2005), pointedly does not consider adaptations of individual plays into films, but takes a look at first one form and then the other in chapters detailing historical influences, formal contrasts, writing, directing, and acting. Many of the critics included in his volume are ones I cite as well, but I do not juggle comparisons nearly as evenly or fairly as that volume. Thoughts on the cinema, for me, inevitably lead to ways to incorporate such thinking onto the stage. This book is not so much about differences between the two media as it is about how to make drama more dynamic onstage, how to think of it visually in light of film, and how to stimulate possibilities for future unforeseen developments.

The chapters, then, are free ranging in order to light upon dramatic and visual problems such as seeing the stage in O'Neill's plays as an existential space of loneliness and isolation, despite the crowded environment of life aboard ship. Relegated to a pleasant drawing room, *The Children's Hour* incites the desire to see that which cannot be seen, while *Cat on a Hot Tin Roof,* set entirely in an upstairs bedroom, challenges an audience to face the dire life-and-death consequences of the central and highly visible bed onstage. *Death of a Salesman,* too, presents a static central scenic image that resonates against the action of a man who cannot walk away.

Who's Afraid of Virginia Woolf?, The Piano Lesson, and *Wit* all attempt to enlarge small scenes into compelling dramas. Bringing the audience onstage in the form of guests in Albee's play expands the domestic drama and gives it a Shakespearean quality in a play-within-a-play format. August Wilson uses singing and music in his plays in order to escape the passivity of his dramas of enslavement. *Wit* makes use of Brechtian dramaturgy to give size and shape to an otherwise intimate drama in which the effects of pernicious cancer are internal and cannot even be seen.

Chapter 8 attempts to pin down what one critic has called the "ineffable power of theatre" of Shepard's *True West.* In pursuit of that same goal, *Glengarry Glen Ross* displays the primacy of action to the exclusion of all else and relates that single-mindedness to concerns of capital and commerce. In sharp contrast, but still in pursuit of the theatrical, the sprawling, chaotic dramaturgy of *Angels in America,* more Elizabethan than contemporary, reinforces and mirrors the play's insistent protest and vehement demand for "more life."

Examples from the film counterparts of all these plays bring these dramatic problems into relief and foster theatrical solutions and possibilities. The answers that I pose underpin my interpretations and are meant as provisional and certainly not definitive. The potential solution of one problem only leads to a better question about a more important problem to be uncovered upon further review of the text. One of the joys of peeling the onion of good plays, aside from the tears, is that you never reach the core of experience, but remain constantly in the process of discovery.

Ultimately, this book is not about adaptation at all. For this reason I don't invoke James Naremore's *Film Adaptation* (2000), since the issues of turning a play into a film are not really central to my thesis. If anything, my book adds a branch to Naremore's fine collection of far-reaching essays by positing that stage productions must adapt from the film versions of plays, even when the dramatic texts come first chronologically. It is impossible to think of theater today without considering the ubiquity of film and television first. Still, I care much more about plays as such in this book than any screen adaptation.

In the chapters that follow, I'm often ambivalent but never unbiased with my viewpoint. All discussions of films are means to approach the subject of stage drama. Some chapters strike an even balance between dramatic texts and film adaptations; in other chapters, I devote much more attention to a particular play or even a group of plays by a given author. The play at hand might be O'Neill's *Bound East for Cardiff,* but my discussion drifts to *The Iceman Cometh* by the end. Similarly, I pick August Wilson's *The Piano Lesson* to discuss at length, but I invoke most of his cycle of African American experience in the twentieth century as part of that chapter. The same holds true for other playwrights who have a significant body of work, such as Miller, Hellman, and Shepard. Still, for Mamet, Kushner, and Albee, equally prodigious playwrights with the aforementioned, there's much less reference to their other works and more attention paid to the screen adaptations of individual plays.

A literary genre with an implied performance, *drama* is not an interchangeable term with *theater,* a performance event that may or may not rely upon a dramatic text. Indeed, some of the best avant-garde American theater today dispenses almost entirely, if not irreverently, with a dramatic text. While it is certainly possible to produce a theatrical event without a text, I think that the best theater profits from the imaginative combinations of words and images. Historically, playwrights from Shakespeare to Molière to Chekhov to Brecht have profited when they wrote for a specific theater group, even particular actors, and a definite place. With all the possible performance venues now available, live and electronic, I intend to show that the theatrical stage remains an important, viable, and powerful option today.

The choice of title for this book deserves final mention. I've focused upon

American plays exclusively because of the quality and diversity of the playwrights. I only wish that I could devote more space to Wallace Shawn, Susan Glaspell, Clifford Odets, Tina Howe, Maria Irene Fornes, Suzan-Lori Parks, A. R. Gurney, Romulus Linney, Adrienne Kennedy, Richard Greenberg, Richard Nelson, and many, many other fine and highly original writers. The phrase "Drama in the Age of Film" steals from both Walter Benjamin and Arnold Hauser. While their respective works from the early twentieth century looked forward, my effort looks back in search of something that I hope is not lost. The title has an intentionally nostalgic ring. If I were to embrace fully the future, perhaps I might more accurately call this book *American Drama in the Digital Age.* Film, the emerging and eventually dominant art of the twentieth century, may well soon become obsolete.

With apologies to Philip Auslander, I couldn't bear to write ad nauseam about "mediatized" culture. In addition to being a bit old-fashioned, I discuss film and television often as if they were the same thing. I am aware, dimly, of cathode rays, but the fine points of the technology do not interest me much. The borders around the rectangular screens compared to the freedom of theatrical space do arrest my imagination, and I organize my critical thoughts accordingly in terms of a big box and a little box. "Life in a box is better than no life at all," Rosencrantz gravely observes in Tom Stoppard's funny play. Theater, alternatively, can invite an audience out of the box.

American Drama
in the Age of Film

I

Revaluations of Virtues

Practically speaking, we want to resuscitate an idea of total spectacle by which the theater would recover from the cinema, the music hall, the circus, and from life itself what has always belonged to it.

—Antonin Artaud, *The Theater and Its Double*

Ask folks to say what makes theater special and they will likely start by spouting something about the differences between stage and screen. Theater is live; film is in the can! But while the earliest films of the last century often did merely record theatrical performances by adopting the same point of view as the spectator in an auditorium, modern cinema discovered techniques so compelling and unique that it liberated itself as an art form and now dominates cultural discourse. The close-up, cut, montage, fade, and many such technologies have entered our collective consciousness and stolen theater's former thunder by making moviegoing more intimate, more real, more palpably visceral than most live events. After first imitating theatrical conventions, cinema subsequently adapted, replaced, and surpassed them.[1] At the dawn of a new millennium, one often-repeated question seems obvious again: Is theater dead?

While it would be reassuring to say that this familiar trope is greatly exaggerated, I, like Twain, can't shake my Missouri attitude and show-me state of mind. To refute the rhetorical question above requires a long, hard look at theatrical form with fresh eyes. I'm sick of the same old saws (live! live! live!) waxing theatrical virtues at the expense of film. Theater has no virtue! Is not the valorization of the stage as live—as opposed to mediated—entertainment a hackneyed, if not highly questionable, proposition? Is the endless human repetition of the same old thing eight times a week necessarily better than the mechanical reproduction of a spontaneous event performed once? The live event, too, is often billed as an intimate experience, but there's no such thing as a close-up in the theater. How much intimacy can there be in a two-thousand-seat house? Theater trades on an aura of exclusivity, vainly seeing itself as an elite forum for serious issues and ideas, but how often does that privilege really translate into more exciting forms than mass-produced entertainment? The magic of theater, according to aficionados, lies in the interactive, though apparently unexplainable, relationship between performer and audience. Belief in such mysticism, however, belies deep-rooted fears about the remarkable irrelevance of drama and theater in American society today. Does the fact that few people actually attend the theater prove its value?

Seeking to revitalize perceptions of theater, I challenge its traditional virtues, using film as a foil, and champion a new critical paradigm. Rather than blindly accepting tired bromides about the theater, I choose to reappraise its characteristics in order to distinguish it truly from cinema. It's time to ask new questions that clarify theater's proper place and that void complacent attitudes about its significance. What things does theater do that film doesn't? How do plays earn their place upon the stage? Rudolf Arnheim identified the formal attributes of cinema long ago in *Film as Art* and argued that problems, such as transposing the three-dimensional world onto a flat screen, sparked imaginative and creative solutions. Acknowledging the limitations of the medium, he suggested, opened a vast territory for exploration and innovation. No similar study has been devoted to drama and the theater.

The brilliant eighteenth-century German critic and playwright Gotthold Ephraim Lessing, whose *Hamburg Dramaturgy* rebelled against French Neoclassicism, also wrote *Laocoön,* subtitled "On the Limits of Painting and Poetry." He didn't address theater directly at all in this work, but rather compared and discussed the aims and capabilities of visual and linguistic art. He illustrated their differences with respect to depictions of beauty on canvas and in verse:

> Physical beauty arises from the harmonious effect of manifold parts that can be taken in at one view. It demands also that these parts shall subsist side by side; and as things whose parts subsist side by side are the proper subject of painting, so it, and it alone, can imitate physical beauty. The poet, who can only show the elements of beauty one after another, in succession, does on that very account forbear altogether the description of physical beauty, as beauty. He recognizes that those elements, arranged in succession, cannot possibly have the effect which they have when placed side by side; that the concentrating gaze which we would direct upon them immediately after their enumeration still affords us no harmonious picture; that it passes the human imagination to represent to itself what kind of effect this mouth, and this nose, and these eyes together have if one cannot recall from Nature or art a similar composition of such features. (74)

Lessing's schema gives painting spatial dominance and poetry temporal supremacy: "succession in time is the sphere of the poet, as space is that of the painter" (64–65). In the example above, he says that painting captures beauty best by presenting it to the viewer all at once at the same time. Seeing such beauty in its totality in one image can take the viewer's breath away. Poetry, conversely, builds an image of beauty from left to right and line by line and therefore cannot be grasped at once. "Parts" that exist "side by side" refer to an image of a beautiful person whose physical features become evident in the artistic representation immediately and in their totality. Verbal description must account sequentially for each feature, and it is impossible, according to Lessing, for the reader to gather a consummate image over time. Painting, then, deals best with the *coexistence* of things, whereas poetry features the *consecutiveness* of speech.

Lessing's comparisons between the genres of poetry and painting make useful, and surprising, analogies for the differences between theater and film. The bias toward the spoken word and the voice of the playwright as the leader of the theater might cause one to suppose that theater is analogous to poetry in Lessing's example. By the same token, film is naturally assumed to be a visual medium and thus similar to painting. This is wrong. Theater is, at heart, spatial, while cinema is primarily a narrative art. Film literally depends upon the interpretation of a sequence of images that flash successively through a projector. Montage theory advocated by Eisenstein and Pudovkin maintained that the meaning of film came not from looking at a single image but in the juxtaposition of two or more images. Whether following such theory or not, all films are made up of images cut from the world and pieced together in a specific arrangement in order to evoke an aesthetic response from the viewer. Anyone who has had to sit through someone else's home movies can attest to the power and need for good editing. Editing includes more than cutting film; it is the cinematic response to the world at the basic level of the shot: what's in, what's out. Films rarely show anything in its entirety—landscapes, rooms, people. There's always the hint of something or someone not seen, just out of the frame, waiting to come into view, perhaps, in the next shot or scene. In any film, the whole world is contingent.

Anything that happens in theater, on the other hand, happens onstage in front of the audience. Entrances and exits may define the action that tells its tale in the course of two hours or so, but theater creates impact through the dynamic use of space. Just as a painting has no other scenes to show, the theater is limited to the space it inhabits. Scenes may travel to rural Russia, the fjords of Norway, suburban California, or Antarctica, but they all occur in homogenous space in front of an audience. Unlike film and television, which might change locales in an instant, theater remains rooted to one place in which everything is seen in its entirety. Whereas a standard two-shot scene in a film cuts between one person and the other, everything *coexists* in the theater. Lessing uses *coexistence* of objects and *consecutiveness* of speech to differentiate the tasks of painting and poetry; I proffer *simultaneity* and *sequence* to distinguish between theater and film. Theater doesn't have the power of editing as a tremendous narrative tool. It must rely upon the space it inhabits, but it has the capability of showing multiple things happening at one time. Things that could occur only through cutting in film can happen at the same time in theater and they can be perceived in their entirety.

Throughout the narrative of this book, I will contrast theatrical *simultaneity* with cinematic *sequence* in a plea for spectacle to fill dimensional space with visual excitement. When I go to the theater, I like to focus on things other than what the director would presumably like me to see. Tension between the directed focus of a particular scene and what I choose to focus on myself creates a stimulating experience. For example, I like to watch the actors who are not speaking and evaluate the performance by looking at them. To add a sports analogy, I like to watch the players who don't have the ball. Televised sports, except in the case of replay isolations on individual players, rarely show anyone except the player with the ball, the immediate and primary focus of attention. One of the reasons that football supplanted baseball as our national pastime is that television simply cannot capture the nuance of the summertime sport. At the ballpark, there is no more thrilling play than a hit to the outfield, runners in motion, the defense lining up for the cutoff, the throw to the plate, slide, and tag. The simultaneity of that action is hard to beat for excitement, yet it is impossible to capture on television cameras. Replays, using several different cameras and cutting between them, piece that play together, but the experience is simply not the same. American football, on the other hand, is made for television, and the rise and dominance of the NFL are tied directly to lucrative network contracts and dedicated home viewers.

The stage's capacity for simultaneous action is analogous also to that of the three-ring circus. These days, the one-ring circus has come into vogue as being more refined than the typical "Greatest Show on Earth," as though fewer rings make the performance less vulgar. It is the vulgarity, the excess of the circus, and the competition between acts in the several rings that never fail to excite me. I'm not claiming that animal acts and clown tricks are preferable to a good play, but the primal elements, though perhaps more base, do provide a thrill that the theater only routinely offers as a Platonic "third remove from reality." Theater requires an imaginative director to juggle competing actions and movements in such a way that the audience can pass informed critical judgments about the stage action. Allusions to the circus hark back to Meyerhold and his rebellion from Stanislavsky and the realistic theater. My emphasis upon physical theater, a circus environment, and the triumph of mise-en-scène does not signal a retreat from dramatic texts. Meyerhold, who played Treplev in *The Seagull* at the Moscow Art Theatre, remained a fan of Chekhov his entire life.[2] At a glance, Chekhov's rural plays in which nothing happens on the estate would seem absolutely anathema to Meyerhold's vision of theater. In fact, Chekhov's plays profit from a physical and theatrical approach. Such strategies help to lift the plays out of the maudlin, sticky goo of social realism, the sanctioned style of the Soviet Union and, oddly enough, the style familiar to most American audiences. Are there funnier moments in the theater than Vanya trailing through the living room of his house while trying to shoot the professor and exclaiming, "Missed him! Missed again! Oh, damn, damn!" (218); or Trofimov, the eternal student, marching out of the room and subsequently falling down the stairs in act 3 of *The Cherry Orchard;* or Treplev's little play "with no living characters in it" (112); or *Three Sisters'* Andrei wheeling a baby carriage whilst dreaming of a distant professorship? Meyerhold's work and his devotion to Chekhov empower us to think of the playwright in new ways and with more profound understanding. All of our received ideas about texts are thus capable of radical shifts and second thoughts.

In *Stage to Screen: Theatrical Method from Garrick to Griffith* (1949), Nicholas Vardac voices the standard view of an evolutionary development of forms in which the need for spectacle was ultimately best met by the visual medium of film. Vardac discusses at length the melodramatic theater of the nineteenth century and the stage machinery and theatrical techniques that manifested the train wrecks, water rescues, explosions, gunfights, and stampedes of that era. He argues that the emphasis upon visual display on the melodramatic stage led directly to the rise and eventual triumph of film: "The film, boundless in its capacity for both spectacular and realistic pictures, naturally fell heir to the cinematic objectives which had been the principal appeal of this form upon the stage" (66). In their more recent book, *Theatre to Cinema: Stage Pictorialism and the Early Feature Film* (1997), Ben Brewster and Lea Jacobs dispute Vardac's assumptions about a seamless transition and handing off of spectacle. Film didn't merely take over the subject matter of the melodramatic stage; more importantly, it studied theatrical methods. The authors show in great detail, for example, how the cinema adapted the tableau, a staple of the melodramatic stage, for cinematic purposes.

The challenge remains for theater to reclaim cinematic techniques to advance the stage as a vibrant visual medium. Practitioners should relish living in a visual culture and not rely upon ancient notions of a dominant theater of the spoken word. As Antonin Artaud observed long ago, the theater is much more than a spoken dramatic text. In terms of a working model, the career of director Sam Mendes might serve as an example. Trained as a stage director, he has now ventured to Hollywood with the lauded films *American Beauty, Road to Perdition,* and *Jarhead.*[3] His sensibility in one medium seems to inform his work in another. A feature article profiled him in the *New York Times Magazine* in 2002 and applauded his artistic cross training by saying that he directs theater cinematically and directs film theatrically (Hirschberg 16–21). He recognizes theater as a visual medium but also sees film as requiring scenic development and not just frenetic cutting and editing. Adding cinematic discipline to the stage with the recognition of distinctive qualities that make a play worthwhile can produce creative and innovative results. The visual vocabulary expands when a director thinks of stage space as having a definite focus (foreground, midground, and background) and thinks of the eye as a camera (crosscutting from one side of the stage to another; zooming from upstage to downstage, and vice versa; panning across the stage from left to right). By making comparisons between the media, by citing similarities as well as differences, theatrical work might achieve true distinction and not be viewed as a minor stop on the way to a full career in film.

Such progressive optimism may seem entirely outmoded in these postmodern times. More than a decade ago, members of the Association for Theatre in Higher Education (ATHE) gathered to hear Richard Schechner, formerly one of the leaders of the American avant-garde and off-off-Broadway theater movement and now a highly paid professor at New York University, deliver the keynote address at the 1992 national convention in Atlanta. Speaking before an assembly of academics, mostly from theater departments, Schechner preached that their profession would soon come to an end. "The fact is," he said, "that theatre as we have known and practiced it—the staging of written dramas—will be the string quartet of the 21st century: a beloved but extremely limited genre, a subdivision of performance" (8). By describing the theater as an "extremely limited genre," he referred to constraints placed upon both producers and the audiences who too infrequently consumed such entertainment due to a lack of physical or financial resources. In short, after an occasionally illustrious 2,500-year career, theater had exhausted itself. Although Schechner specifically attacked the text/performance model with its implied hierarchy of playwright, director, actor, he did envision a new collective and collaborative performance tradition emerging to dominate in the new century, an exception that no doubt stemmed from his own background as the leader of the Performance Group in the 1960s, with celebrated productions such as *Dionysius in 69,* often still catalogued in today's theater history books.

I listened to his words in Atlanta after I had just accepted my very first full-time teaching job (albeit with no health insurance) in a traditional theater department. Eleven years of college down the drain! I was surprised to read later in the *Drama Review,* Mr. Schechner's journal which subsequently published his remarks, that his speech had been "enthusiastically received." Perhaps memory failed me. All my petty protests can't hide the fact, though, that as W. B. Worthen pointed out in 1998, Schechner's mostly right about the state and future of traditional theater, not mostly wrong. And his is not the only voice to speak of the end in sight. In the early pages of his book on contemporary drama and theater, Stephen Watt poses the question, "Is it doomed to go the way of the epithalamion or serials on the radio, possessing merely an antiquarian interest and playing no viable role in postmodern culture?" (6). You don't need a weatherman to know which way the wind blows, and you don't need Schechner, Watt, Worthen, or me to tell you that the age of theater has passed. The importance of drama today pales compared to Renaissance drama of the sixteenth and seventeenth centuries. If Shakespeare represents the zenith of dramatic accomplishment (and few could doubt it), why didn't subsequent writers copy his art? Instead, the rise of the novel in the eighteenth and nineteenth centuries eclipsed the drama and theater as a dominant form. It is not by accident that a narrative and descriptive genre ascended to prominence at the precise moment that societies were becoming more democratic and less aristocratic and the heterogeneity of society needed full representation. Times reversed the often-told tale of the One and the Many, and now demanded individuation to account for society's vicissitudes. Hamlet no longer stood for all the people. The twentieth century ushered in the technological age, and the possibility of reproductive art and film, reliant upon machinations, rose in popularity among the masses. The present century might well be later described as a visual and virtual age. Photographs formerly assured the viewer that something actually existed in front of a camera at the time of the shot. In the era of digital technology, such certainty is no longer secure. In a visually oriented world inundated with computers and computer-generated images, in a world full of technological wonders, how can anyone accept with a straight face the simple art of three boards and a passion?

The future of live performance does appear bleak. In his landmark essay written in the 1930s, Walter Benjamin explained, "that which withers in the age of mechanical reproduction is the aura of the work of art" (223). The aura, a key term of Benjamin's, is produced by notions of authenticity and originality. In a mediatized culture, led by film and taped television events, a "plurality of copies" substitutes for "a unique existence" (223). The acceptance of this substitution and its ubiquity is the genesis for Philip Auslander's book *Liveness: Performance in a Mediatized Culture* (1999), which makes a convincing argument that the live, or original, event is not even that which audiences seek. People, surrounded by picture screens, monitors, mikes, and speakers of every size and shape, actually pursue and prefer the *copy* to the *original*. Auslander writes about much more than theater in his book, and some of his best examples about performance refer to the music and sporting industries. He points out the fact that most fans watch concerts and see sports by craning up to the JumboTron, which magnifies the live performance and offers a much better view of the performers than the naked eye alone permits. Auslander also observes a historical change in how the music industry promotes its performers. Formerly, it booked concert tours and live performances to boost record sales. Now, more and more, producers orchestrate live performances to duplicate the studio sound of recorded music. Concertgoers expect live performances to sound like the recordings they listen to at home or in the car and measure the authenticity of the original against the standard of the copy.

What even constitutes a live event remains a question. The Rolling Stones' concert filmed "live" in Madison Square Garden by HBO at the end of their Licks tour on 18 January 2003 provides a case in point. During the course of the concert, which has since been rebroadcast many times on the cable network, the band members acknowledge and play to various cameras stationed around the stage. Roving camerapeople frequently catch each other in their sights to add to the sense of spontaneity. The audience, too, acknowledges the red light, but it also watches the concert on the giant video screen that backs the band. Mick Jagger sings "Angie," "Brown Sugar," "Can't You Hear Me Knocking," and all the familiar oldies but goodies, but the huge image of him and his lips looms even larger and more compelling above and beyond him. Transfixed by the TV from the comfort of my suburban couch, I, too, enjoyed the picture within the picture. The event also featured the use of Ron Wood's famous "guitar-cam" positioned atop his Fender Stratocaster to enable fans to see the stage from his point of view; but really, upon reflection, this provided just another angle for fans to see themselves and promote their own narcissism.

As for the sound, Millennia Music and Media Systems issued a press release after the concert to promote one of its products. Referring to how the event was recorded, an engineer said: "'we used a total of 82 channels of HV-3s [Millennia's microphone preamplifiers] on stage to drive about 800 feet of wire down to the Remote Recording Services' Silver Truck, five stories below. We took the inputs in line level to our Neve VRM and Studer 961 series Consoles and mixed them down to Dolby Stereo for broadcast. We also recorded the show to Studer D-827 Digital 48 Track Recorders for later remix'" (Millennia). This live event was later packaged as part of a four-DVD set, involving three taped concerts in all parts of the world and marketed for Christmas at the end of 2003.[4]

Expectations of technical perfection have had a profound effect on live performance in the theater, too, where audiences flock to long-running musicals having already bought the "original cast album" in Boise. "It sounds just like the CD!" serves as the highest possible praise. My own experience as one of the last people in the whole entire world to see *Les Misérables* is noteworthy in one respect. I sat far away from the stage, high up in one of the last rows of the mezzanine, and could barely interpret the body language of the performers, but I could hear perfectly well thanks to a generously large set of speakers located immediately behind me. The performance created a schizoid split of sensory impressions. On the one hand, I sat in what could almost have been a separate area code from the actual performance onstage. On the other hand, and in both ears, the sound nearly drove me out of my seat. The sheer amount of mixers and amplifiers and other stuff that technicians use to make things happen at a Broadway theater is definitely impressive, but still it does make me wonder: how *live* is the live performance I'm paying a premium price to see?

By far, though, the greatest threat to the theater comes from film and television. The HBO series *The Sopranos,* a hybrid form of cable programming which combines the best of both television and film ("It's not TV, it's HBO"), has put the latest hit on stage drama: the show provides a quality, realistic narrative performed by excellent actors; compared to a theater ticket, it's very inexpensive to watch; the living room is much more accessible than an uncomfortable seat in the theater, and most people do not have access to good live theater anyway; and the cable show offers an intimate look into a range of characters' lives in a serial format over a long period of time (the show has completed six seasons). Viewers such as me are part of the problem, as a letter to the *New York Times* pointed out in late 2001:

> If the American public wants *The Sopranos,* new playwrights (or frustrated screenwriters posing as playwrights) will write like *The Sopranos* or *Sex and the City,* and artistic directors will produce these plays, and the audience will compare the prices. I'm tired of watching the latest movie of the week on stage. (Rebecca Gilman comes to mind.) Give me risky work, even work that isn't quite successful (because that's interesting, too), something that can engage me as a person who's living in the world, and not in front of a screen. (McKevitt)

This angry letter writer fervently believes that theater is better than television and that any right-thinking adult would be hard-pressed to disagree with her. I'm not sure, though, that I see the difference between "living in the world" and "living in front of a screen." Philip Auslander might argue that contemporary life is "living in front of a screen." Whether it's crunching numbers on a spreadsheet, word processing on a PC, scheduling and avoiding conflicts on a PDA, competing on a Playstation ("Live in your world, play in ours"), or lounging in front of the tube, most people spend a remarkable portion of their lives in front of various screens trying to bring images to order.

Contrariness aside, though, I do agree with the sentiments expressed above insofar as theater ought to provide a different experience than film or television but too often doesn't. My chief complaint against theater arises when it tries to present subject matter in the same way as the other media and can't do it as well.

"For the theater to survive the 21st century," lamented critic Clive Barnes of the *New York Post,* "it will have to do what it singularly failed to do in the 20th century: take note of its competitors, and not attempt to do badly what they can do better" ("Theater Must Do"). Film and television are more "worldly" media than theater and are therefore better equipped to present realistic portrayals of human lives and events. The only purpose of theater, to borrow from Brecht, is to give pleasure and issue "no other passport than fun" (*Brecht on Theatre* 180). If theater offers that, people will attend. But if it offers the same experience as film and television, audiences will stay away in droves. Why should people go to all the trouble of attending the theater, and pay all the money it takes to get there, in order to see the same kind of entertainment that they can watch more easily and affordably in the comfort of their own homes?

Unless it presents something substantially different than can be offered by the other media and, at the same time, something vital to consumers, today's theater might disappear as quickly and quietly as the superfluous characters on a Chekhovian estate. In *The Seagull,* Sorin responds to Treplev's diatribe against the conventional theater by saying, "We can't do without the theater" (109). It's time to ask, "Why not?" Edwin Wilson, writing about one hundred years later and evoking Gaev's salutation to a bookcase in *The Cherry Orchard,* pines for the past and future of theater when he concludes the seventh edition of *The Theater Experience,* an Introduction to Theater class textbook, one of the best and certainly most used (a tenth edition is scheduled for 2007) of its kind. Attentive readers might hear the distant strain of Schechner's string quartet:

> The one thing we do know is that theater will continue; it has already demonstrated this in the way it has met the challenges of film, television, and other electronic innovations. The reason is that when we go to the theater, we become part of a group with a common bond: an audience sharing an experience. In the exchange between performers and audience, we take part in a direct human encounter. From the stage, we hear the dark cry of the soul, we listen to the joyous laughter of the human spirit, and we witness the tragedies and triumphs of the human heart. As long as people wish to join together in a communion of the spirit or share with one another their anguish and suffering, the theater experience will provide them with a unique way of doing it. (441)

It's high time to dispel the attendant nonsense that clings to the nature of the theatrical experience. Wilson begins his book in the same key as he ends it: "At the heart of the theater experience, therefore, is the performer-audience relationship: the immediate, personal exchange whose chemistry and magic give theater its special quality" (19). It is very difficult to know what "chemistry," "magic," and "special quality" are, and yet the theater world is filled with such empty medieval rhetoric. Milly S. Barranger, another Introduction to Theater author, upholds the party line of liveness and immediacy in the fifth edition of *Theatre: A Way of Seeing:* "It is theatre's *immediacy* that makes it different from other arts. Theatre presents human beings playing fictional characters who move, speak, 'live' *before* us, creating recognizable people, events, and places. For a short time we share an experience with actors that is imitative, provocative, entertaining, and magical. Theatre's *living quality* sets it apart" (5). For the general theater enthusiast, David Black's *The Magic of Theater: Behind the Scenes with Today's Leading Actors* purports to answer a serious question—one historically that fascinated both Diderot and William Archer—about who exerts a greater effect upon an audience: "the actor who actually feels an emotion or the actor who successfully imitates it?" (xiv).[5] Unfortunately that interesting question goes unanswered by Black in the pages that follow. Instead, statements such as these by actor William Hurt fill the pages: "The mystery opened up through the theater is the imagination itself. That's the hero" (63). What does this mean? It suggests, maybe, that Hurt valorizes the relative poverty of theater compared to film and celebrates the suggestiveness of the theatrical medium over the realism of cinema. That's only speculation. The fuzziness surrounding all the above statements begs the question whether there really is something special at the heart of the theatrical experience. Does obfuscation, as a result of direct motive or a product of inarticulate expression, hide the fact that nothing lies underneath the verbiage?

If theater is worth saving, if it is worth having and doing, then it must be recognized as a distinct experience with its own properties and qualities that set it apart from film and television. In her book *Unmarked,* Peggy Phelan valorizes the concept of performance as that which cannot be reproduced. Performance, in her analysis, exists only in the moment of utterance and therefore resists capital drives for reproduction, mass distribution, and consumption. She argues, "Performance honors the idea that a limited number of people in a specific time/space frame can have an experience of value which leaves no visible trace afterward. . . . Performance's independence from mass reproduction, technologically, economically, and linguistically, is its greatest strength" (149). Phelan's prejudice against written texts echoes Antonin Artaud's "No More Masterpieces" and his conviction that "the theater is the only place in the world where a gesture, once made, can never be made the same way twice" (75). Performance in Phelan's terminology does not concern the production of established plays. She would have little use, I suspect, for the kind of drama that I will continually talk about throughout this book. She sees the idea of performance as an escape from the strictures of capitalist society. That which is never repeated cannot be co-opted to serve a capital economy. Yet even Phelan admits that once you begin to talk about performance, the act of talking, the fact of words, reintroduces the idea of performance into play as a commodity to be shaped, repackaged, and sold.

Against Phelan's resistance politics, Auslander argues that there is no basis to make an ontological distinction between theater and film. Early on, he says instead that "the relationship between the live and the mediatized is one of competitive opposition at the level of cultural economy" (11). Later, he adds, "To understand the relationship between live and mediatized forms, it is necessary to investigate that relationship as historical and contingent, not as ontologically given or technologically determined" (51). Given the various forms, live and mediatized (in other words, television, film, digital), fighting for cultural supremacy in a Darwinian survival of the fittest, it is not surprising to read that Auslander's theatrical forecast is pretty dismal. From a historical perspective, theater's glory days reigned four hundred years ago. Looking at the contingent forces impinging upon it today, the vast number of entertainment choices available and the technological sophistication evolving for those same choices, it's very hard to predict a bright future. Auslander makes many keen observations and persuasive insights in his book, and perhaps time will reward him for ringing the death knell of live theater. My project resists his fundamental premise with a firm conviction that theater does constitute an "ontologically" distinct art form.

Theater offers a potential spectacle filled with movement and the whole-bodied presence of human figures; features simultaneous action unfolding throughout the playing area; reverberates with sound and rhythm. Such images are not the means to an end; they are the essence of dramatic art. It is a great shame that dynamic Plato did not write the *Poetics!*[6] Instead, we're saddled with his pupil's dry as dust lecture notes, delivered in antiquity more than 2,500 years ago, which still continue to plague the modern dramatic imagination. Aristotle's six elements of drama, in hierarchical order no less, have become writ in veritable stone: plot, character, thought, diction, music, and spectacle. His legacy, despite Artaud's and Brecht's welcome caveats in the twentieth century, has led to plot-dominated drama in which the goal of reaching the end has been approached as Holy Grail. Getting to the end, tying and untying the various complicated knots of the plot, is not the most important part of a play. Plot is merely an excuse for something interesting to happen along the way. And, contrary to Aristotle's list, I consider spectacle as the most, not least, important element in today's theater. If we have become a visual culture, immersed in the daily rituals of film and television, then an opportunity exists for theater to exploit such heightened visual acuity.

Drama is, according to Aristotle, an "imitation of an action," and it follows then that "the structure of events, the plot, is the goal of tragedy, and the goal is the greatest thing of all" (27). The linguistic roots of drama (to do, to act) denote an action in time and space with a beginning, middle, and end unfolding in one direction from first line to last. Plot is "the basic principle, the heart and soul, as it were, of tragedy" (28). Aristotle proceeds to define the remaining aspects of drama and ends the section by asserting the relative unimportance of spectacle, admitting that "the visual adornment of the dramatic persons can have a strong emotional effect but is the least artistic element, the least connected with the poetic art; in fact the force of tragedy can be felt even without benefit of public performance and actors, while for the production of the visual effect the property man's art is even more decisive than that of the poets" (29). Here, then, Aristotle makes a clear distinction between drama as literature and as theatrical performance. He valorizes the word of the playwright over the visual spectacle of performance that he considers decorative and not an essential aspect of it. He asserts, too, that the playwright is not responsible for the visual effects and implies that the "property man's art" is servile to the playwright's and that it indulges the base impulses of the theatrical crowd. Aristotle is only the first to separate drama from performance and view the text as primary and performance as secondary, derivative, and parasitic to the host text.

"Wake me up when they kill themselves," I still vividly remember saying to my parents when I attended the ballet in St. Louis to see Nuryev dance *Romeo and Juliet*. Even as a young boy I exhibited a keen Aristotelian bias with my steadfast devotion to the end of the story. I knew where the action was headed, and I was prepared to skip the necessary dalliance in between. (I'm sure that I was tired and bored and thinking about the Cardinals as well.) I didn't have patience for Aristotelian suspense, the arabesque pattern of the plot changing directions with each recognition (e.g., "my only love sprung from my only hate") and reversal (e.g., Romeo seeks peace with Tybalt; Tybalt kills Mercutio; Romeo slays Tybalt) and winding inexorably toward an inevitable conclusion. Unfortunately, I slept through it all, but if I had been awake I would have really seen something! Aristotle actually says very little about catharsis. Defined variously as purification, purgation, or clarification, catharsis results from undergoing an intense experience (real or fictional). In drama, it is an emotional response and release to pent-up feelings borne by the plot along the way. After Romeo toasts Juliet's body with a vial of poison and dies, Juliet awakens, grieves, kisses Romeo's corpse, and then kills herself. Catharsis and denouement follow when, soon after, the friar, the prince, and respective families enter the vault, discover the lovers, and lament their deaths. The audience grieves with them and mourns the loss with realizations of the actions that caused it. The calculated ebb and flow of the plot, replete with a series of recognitions (e.g., she's dead; he's dead; it's our fault) and reversals (she's not dead; let's be friends), produces an intense emotional response precipitated by the action which builds and builds and builds and finally climaxes like a male sex fantasy.[7]

In search of an alternative theater that could explore the whole range of theatrical experience beyond the masculine endings of Aristotelian plots, Antonin Artaud's metaphysical theater of sounds and gestures and Bertolt Brecht's political theater of clarity and insight both made a plea for a spectacular theater instead of a merely literary one. The "Theater of Images" today refers to the works of such avant-garde artists and collectives as Robert Wilson, Richard Foreman, Mabou Mines, and The Wooster Group. For these artists, the text is only part of the total theatrical experience. When I saw The Wooster Group's production of O'Neill's *The Emperor Jones* a few years ago, several striking images in the performance, notably a soft-shoe minstrel dance and a crude finger shadow projection of slave ships crossing the ocean, stuck in my consciousness. I can't remember O'Neill's play very well, but those images from the performance have stayed with me.[8] A popular culture phenomenon such as Cirque du Soleil has capitalized on the avant-garde's push for a theater of images. It has successfully aestheticized the vulgarity of the circus and developed a theater of images palatable to a mass audience. Music, costuming, feats of great skill and daring, and traditional clowning have all effectively dispensed with the need for narrative. Themes remain perhaps, but an understanding of them is not required in order to enjoy a performance.

Artaud argues the loudest and most passionately against Aristotle and the narrative theater. In his most famous work, *The Theater and Its Double,* he argues persuasively that theater does not fundamentally concern dialogue. He seeks to replace the theater of words with one of sound, incantations, gestures, and movement in theatrical space. Instead of a canonical theater, reverential to the playwright and the written word, Artaud issues his signature phrase when he concludes that we should not dally with dramatic forms, but be "victims burnt at the stake, signaling through the flames" (13). Peter Brook labeled Artaud's vision the "Holy Theatre" in his still influential *The Empty Space* (1968). Brook described Artaud's intentions to create spiritually spectacular events: "a band of dedicated actors and directors who would create out of their own natures an unending succession of violent stage images, bringing about such powerful immediate explosions of human matter that no one would ever again revert to a theatre of anecdote and talk" (53).

Artaud sought to create a language in space and in movement to replace the written text of the playwright, and he named this language the mise-en-scène, a term he applied to the physical space of the theater that he said needed to be filled with something much more than the words of the playwright. Artaud's own descriptive language, however, remained somewhat mystical regarding his new terminology: "It is in the light of magic and sorcery that the *mise en scène* must be considered, not as the reflection of a written text, the mere projection of physical doubles that is derived from the written work, but as the burning projection of all the objective consequences of a gesture, word, sound, music, and their combinations" (73). If language fails Artaud, however, as language has often failed the theater, his striving for a more powerful and evocative and visually, viscerally effective theater remains laudable and idealistic. In a letter to a friend in 1932, Artaud concludes, "The true purpose of the theater is to create Myths, to express life in its immense, universal aspect, and from that life to extract images in which we find pleasure in discovering ourselves" (*Theater and Its Double* 116). Joseph Chaikin, a pioneer of off-off Broadway in the 1960s in America and a disciple of Artaud in the sense of working for an ensemble-based theater independent of a prescribed text by an outside author, echoed a similar formulation of the purpose of theater in his chronicle *The Presence of the Actor* (1972): "The theater, insofar as people are serious in it, seems to be looking for a place where it is not a duplication of life. It exists not just to make a mirror of life, but to represent a kind of realm just as certainly as music is a realm" (25). In retrospect (with an established end of the narrative in sight), it's easy to categorize the spirit of the '60s as an attempt to discover a ritualistic theater based on essences as opposed to appearances, one that transcends everyday experiences and addresses the spiritual vacuum left by the materialism and greed of modern life. Equally important, though, and often overlooked, is the desire to discover what belongs to the theater as purely theatrical, a pursuit that the pervasive dominance of narrative obscures.

I have distinguished between Aristotle's theater of plot and language and Artaud's mise-en-scène in order to separate two radically different impulses. The practical application of Artaudian theory, however, has always been a bit suspect. Always passionate and inspirational, his voice is very rarely clear. How exactly do those signals through the flames look? A fine actor in film, Artaud's artistic credentials as a director are limited to a few productions, most notably Shelley's *The Cenci*. Even Artaud himself didn't know how to translate his theory into actual practice.[9] Although it is possible to see how Shelley's play would lend itself to radical production ideas, Artaud discovered that it was quite difficult to discard words altogether and that an established plot provided a structure with which to work.

While Brecht agrees with Aristotle that "narrative is the soul of drama" (*Brecht on Theatre* 183), he argues that the method of construction should be wholly different. He calls his theater the "Epic Theater" because it emphasizes the big picture of the world that the audience can see as opposed to the limited events portrayed in an Aristotelian play. While the dramatic theater emphasizes plot, the

Brecht play tells a story, or narrative. And while the Aristotelian plot immerses the spectator in the action, the Brecht play turns the spectator into an observer in order to evaluate better what happens. Alienation, that famous Brecht term, is a means of creating distance from the action in order for the spectator to see and evaluate what's happening. Brecht's theater is above all else a theater of vision. All the famous and familiar techniques, the signs, the songs, the exposed theatrical trappings, are theoretically supposed to help the spectator see the play. The Aristotelian plots, as I described them earlier, attempt to deceive the viewer along the way in order to make grand revelations at the end. In such plots, the viewer, according to Brecht, gets swept away in the current of events and the machinations of the plot make all events seem inevitable. Such a theater repulsed Brecht. His interest in social and political change prompted him to create a style of theater in which the plot seemed in no way inevitable, but subject to the decisions and actions of particular characters in specific situations. Brecht charges the actors in his company with making attitudes clear to the audience. Gest, a key term in Brecht's visual theater, pertains to the physical, psychological, social, and economic relations between human beings. He asserts that "the grouping of the characters on the stage and the movements of the groups must be such that the necessary beauty is attained above all by the elegance with which the material conveying that gest is set out and laid bare to the understanding of the audience" (200–201). In the new scientific age of learning, according to Brecht, pleasure comes from understanding, but understanding is possible only in a theater that presents a dramatic situation as clearly as it can.

A good theatrical performance can be understood in any language because sound and movement function independently onstage. The ability to see everything simultaneously in relation to all parts in the theater creates a full and understandable visual text apart from and supplemental to the written text. The same is not true in film, where the whole world is contingent and often out of the frame and just out of view. Referring to the interdependence of word and gesture in film as the "principle of coexpressibility," Erwin Panofsky specifies, "that which we hear remains, for good or worse, inextricably fused with that which we see; the sound, articulate or not, cannot express any more than is expressed, at the same time, by visible movement" (237). Without sound, a film is virtually unintelligible. Why do the airlines offer in-flight films for free but sell the headphones to passengers for movies on long-distance flights? It is quite educational to watch the many monitors throughout the cabin without a headset and attempt to piece the action together. It's almost always futile because the silence denies an identifiable context for the series of momentary images. It's difficult to locate the images without a soundtrack. Subtitles are crucial for the enjoyment of a foreign-language film, too, in a way that has no analogy to theater practice.

The two theatrical tracks—one of plot and language, the other of spectacle and gesture—work independently, but they are not mutually exclusive. The imaginative combinations of words and movement can create extraordinary events.

Perhaps, then, we shouldn't do without Aristotle, but we certainly do need more than just him. The amusing premise of Umberto Eco's novel *The Name of the Rose* places a single copy of Aristotle's second book of dramatic criticism, a serious treatment of comedy that represents a follow-up to his discourse on tragedy, in a medieval library.[10] In the novel, the church views the treatment of comedy as an attack against the Word of God and therefore keeps the work under wraps and out of sight. The authorities fear that laughter, the goal of comedy, frees humankind from the fear of God and undermines the authority of the treatise on tragedy. Eco, the Italian semiotician and author of such academic works as *The Open Work,* which advocated ambiguity as a virtue of texts, wrote a novel about the dangers of curtailing knowledge and the threat of univocal authority. At the same time, the novel functions as a murder mystery and reveals the discovery of Aristotle on comedy near the very end! Thus, Eco's book adheres faithfully to Aristotelian plotting!

Lawrence and Lee's old chestnut *Inherit the Wind* concludes in praise of plenitude and perfectly sums up my attitude regarding Aristotle. Their play puts in dramatic form the Scopes Monkey Trial of 1925 that pitted Clarence Darrow (Henry Drummond in the play) against William Jennings Bryan (Matthew Harrison Brady). The argument in the play, one that still carries weight even today, is whether to teach creationism as found in the Bible or evolution as theorized by Charles Darwin. At the end of the play, Drummond, having lost the case as a formality, but essentially having won the argument and carried the day, remarks, "The Bible is a book. A good book. But it's not the *only* book" (123). In his final gesture, Drummond takes both books in hand, the Bible and *The Origin of Species,* and balances them as though they were weights upon a scale. Then, he slams them together and tucks them both side by side into his briefcase.

There is no need to discard Aristotle. His curse on us is not that his work endures, but rather that it often seems to exist alone. His first words on drama should not be our last. In the beginning was the word, but the word described an image of the world.

2
Dramatic Projections

On a screen the study is projected; on a stage the actor is the projector.
—Stanley Cavell, *The World Viewed: Reflections on the Ontology of Film*

Projecting one's voice as an actor, modulating volume and articulation such that people far away hear clearly yet those close by are not blown away, is a tricky task, but acclaimed British voice coach and author Patsy Rodenburg attacks the problem with refreshing candor and simplicity. She adopts "breathing the space" as a phrase to emphasize the naturalness of the activity, the importance of breath support for vocal power, and the mental preparation necessary for the job: "Whatever space you are performing in, stand on the stage when it's empty and breathe to the perimeters of the theater or room" (*Actor Speaks* 57). This exercise requires the speaker to measure and match energy output to the specific configurations of the room. It is therefore much more challenging to breathe to the perimeter of a large house than an intimate theater of 150 seats. Performance demands grow exponentially with the size of the space.[1]

Just as increased size of the playing space requires greater skill from the actors, a bigger playing space requires more from the drama in order to be seen and heard. A "bigger" drama is a more powerful drama, a more compelling drama, a more emotionally rich drama than can be contained within a smaller, more intimate space. The "big" plays that I champion require huge emotional commitments from the actors who play them. Rodenburg again relates the emotional demands of a dramatic text to the vocal demands placed upon the performer by saying that "the greater the pain or passion, the bigger the sound needed to purge it. The bigger the conflict, the more clamorous the voice" (*Right to Speak* 225). This louder, more emotional, ringing voice carries the message of the play, though it might not be in easily understood words. Harold Pinter observed an inverse relationship between emotion and speech years ago: "The more acute the experience the less articulate its expression" (11). The actor, then, in the great pitch of a turbulent drama, relies upon the emotional intensity of vowels to convey depths of feeling at the expense of intellectual consonants. As King Lear carries the dead Cordelia onstage and bellows "Howl! Howl! Howl!," each exclamation and exhalation taps the outrage and pathos of Shakespeare's great tragedy.

By analogy to the actor's vocal challenge in the theater, drama, too, projects its image to an audience. The intentional pun on "projection" with respect to film ties the very different experiences of the two forms into a bundle of contrasts. Whereas the camera draws the viewer into the world and offers an extremely compelling illusion of reality, the stage drama must always bridge the distance between the performer and audience. Projection addresses the need for size and volume in the theater in order to be seen and heard as opposed to the camera's and microphone's ability to zoom in on the actor's face and amplify the voice. In his comparison of theater and film, Roger Manvell identifies the playwrights' call to "speak up" with their writing: "The skill of the dramatist lies in writing 'projectable,' theatrical dialogue; in this sense, the dialogue of most plays is written 'up,' pitched beyond normal speech, in order to become effective as spoken by actors and actresses. . . . However realistic dialogue may seem when first heard, underlying it always is the fact of projection, a continuity or significance of speech alone that commands attention from an assembled audience" (32). Projection in the theater requires human labor, whereas cinematic projection is mechanical and technological. "Plays are performed. Movies are made," observes Michael Caine in his book on film acting (16).

Stage and film director and teacher Patrick Tucker distinguishes acting styles in the two media by comparing the distance of a stage actor from the audience with the distance of a movie actor from the camera. Actors project theatrical performances according to the size of the space in which they're working. In films, though, actors constantly adjust their performance within a single film according to the size of the individual shot. In Tucker's schema, a mezzanine view in the theater is equivalent to a long shot in the cinema in which the entire human figure is visible; an orchestra seat in the middle of the house is akin to a midshot in which the human figure is seen from the waist up; a front-row seat is similar to a medium close-up shot from the chest up; and, finally, an extreme close-up shot has no parallel in the live theater (5–9).

The long shot requires a "bigger," more melodramatic acting style, since the camera is farther away. At the other end of the acting spectrum, the extreme close-up requires the actor to do nothing but "think" the thoughts (9). Accepting Tucker's breakdown for a moment, film acting would seem to have much greater flexibility (changing from shot to shot) and range (the close-up is not even an option for the theater) than acting onstage. The problem with his analogy is that while the film actor adjusts a performance for each shot, the eventual audience sees only one shot at a time during the sequence of the film. In the theater, the actor must scale a performance for the size of the theater, surely, but in any space, big or small, the actor has to convey the honesty and integrity of the performance simultaneously to the person sitting in the orchestra pit as well as on the back row of the theater.

The stage actor projects a performance to the witnesses of the event, while the film actor performs for the camera. Michael Caine, an accomplished actor on both stage and screen, offers a useful comparison: "On stage, you have to project your voice or the words will sink without a trace into the third row of seats. On stage, the basic premise is action; you have to sell your attitudes to the audience. In movies, the microphone can always hear you, no matter how softly you speak, no matter where the scene is taking place. In movies, it is *reaction* that gives every moment its potency. That's why listening in films is so important, as well as the use of the eyes in the close-up" (11). The film actor does less, exerts less energy, reacts instead of acts because the audience, the camera, rests nearby. Despite the variety of shots that may require a separate style of acting, more melodramatic or more intimate, the majority of shots are what Tucker calls the "intimate" theater style which translates, not coincidentally, into the standard style of realism. Such shots are perfect for capturing the facial responses of actors and their visible reactions, what's vital for Caine, within the intimacy of the shot. It's very difficult to gauge how tall an actor is in a film because the entire body is rarely visible in context with surroundings and, more importantly, with other characters. Most of the shots cut the actor off just above or just below the waist in order to achieve the desired intimacy. The close proximity of the camera to the actor means that the personal qualities of the actor supersede technical training. This is immediately true when one reflects upon the movie star's performance onstage, and the stage actor's appearance in film. A film actor with no ability to project is lost on a stage before an audience in a two-thousand-seat house.[2] Likewise, the stage actor who cannot modulate a performance to fit within the frames of the various shots appears ridiculous and absurdly histrionic.

In his highly popular book, *Acting for the Camera,* veteran screen and television acting teacher Tony Barr insists upon the very different scales of performance for stage and film: "Therefore, the greater-than-life style necessary for naturalness in the theater is unnecessary—and even undesirable—for film. Moreover, anything you do that is dishonest in relation to what the character is thinking or feeling will be noticeable to the audience. The camera allows no deceit. Either you are truthful or you are not" (4–5). The camera doesn't really lie. It merely records. But because it can record action at close range to the subject, any movement has the possibility of seeming huge. The scale of performance is entirely different than in a stage play. A flicker of a smile in an extreme close-up shot may represent much greater actual movement than an actor's vault across the width of a proscenium in the theater.

Finally, too, whereas the actor onstage controls his or her performance, the film actor has no way of knowing how he or she is acting. The camera, after all, provides no feedback. Its blank eye never even blinks. The director and film editing teams collate so many takes of so many shots to assemble an actor's performance. Furthermore, since the sequence of shots will most likely not correspond to the chronology of the movie, the film actor will not be able to see how any one shot or scene will relate to the previous one, the one after, or, indeed, the arc of the entire film.[3]

While the actor projects a performance to the audience, a film is projected upon a flat screen. The relationship of the active to passive voice here is analogous to the exterior and interior modes of performance dictated by theater and film. Dramatic projections possess both direction and dimension. A dramatic performance takes place in front of the audience and moves toward it. In cinema, by contrast, the movie projector is located behind the audience and directs its focus literally over the heads of the audience. In the movement, too, from page to stage, the theater transforms from two dimensions to three. The process of moving from models and renderings on paper to technical drawings and plans to fully realized scenery and costumes in a theatrical space is part of the supposed magic of theater—tied closely to make-believe, dress-up, and playing with dolls. The theater resembles the world in exactly the same way as a toy theater resembles the world for a child. The analogy of theater to world is the source of much of the theater's resonance and power.

The cinema works quite differently and moves in the opposite direction from three dimensions to two. Film begins in the world, an immediately apparent fact borne out by a visit to any location shoot. Walter Benjamin, in his famous essay on art and technology, claims that the painter is to the cameraperson as the magician is to the surgeon. One lays on hands, the other penetrates the body. The painter makes up his subject out of thin air (like a magician) and applies various pigments to the canvas. Benjamin suggests that the painter (and, by extension, the playwright) extracts from the world in order to create the illusion of life in two dimensions. The filmmaker, on the other hand, always remains immersed in the world: "Film penetrates into reality, a thorough permeation which offers, paradoxically, an aspect of reality free of equipment" (235–36). The cameras, booms, microphones, dollies, tracks, trailers, and buffet tables disappear from the final cut. The finished product wipes clean the chaos from the film site. Theater may be of the world, but cinema is rooted in the world. Turning Shakespeare's metaphor into literal fact, Gilberto Perez remarks, "All the world, because of the camera's access to it, may be enlisted as a stage for films" (38).

The theater, compared to film, seems at a glance to operate at a severe disadvantage. The entire theatrical event unfolds within a single space in front of the audience, and the action is progressive, to borrow one of Goethe's terms, moving from beginning to end without temporal interruption. In the cinema, the ability to edit, to juxtapose one sequence of shots with another, alters the categories of time and space such that a story loses, in the words of Arnold Hauser, its "uninterrupted continuity" and "irreversible direction" and becomes dynamic rather than homogenous: here, there, far away, up close (240). The theater lacks cinema's agility to jump, cut, repeat, skip, accelerate, flash forward, flash back, or retard. Plays such as *Rashomon,* in which the same crime is presented from four different points of view, remain novelty acts in the theater primarily because of the clumsiness of presenting four perspectives. Each one has to follow in sequence and be presented in its entirety. A cinematic treatment, on the other hand, can juggle four versions by cutting back and forth between each one. Similarly, while many films alter the temporal sequence of events between past, present, and even future, most plays adhere to chronological order. In part this is due to the fact that theater seems to need a building of events to achieve desired effects (such as catharsis), but more importantly it is because theater, once moving in a single temporal direction, finds it very difficult to reverse directions.

There are remarkably few plays that experiment with altering chronologies, while such techniques are standard practice for the cinema. Playwright Donald Margulies offers exceptions to this rule in *Sight Unseen* and *Dinner with Friends,* though his attempts to alter chronology prove difficult to achieve on stage. The first play concerns an artist contemplating his integrity, but the temporal span of the play, highlighting a few key moments in his life, might be better served in a medium that could encompass more such events and weight them, in length of time of representation, differently according to their importance. Norman Jewison directed a film adaptation of *Dinner with Friends* for HBO in 2001 which remained largely faithful to Margulies's play, but a color filter change gave a different look to the one scene that flashes back in time and helped indicate temporal displacement. In the stage version, the scene which flashes back over twelve years to a little house on Martha's Vineyard is placed at the start of the second act, presumably to allow the actors to change makeup. The stage directions indicate "Everyone has more hair" (40). Presumably, they "take it off" after the scene. All in all, the film version accommodates shifts in time much easier and more efficiently than the play.

Film editing gives the cinema a flexibility that is unheard of in the theater. The camera creates multiple points of view and variable distances from the subject, impossible to achieve in a theater in which the audience sits in a fixed seat in front of a stage. Following the Russian school of montage theory, Susan Sontag further notes that "the distinctive cinematic unit is not the image but the principle of connection between the images: the relation of a 'shot' to the one that preceded it and the one that comes after" ("Theatre and Film" 108). If the relation between shots is the key element, then time is crucial, and, in general, the shot remains very short in order to juxtapose two or more shots. Multiple shots make up a single scene in a movie. Each scene accommodates the "master shot," multiple points of view, and the close-ups for each actor. A play, conversely, breaks down into acts and scenes that are comparatively much longer units of action. Whereas the meanings of a sequence of film may lie in the perceived relations between one shot and the next, the meanings of a play on the stage occur in the unfolding action witnessed by the audience.

Cinema brings out the brevity of the shot, but theater counters with the development of the scene in which entrances and exits determine the basic units of action. Directors frequently divide a script into acting scenes or "French scenes" delineated by the comings and goings of the major characters. All plays break down into a succession of entrances and exits. The actors are onstage or off, whereas in film the actors are in the shot or not, but they might be in the next one depending on what the camera focuses upon. Each scene in a play provides an "entrance" followed by a period of development in which something happens that furthers the action and then ends with an "exit" from the stage. Dramas strand actors onstage for the duration of the scene. In play after play, playwrights devise tactics to bring characters on and get them off. The false exit—an actor turning back for one last word—does not really even exist in real life, but it is a staple of the theater. Playwrights know full well the power of the door to create interest and dramatic tension. The door is the most important element in any scene design, and directors spend a great deal of time with designers plotting where to place the various entrances on the set. "Making an entrance," so vital to theater lore, and a necessary skill for an actor to develop, is simply not an issue in the movies, where, through the power of editing and the mobility of the camera, an actor merely appears when needed.

After stacking the deck against theater in comparison to film, it's time to flip the terms of discussion. There probably hasn't been a better and more important theater book written since Peter Brook's *The Empty Space,* in which the eminent director lauds the visionary work of Stanislavsky, Artaud, Grotowski, and Brecht in praise of an immediate theater. Brook argued in 1968 that theater possessed distinctive and vital qualities that could not be duplicated in other media: "Compared with the cinema's mobility, the theatre once seemed ponderous and creaky, but the closer we move towards the true nakedness of theatre, the closer we approach a stage that has a lightness and range far beyond film or television" (87). The "lightness" and "range" Brook mentions refer to the freedom that a theatrical audience enjoys by seeing an event with its own eyes. In film, the camera looks for an audience and tells it what to see by virtue of focus.

Gilberto Perez cites the lines of perspective in photography as mainly indicative and bluntly labels the camera a pointer: "From among the world's innumerable number the camera specifies a particular sight it captures for our looking" (397). In the cinema, every image has been previously wrought and processed and reproduced for the viewer's consumption. An audience sees what someone else has already seen and appreciates everything that has been placed in the frame on its behalf. The responsibility of the audience to see for itself in the theater requires the viewer to scan the stage and pick up on everything that he or she sees. Such liberty creates the possibility for an aesthetic experience very different from that offered by the mediated arts. Favoring the freedom of the viewer to see many things at a theatrical event, Martin Esslin has compared the two forms: "The sense of complexity, of more going on than one can take in with one glance, the richness of an intricate counterpoint of human contrasts, will inevitably be reduced in a medium which clearly leads the eye of the spectator rather than allows it to roam at will" (80). Good theater, too, always sparks the sense that there is more to see than can be perceived entirely at any one time. Stage directors try to frame the stage action and focus attention to key elements, but in no way can they focus attention with the same degree of precision as their film counterparts. But, by giving up the hope of doing so, the stage director can offer a multiplicity of happenings onstage.

If film offers the possibility of being "here" one second and "there" the next, the stage can thrill an audience with simultaneous action within the confines of its allotted, homogenous space. The fact that the theater is limited to one place can turn into an artistic advantage as plays boast about everything happening before the audience's eyes. The prologue to *Henry V* sets the stage for this kind of virtuoso theater of the imagination, but modern plays can take similar advantage of theater's exclusive "hereness," its heavy anchor that drops the event in front of the audience's face. Susan Glaspell's *Trifles* plays effectively because the audience sees the entire downstairs interior of the household. All the clues to the murder remain in the room, and the audience follows the two women characters as they discover crucial evidence. Significantly, the men look for evidence upstairs out of sight, and the audience only hears their plodding efforts as they toss things and move furniture about and above the main playing area. One key to the successful theatricality of the play resides in the fact that all the evidence is available for anyone to see and read, but only the sensitive and sympathetic women can piece such "trifles" together. The clock in Marsha Norman's *'night, Mother* provides the constant visual reminder that Jessie's suicide is imminent. Without its presence in that play, the action, most of which is mundane conversation, loses urgency and dramatic interest. There's an old acting exercise about dramatic action in which a student first sits in a chair and does nothing. The class quickly agrees that such a "scene" is not very interesting, but then the actor discovers a bomb underneath the seat, and, very quickly, the little scene without words or movement gains potent dramatic interest. The clock in *'night, Mother* functions as a bomb set to detonate in sync with the end of the play and Jessie's final exit to her bedroom.

A. R. Gurney's *The Dining Room* champions the "hereness" of drama by staging an anthropological study in which people come and go, live and die, but furniture remains through the ages. His play chronicles almost a century of life of a dining room table passing from one generation to the next. The constancy of the table resonates with lives lived differently over the years and space used differently: a main room of pride, a setting for a formal dinner, a casual family gathering place, a place to do homework, a storage facility, an extraneous room. In all of the changing scenes, the table remains as a reference point. Technically, the presence of the table allows for all the significant changes to be accomplished through costuming alone. Thus, the scene changes move quickly with one scene beginning from one side of the table as the previous scene clears from the other side.

Audiences can anticipate the kind of show to be performed by simply counting the number of doors or entrances on the set. If there are only a few, look out: tragedy tonight! If the set seems to have a lot, it's a comedy, and if it has very many, perhaps even a farce! In farce characters enter and exit simultaneously, and a character comes in on one side as another character goes out the other side. The timing of this mechanical operation can be appreciated only if the audience can see the whole stage. Here's how Kaufman and Hart describe the Vanderhof living room in *You Can't Take It with You:* "The every-man-for-himself room would be more like it. For here meals are eaten, plays are written, snakes collected, ballet steps practiced, xylophones played, printing presses operated—if there were room enough there would probably be ice skating" (233). As the action builds in the play, the various characters perform their tasks at their stations in this room and more and more characters enter the stage from various portals, including stairs from above, and the cellar below. In addition to capitalizing upon the "hereness" of drama, theater can exploit simultaneous action on the stage for comic effects as the audience tries to follow the happenings.

The stage can also be split left from right, upstage from downstage, and above from below to show different action on different parts of the stage. The most theatrical scene in Richard Nelson's *Two Shakespearean Actors* places American Edwin Forrest on one side of the stage and Englishman Charles Macready on the other. By so doing, the playwright presents each style of acting simultaneously and the audience can make an immediate and visceral choice about whom it prefers. This is important in a play that describes events leading up to the Astor

Place Riot in 1849 and makes a case for why acting and theater were significant at that time. In Clifford Odets's one-act *Waiting for Lefty,* the stage is bare and all scenes take place within a ring surrounded by union men sitting in chairs observing the action. The audience sees past the performed action to the powerful men upstage who control the fate of the play and dictate its outcome. In this play, those controlling men are the dominant and only scenic elements. It is crucial, then, that the audience sees the powers-that-be at all times, and that the action reveals the "man behind the curtain." Both O'Neill's *Dynamo* and Sam Shepard's *A Lie of the Mind,* two plays separated by about fifty years, divide the stage to show one family on one side and the rival family on the other. Another O'Neill work, *Desire Under the Elms,* creates a second floor for the family house and creates scenes in which action on the stage floor contrasts with movements that take place in the upstairs bedrooms. Whereas the tendency in film would be to juxtapose one scene with the other by cutting between them, the theatrical solution presents scenes simultaneously and forces an audience to choose what it wants to see.

Probably in part because of her interest in absurdism in general and Ionesco in particular, the mise-en-scène in many of Tina Howe's plays presents the kind of simultaneous staging that represents a hallmark of theatricality. *Museum, Coastal Disturbances,* and *The Art of Dining* all take place in very public spaces and liberally scatter the inhabitants of each locale across the stage. The paintings and artworks spread the stage in the first, the endless sand and the sunbathers' search for privacy take the stage in the beach play, and the dinner patrons and the kitchen fill up the playing areas in the restaurant. The setting in each play requires that simultaneous events happen in different areas, and all the plays offer madcap, often farcical action.

Compared to film, theater is wholly artificial. Whether in Joplin, Missouri, or New York, New York, an audience applauds when the houselights dip and the stage lights come up on a scene that looks "real" and recognizable. In the nineteenth century, Americans paid money to see moving dioramas of familiar places, so the trompe l'oeil standard of scenic art should surprise no one. Audiences applaud that which looks very much like something they have already seen. It must be hard to duplicate real life, such applause seems to suggest. In film, that which looks lifelike receives no approbation. Instead, viewers check to see whether or not they have been there! The worldly spectator proudly announces—sometimes impressively, but more often obnoxiously—the exact location of a particular shot. Film takes place in the world; theater is of the world.

I saw *Three Days of the Condor* again recently on cable TV late at night and bolted upright when I discovered that the CIA office in the movie is located high in the World Trade Center. The movie has establishing shots of the towers, of course, so familiar in countless other films and television programs, but it also offers several shots at the base of the towers as well as a long scene that occurs up in the World Trade Center itself with shots of the surrounding tri-state landscape taken through the characteristic oblong, rectangular windows. With an obscure plot involving oil fields in the Middle East, the movie, which works off a certain level of paranoia about what our government may be up to and what it's capable of doing, played pretty eerily to me and, for a product of the 1970s, seemed absolutely prescient about the world condition. As Benjamin says, the penetration of reality seemed real and convincing and complete mostly because of photographic roots, which insist that something was there and did exist at one time before the camera. In the case of *Condor,* I watched with fascination something I had seen and visited, but also with painful and powerful awareness that it exists no longer.[4]

Photography records a worldly "then" and "there" context that theater simply does not possess. The human figure blends in with the scenery in two-dimensional film precisely because the projected shadows have the same value. Everything is of the same material. In the theater, however, the human figure attracts primary focus. In the cinema, the camera moves and everything else moves with it. On the stage, though, the audience sits still, and only the actors move and attract attention (I'm not counting the occasional falling chandelier or hovering helicopter that may land on American stages). The actor stands out literally in contrast to the scenery, which is, by and large, an imitation (how Platonic!) designed to fit in the dollhouse. The human figure contrasts with the surrounding scenery, and historically this has been one reason why the actor has performed in front of scenery and not around it. The history of theater can be taught as the gradual integration of the actor with the surrounding scenery. The invention of perspective scenery in the Renaissance, for example, created new opportunities for realistic scenery, but the illusion worked only insofar as the actor did not stray too close to the scenery and thus destroy the perspectival relationships. As scenery became three-dimensional instead of two-dimensional painted as three-, and as it encroached upon the ground formerly reserved exclusively for the actor— that is, as the scenery began to take up acting space—it began to interact with actors and compete with the actors for attention.[5] This resulted, ultimately, in the dramatic style of realism, but the invention of film has clearly obviated a need for such a style in the theater.

Theater views humanity in relationship not to the world "out there" but to the world of the stage. This phenomenon allows theater to focus exclusively on human affairs and makes the actor primary. This also provides another opportunity for theater to capitalize on its relative poverty in comparison to film and to make virtue of necessity. Beginning with *The Empty Space,* Peter Brook has long argued for such a "Holy Theatre." As late as 1993, he was still arguing for a theater that emphasized the human body and not the scenic details. In *The Open Door,* he writes, "If all you do is place two people side by side in an empty space, each detail comes into focus. For me, this is the great difference between theatre in its essential form and cinema. With cinema, because of the realistic nature of photography, a person is always in a context, never a person outside a context" (31). An ideal theatrical performance isolates the human figure, Brook intimates, and strips away the trappings of the mundane world. By making the familiar strange, as the Russian formalists said, an audience sees itself anew and emerges from the darkened theater refreshed and ready to meet the harsh light of day. Antonin Artaud envisioned the theater as a cathartic assault upon consciousness and being. In his evaluation of one of the great thinkers of the twentieth century, Brook observes Artaud's noble intentions for the theater: "Artaud maintained that only in the theatre could we liberate ourselves from the recognizable forms in which we live our daily lives" (*Empty Space* 53).

The theater does something quite different, then, from cinema, whose photographic essence works upon human memory and cuts into the nostalgic revelry of everyday life. Theater shares none of the worldliness of film. To the extent that it succeeds, it works in a diametrically opposed direction, as film historian André Bazin elaborates with several contrasting analogies: "Whether as a performance or a celebration, theater of its very essence must not be confused with nature under penalty of being absorbed by her and ceasing to be. Founded on the reciprocal awareness of those taking part and present to one another, it must be in contrast to the rest of the world in the same way that play and reality are opposed, or concern and indifference, or liturgy and the common use of things" (104). The stage cannot compete with film or television for the realistic depiction of events in everyday life. Instead, it removes itself from the world in order to see the world better. Even if the illusion appears to be realistic, the presentation of surface reality is rarely the goal of the theatrical event. Everything on the stage has the capacity to stand for something else and to resonate with private and collective experiences.

Bazin considers theater in a wholly nonrealistic fashion—as illusory, as ritualistic, as otherworldly. Two excellent examples of this alienating process of rebelling against realism and highlighting the human figure come from such disparate sources as Thornton Wilder and, much more recently, Suzan-Lori Parks. The former playwright voiced his dissatisfaction with the realistic theater in a preface to his published plays: "When you emphasize *place* in the theatre, you drag down and limit and harness time to it. You thrust the action back into past time, whereas it is precisely the glory of the stage that it is always 'now' there" (xi). Cinema, the mediated form rooted in photography, offers a "there" and "then" quality, but theater's "here" and "now" emphasizes immediacy and focuses attention upon human interactions. The absence of scenery in favor of pantomimic action in *Our Town* earns dramatic significance precisely because the theme of the play is that people don't notice and cannot see what is truly important about life while they're living it. Stripping everything away except the human figures points out beautifully that the only things that do matter are love and human relationships. There isn't a more moving scene in American drama than the final act in which George falls prostrate before Emily's "grave" on the stage floor.

The dramaturgy in the plays of Suzan-Lori Parks also dispenses with dramatic realism quite effectively and in complete concert with her dramatic message. In "Possession," one of several short essays that precede the published version of *The America Play,* she states,

> A play is a blueprint of an event: a way of creating and rewriting history through the medium of literature. Since history is a recorded or remembered event, theatre, for me, is the perfect place to "make" history—that is, because so much of African-American history has been unrecorded, dismembered, washed out, one of my tasks as playwright is to—through literature and the special strange relationship between theatre and real-life—locate the ancestral burial ground, dig for bones, find bones, hear the bones sing, write it down. (4)

The scene of *The America Play* is "[a] great hole. In the middle of nowhere. The hole is an exact replica of The Great Hole of History" (158). Realism validates an objective appreciation of events, but Parks argues in her dramas that no such experience exists. The void is the blank space upon which a new history is written because the old one is simply not useful or true. Even in her recent work, the "accessible" *Topdog/Underdog,* the apartment has largely been stripped of detail and the urban setting is relatively unimportant in the action that is, by virtue of the characters' names, Booth and Lincoln, fated to end with an obvious result. The fatality of the play leavens the possibilities of creating new histories and new identities with the inevitabilities of human urges to fall into old and familiar patterns.

Nothing is what it seems to be once it appears on a stage. A cigar may sometimes be a cigar, even to Freud, but onstage a cigar is never just a cigar. It is probably many things. The dynamics of the stage, of people watching other people from a certain distance, magnifies everything and endows all things with latent meanings. A door is not a door, but a portal, a gateway, a limit, a horizon, a barrier, a threshold, a rite of passage. It is everything except just a door. Realism as a style tries to curtail the play of meanings and connotations with an over-abundance of objects and images. The more that is visible, the more "full" the illusion is, the less "meaning" individual objects accrue. Film, quite clearly, can far surpass the realism possible in the theater, and it can produce that style in an effortless way. In the cinema, objects are just as important as human figures. In film everything is an object, and therefore a subject, whereas in the theater the environment serves to frame the action of a play around the human figures. Rudolf Arnheim observes, "In film inanimate properties are just as useful as the human actor to show psychic states. A broken windowpane may be as good as a quivering mouth, a heap of dead cigarette stubs as the nervous drumming of fingers. Once again the classification—so characteristic of film—of man as one among many objects is plainly revealed. The traces of human strivings are as visible on inanimate objects as they are on the body itself" (*Film as Art* 143). Indeed, the equivalence between animate and inanimate objects in film stems from the fact that projected images upon a flat screen are all the same.

Although theater takes the human body out of a worldly context, it presents that same body in full view of the spectator. Another aspect of seeing for one-self as opposed to seeing through the eyes of the camera has to do with whole-bodied performances. Actor Jim Dale told David Black in an interview, "I love the fact that on the stage you can control what you are doing with the full length of your body, whereas in film it's the director's medium" (Black 246). Obviously, film directors don't control an actor's legs or arms. What Dale clearly means, though, is that the director dictates what the audience will eventually see. An actor in film does not know what an audience will see on the screen after the film has undergone the editing process. Rarely does film capture the entire human figure. Most shots divide the body into segments from the neck up (close-up), from the waist up (medium shot), from the knees up (medium-long shot), and entire body (long shot). Of course, on the stage the body is on full display at all times. What a shame, then, that most plays waste such a splendid opportunity to show off the body in favor of chitchat for two hours. The most exciting theatrical events are those in which the human body undergoes an experience and transfor-mation in the dramatic action. Ian McKellen's performance as Edgar in *Dance of Death* in 2001 became extraordinary when he rose from his chair and performed a little jig. The whole-bodied nature of the dance is something not regularly seen in film and, onstage, reveals the whole human form in motion. Helen Mir-ren's seduction of David Strathairn as Kurt similarly revealed the thrilling the-atricality of seeing the woman manipulate her man in complete and full-bodied view. As a kind of pretense, her actions created a play within the play and mag-nified the onstage drama with daring excitement.

Unlike in films, too, the theater frequently casts actors as nonhuman subjects such as animals. Bert States has written well about the phenomenon of the dog onstage and suggests that playwrights and producers consider wisely before allowing them before an audience.[6] A. R. Gurney's play *Sylvia* concerns the relationship between a middle-aged man and his new canine acquisition, but the dog is played by a young woman. Sarah Jessica Parker originated the role and clearly was responsible for much of the play's success. In a film, of course, the realistic prerogative would take over and a nationwide talent hunt would find the most personable dog, a trainer would give it direction, and take after take would capture the spontaneous cuteness of the animal. A big star, perhaps even Sarah Jessica Parker, would perform the voice-over for the pooch. But such a move would ruin Gurney's witty satire. The play shows the man in a midlife crisis, the dog is a substitute for a younger woman, and he indeed goes a little crazy and conducts a kind of love affair with the dog. With an attractive and charismatic woman cast in the part, the duality of what's going on is always visibly apparent and the man's obsession is both more comic and completely understandable. The fact that Parker later blossomed into stardom with her HBO series *Sex and the City* makes the point of the play even more explicit.

In an entirely different vein, Tina Howe casts the young boy in her play *Birth and After Birth* with a very hairy older man. Again, a movie would cast the perfect child actor in the part and, in so doing, would ruin the play. The play scathingly critiques modern parenting, and the casting highlights the absurdity of the play. The parents in the drama completely lose themselves with an obsessive infantilizing of their child. The older man in the child's role visually reinforces the fact that the child will grow up and leave and that, in fact, the parents need to plan their own obsolescence. It's probably wise not to have a small child or a dog onstage, but in these two cases, the humor and serious themes of each play would not even be apparent with realistic casting.

Mere liveness does not distinguish the theater; theater must be bigger than life. How often is "theatrical" used as a pejorative term to describe human behavior? "Histrionic" derives from the Latin word for "actor." People become insufferable when they act histrionically offstage. The dynamics of stage expression, however, require a histrionic presence pitched to bridge the gulf between the stage and the audience. The "theatrical" person is so because of gestures too large, a voice too loud, and expressions too grand for normal, intimate dinner-party conversation. But within the context of the stage, the same mannerisms might be perfectly suited for the occasion. Drama deals with emotions that exceed the normal boundaries of everyday life. An audience wants to see those things that it may have felt before but not necessarily felt to the degree to which such experiences are presented onstage. Stage drama puts the actor in a vulnerable position. To recall the whole-bodied nature of theatrical performance already discussed, a good drama places that body at tremendous emotional and psychic risk to the extent that the audience sees the effect of the drama played out upon the actor's body. Frequently, I've heard the amateur actor stand up for a character's rights with something such as, "My character wouldn't do that," or, going one step further in protecting the sanctity of the character, saying, "I'm not comfortable doing that." All such responses fit into the comfy confines of what is "normal," "realistic," and "acceptable" behavior. But why should a dramatic performance be comfortable? The audience is comfortable sitting in its chairs. I don't think that it wants to see an actor who also looks comfortable. The actor must submit to that which is uncomfortable, psychologically speaking, or how else does that actor justify a position on the stage and the attention of the collective audience?

A theatrical performance begins and ends with the courage of each individual actor. The actor is a surrogate for the audience, standing in for it and doing that which it is afraid to do.[7] Actors address the hopes and fears of the audience and submit to uncomfortable tasks in order for the audience to live vicariously through them. They have no other reason to be on the stage. They must embrace those sitting near and far from them in order for all to identify with their performances. An audience expects to see grand gestures, deep emotions, and heightened physicality during a performance, and the actors must find a way to satisfy such demands. The best plays demand that actors fully commit to actions that evoke powerful emotional experiences: grief in Donald Margulies's *What's Wrong with This Picture?*; mourning in Paula Vogel's *The Baltimore Waltz*; falling in love in Tina Howe's *Coastal Disturbances,* in which Leo and Holly spin faster and faster around each other on the beach; confession in the assaulting monologues of Wallace Shawn's *The Designated Mourner*; confrontation between father and daughter in Romulus Linney's *Childe Byron*; violent sexuality and sadism in Maria Irene Fornes's *The Conduct of Life*.

Theater radiates from the actor onstage, but the stage director is the person in the theater most responsible for assuring the success of a theatrical event. The visionary modernist Adolphe Appia defined directing as "the art of projecting into space what the dramatist has been able to project only into time" (57). Like Molière's M. Jourdain, who joyfully discovers that he has been speaking prose all his life, playwrights, practitioners, and critics now realize that the best theater has always been a visual medium. By focusing on the dynamics of human figures moving and speaking in time and space on a stage in view of an audience, directors discover the riches of the poor theater and encounter an original vein of theatricality as powerful as any movement in history. Ultimately, then, the director balances poetry and painting, deals with the coexistence of objects onstage as well as the consecutiveness of the dramatic text, deals with simultaneous events in three-dimensional space as well as the sequence of events that happen in the course of time. Labels such as "realism" or "symbolism" or "expressionism" are shortcuts at best and obfuscations at worst for a true understanding of a work. Referring explicitly to painters in *Art and Visual Perception,* Rudolf Arnheim says that "[t]he utterances of artists make it clear that they think of 'style' simply as a means of giving reality to their image. 'Originality' is the unsought and unnoticed product of a gifted artist's successful attempt to be honest and truthful, to penetrate to the origins, the roots, of what he sees" (138). The director exploits the theatrical medium to bring life to a drama. Authentic style results from an honest engagement with material. Style, then, is not something applied, extrinsic to the work, but something discovered as intrinsic in the process of staging the event.

Film directors, unlike their theatrical counterparts, usually receive top billing as "authors" of the film, and the screenwriter(s), cinematographers, designers, and actors fall in line underneath. In theatrical practice, the playwright gets the top position, usually followed by the director and the designers and actors in descending tiers. In the case of theater, there might be a more productive way to look at relationships between the creative team that escapes the phallic hierarchy of tradition. Such repositioning begins with directors reimagining their responsibilities and broadening their perspectives. Robert Edmond Jones once spoke of the designer as "an artist of occasions" (*Dramatic Imagination* 69), but I'd like to co-opt his term to state that directors are also true artists of occasions because they are responsible for staging an event which takes place in a certain time and space. The stage director hosts a gala event with responsibilities that include seeing that everything runs smoothly and, more importantly, that everyone has a good time. The generous director considers the needs of the paying audience as well as the working actors, designers, and technicians. How do audience members perceive the show? Are they getting enough information? At the right time? Is the pacing acceptable? Too fast? Too slow? Are the words audible? Is the work worth their time? Terry McCabe's recent book *Mis-directing the Play* (2001) poses many useful correctives to current abuses in contemporary theater, but he interprets the job of the director entirely too narrowly. His clarity and conviction are impossible to miss when he states, early on, "the object of directing is rather to make clear the director's best sense of what the playwright had in mind" (8). The director as host faces many obligations in addition to appeasing the playwright. The voice of the playwright, certainly an important one, can't be the only voice that the director hears. A director's concern for the event exceeds that for the text. By addressing the needs of others—everyone involved, not exclusively the playwright—the director creates an environment for a successful event.

The director as host sparks a great party to help guests forget the workaday world and to enjoy the holiday spirit of theatrical escape. Fabian, the accomplice of an original party animal, Sir Toby Belch, speaks as a theater critic in *Twelfth Night* when he comments upon the action in that comedy: "If this were played upon a stage now, I could condemn it as an improbable fiction" (3.4.128–29). Why do we still today too often behave as neoclassicists who demand that action be probable and necessary? Is verisimilitude truly virtuous? Should art really be less interesting than life? Shouldn't it be the other way around? Shouldn't we benefit from surprises at the theater? Shouldn't it really be like a party, an evening with friends, and an event from which we emerge refreshed, capable of seeing the world with new clarity and energy? Theater can stimulate and delight the senses of an audience and create experiences that heighten the nuance, complexity, and ambiguity of real life. Then it can stop wearing black and have some fun again and get out from the shadows of film. Theater has been done regularly in the dark only since the advent of gas and electric lighting in the late nineteenth century. Instead of staring in blind and blank wonderment at the cloaked illusion, it is time to draw back the curtain and study a few tricks behind it.

3
A Vicious Cycle at Sea

Fog, fog, fog, all bloody time. You can't see vhere you vas going, no. Only dat
ole davil, sea—she knows!

—Eugene O'Neill, *"Anna Christie"*

Eugene O'Neill didn't like the theater very much, but he liked the cinema even
less. Ironically, among all the screen adaptations of his work, he truly loved John
Ford's *The Long Voyage Home*. First of all, the movie derived from four humble
one-acts written very early in the playwright's career, not from such later splashy
successes as *Strange Interlude, The Great God Brown,* or *Mourning Becomes Electra.* Second, although O'Neill always insisted that theatrical productions follow
his texts faithfully, Ford's film hardly paid slavish attention to the source material. Surprisingly, perhaps, in this case O'Neill responded very enthusiastically
to the liberal treatment given his little plays. After reading the script in advance
of the film's release in 1940, O'Neill congratulated screenwriter Dudley Nichols
in a letter which included the following statement: "I believe a picture of a play
should concentrate on doing those things which the stage cannot do. Then a balance can be struck in which the picture medium brings fresh drama to the play
to take the place of the stuff which belongs to the stage and cannot be done as
well in pictures" (*Selected Letters* 503). The fact that O'Neill clearly loved the
film yet felt entirely unthreatened by its success suggests that he believed the two
enterprises were entirely separate. A synergistic relationship between theater and
film, O'Neill says, works to strengthen the understanding and independence of
both forms.

Comparing *The Long Voyage Home* to the source plays from which the movie
is taken builds a case for the unique properties and capabilities of drama. It is
commonplace to assume that film adaptations "open up" a drama with a more
expansive treatment of space and time. Surprisingly, Ford's film defies that expectation and, in the process, shows what O'Neill's little plays do. And thus
the source plays of the fine Ford film, all written when O'Neill was a relatively
unknown talent, reveal the early signs of later techniques perfected in a mature masterpiece such as *The Iceman Cometh* and strive to transcend theatrical
limitations.

In his letter to Nichols, O'Neill did not elaborate further about those things on film "which the stage cannot do," or which aspects of theater "cannot be done as well in pictures." Several years later he maintained that the "talkless parts" were the high points of the film for him. That he liked it at all is truly remarkable. Although America's only Nobel Prize–winning playwright liked the *idea* of theater and film very much, the practice of the commercial Broadway "Show Shop" and popular Hollywood claptrap appalled him. As early as 1924, he announced, "I don't go to the theatre because I can always do a better production in my mind than the one on stage. I have a better time and I am not bothered by the audience" (qtd. in Cargill, Fagin, and Fisher 112). While he regularly failed to attend the opening nights of his own plays, he did work on productions during their rehearsal periods. He had nothing whatsoever to do with the film adaptations of any of his plays and regarded Hollywood as merely a source of income. Even this detached demeanor, however, did not come without regrets. O'Neill tried to barter the sale of *Mourning Becomes Electra* for $150,000, the price for which he was apparently willing to suffer the consequences of having to endure the film. In his letter to Theresa Helbrun in 1944, O'Neill appealed to her memory of the play's stage triumph at the Theatre Guild: "Do we want to let Hollywood debase (as it must, being at heart, even with the best intentions, merely a commercial mob amusement racket) the *Mourning Becomes Electra* in our memories, the achievement that had great significance, whereas the picture will have none?" (*Selected Letters* 558).[1] About the filming of *The Hairy Ape,* O'Neill expressed further regrets about relinquishing the rights to one of his very favorite plays and fondest memories in the theater: "I didn't really want to sell because I knew no one in Hollywood had the guts to film *my* play, do it as symbolic expressionism as it should be done, and not censor it into imbecility, or make it a common realistic stoker story. . . . So when I tell you *I am not* going to see the film—nor read one word written about it—nor even ever admit that it exists, I sure mean it!" (*Selected Letters* 558).

The films of *The Hairy Ape* (1944) and *Mourning Becomes Electra* (1947), the last movie of an O'Neill play made during the author's lifetime (1888–1953), immediately succeeded *The Long Voyage Home.* Prior to those films, according to John Orlandello, "There is no indication that O'Neill ever saw any of the films made from his works during the 1930s—reports from friends and reviews of the films dissuaded him from seeing them" (12). Anyone who has seen the execrable film version of *Strange Interlude* (1932), starring Norma Shearer's amazing eyebrows, can surely empathize with the playwright's position. O'Neill liked very much the silent film version of *"Anna Christie"* (1923), but he hated the idea of Garbo in the role of her first talkie in 1930 and her immortal opening line: "Gimme a whiskey—ginger ale on the side. And don't be stingy, baby." Garbo had none of the hardness of Blanche Sweet in the earlier adaptation, the sea as fate lost all its significance, and the love story wallowed the whole thing into a happy ending, the very ending that O'Neill had wanted to avoid in the play, but that had always plagued interpretations of the work.

By contrast, O'Neill claimed to his daughter, Oona, that *The Long Voyage Home* was "an exceptional picture with no obvious Hollywood hokum or sentimental love bilge in it" (*Selected Letters* 513). He even owned a 16mm print so that he could watch the movie at home whenever he wished. The film, however, did not copy the stage play. O'Neill, always previously a stickler for theatrical productions adhering to his scripts and stage directions as closely as possible, accepted the changes to accommodate a new medium. Addressing the challenge of adapting O'Neill's plays to the screen, Kurt Eisen eloquently states, "To capture the spirit of an O'Neill play in cinematic form requires not a literal fidelity to the original stage version but a comparably defiant attitude towards easy formulas— to film against the grain of Hollywood, just as O'Neill always tried to write against the prevailing norms of Broadway—including the very norms his own work helped to establish" (120). A director must recontextualize the radical in one medium as radical in a new medium. Distilling the essence of the source work, different means gain different ends.

The Long Voyage Home achieves narrative coherence by tying together four disparate one-acts of the sea: *Bound East for Cardiff* (1914), *In the Zone* (1917), *The Long Voyage Home* (1917), and *The Moon of the Caribbees* (1917). O'Neill didn't write the plays consecutively or envision them, initially at least, as part of a set. They were all produced separately. Some of the individual plays feature the same characters, but each play carries its own independent action. *Bound East for Cardiff* was the first O'Neill play ever to be performed, and it concerns the last dying moments of an injured sailor, Yank, and the tender ministrations of his friend, Driscoll. *In the Zone* is a well-crafted melodrama that leads to a surprise ending as it follows the heartbreaking story of Smitty, whose wife left him because he could not quit drinking. *The Long Voyage Home* features the struggles of the Swede Olson to leave the sailor life behind and return to his native homeland. Finally, *The Moon of the Caribbees* once again depicts Smitty's loneliness, but this time in counterpoint to the drunken and celebratory spirits of his less refined shipmates. Stylistically and artistically, each play is distinct as well. While *In the Zone* has the most straightforward narrative, the last play has virtually no plot and succeeds through its creation of atmosphere, its panorama of ensemble characters, and its evocation of a mood. O'Neill himself felt that the former drama is representative of the best plays of the past, while *The Moon of the Caribbees* contains elements of drama's future.[2] Despite the differences within the plays, they were first grouped together on a single bill in 1924 at the Provincetown Playhouse under the direction of James Light with the title *S.S. Glencairn,* the name of the tramp steamer on which the sailors serve. The plays have been presented several times since then with that title. O'Neill, too, later referred to the plays as his Glencairn Cycle and envisioned an O'Neill repertory producing it regularly.

Dudley Nichols's screenplay incorporates all the plays in one central action: Olson's last voyage, a dangerous transatlantic crossing from the United States to London on a merchant marine vessel, the *Glencairn,* loaded with ammunition to aid the war effort against the Nazis in 1940. The time is updated from the First World War to the next, and, whereas only *In the Zone* takes place during wartime, Ford's film fits entirely within the context of the war environment. The order of the plays is changed such that action begins with *The Moon of the Caribbees,* followed by *Bound East for Cardiff* and *In the Zone,* and ending with *The Long Voyage Home.* The action remains episodic, and the shift from one play to the next is still detectable, but there is a sense of movement as the sailors go from enjoying liberty, anchored in the West Indies (the setting for *Moon*), to crossing the ocean (*Bound East for Cardiff* and *In the Zone*), to reaching port in blacked-out London (*The Long Voyage Home*).[3]

Several episodes in the screenplay depart from the source material to bridge the action from one play to the next and to reinforce thematic significance and structural integrity. I'll outline many of those changes and additions below, but a couple deserve special mention here. The well-educated Smitty is killed by German aircraft in the movie, and the refrain "Smitty's going home" resonates with the preceding death of Yank (from *Bound East for Cardiff*) and also amplifies the title of the film and the decision to put *The Long Voyage Home* in the anchor position among the four plays. The film ends quite differently than the one-act. In O'Neill's play, unscrupulous money-grubbers drug the sailor Olson and crimp him aboard the *Amindra.* Once again, Olson fails to get home. In the film, Olson's shipmates save him, but sailors from the *Amindra* knock Driscoll out in a fight and press him into service to replace Olson. The final scene shows one of the *Glencairn* shipmates reading a headline in a newspaper proclaiming that a German U-Boat has sunk the *Amindra* and that the entire crew has been killed. In the play, Olson says that he wants to go home, yet he continually makes decisions that force him back out to sea. He tries to stop himself from drinking, but he finally agrees to a drink anyway in spite of past experiences. The irony rests entirely with the individual. In the film, Olson and Driscoll function as interchangeable parts. Either one will serve the ship. It doesn't matter which one. Here, the irony of the film involves the social exploitation of these relatively "faceless" men upon whose backs war is waged and won.

The "talkless" parts of the film, gorgeously photographed by Gregg Toland, portray the sailors aboard ship and the ship in action. These moments would be impossible to achieve onstage: the *Glencairn* loading cargo in port; the gangplank raised and lowered; smokestacks belching steam; the ship leaving harbor; sailors battening down a tarpaulin; a violent storm at sea and Yank's fall from a ladder (a scene only alluded to in the play); Yank's burial at sea, with rear projections of the waves and whitecaps in the background and ocean spray drowning out almost all the words of the quick funeral service; the aircraft raid that kills Smitty (the viewer never sees the planes overhead—only the effects of the attack, such as bombs splashing in the water and an array of bullet holes from machine guns); Smitty's grieving family greeting the ship at the dock; sailors departing from the ship and walking down the gangplank for shore leave; sailors traipsing through the wet, dark streets of London looking for an appropriate watering hole; the men returning to their ship, broke, with no options left except to sign up for another tour of duty. While each play limits scenic space to a single area, the ability of the camera to film the sailors in time and space, to show them performing their work rather than merely reporting it, gives tremendous insight into the pathos of their struggle.

All of O'Neill's plays are written for a proscenium theater, and his detailed, often mocked, stage directions indicate various stage positions, including stage left and right, upstage and downstage. It is assumed that the audience sees the play "frontally." Yet the film exploits the fact that the camera can lead the viewer to multiple positions. From its opening, the film distinguishes the possibilities of stage and film action. In *The Moon of the Caribbees,* O'Neill presents a cross section of the ship as the focal point in the action. The ship is anchored off of an island, and throughout the action distant singing from that island can be heard. O'Neill places that island upstage, and his stage directions make clear that it is represented scenically on a perspective drop showing the horizon line: "In the rear the dark outline of the port bulwark is sharply defined against a distant strip of coral beach, white in the moonlight, fringed with coco palms whose tops rise clear of the horizon" (*Complete Plays* 1:527). The upstage area is only scenic space. If a figure were to stand against the backdrop, the illusion of the perspective would be ruined. All the action takes place on the downstage "boat." The film, on the other hand, faces no such restrictions. The opening sequence cuts between the native women on the shore, undulating to the rhythms of the music with the ship's outline in the distance, to the sailors on the *Glencairn,* looking back toward the island and restlessly responding to the sounds of the music and the expectations for the night. The wordless cutting between both locales builds tension beautifully in preparation for the eventual meeting of men and women on deck.

The camera's ability to achieve close-ups on the actors' faces also gives it a significant advantage over the stage at key moments. *Bound East for Cardiff* becomes very intimate once Driscoll decides to stay by the bunk of the dying Yank. O'Neill's stage directions concerning the dying sailor become similarly intimate: "A spasm of pain contracts his pale features. He presses his hand to his side and writhes on the thin mattress of his bunk. The perspiration stands out in beads on his forehead" (1:193). In a theater, who would actually see this stage picture? O'Neill describes something that is simply not visible to an audience from any appreciable distance. His directions orient to the printed page and a reading public.[4] In the film, however, those same directions are quite readable as the camera comes in within just a few feet of Yank. The perspiration on his face is visible; his pain is palpable as he writhes on the bunk. The perspective achieves such intimacy that the final moments leading to his death are painful to see. There is none of the detachment that a stage view mandates. The audience is with the men surrounding Yank. Similarly, in *In the Zone,* O'Neill solves the problem of intimacy by having Smitty turn his face to the wall as his shipmates read aloud his very personal letters. In the film, however, the camera cuts back and forth between the letter reader and a tight close-up of Smitty's tortured face as he hears the spilled contents. The proximity of the camera to the victims greatly intensifies both scenes.

Overall, however, much of the camera work in the film re-creates stage compositions, due to the fact that photographer Gregg Toland relied extensively upon a low-angle camera and a wide-angle lens. For the viewer, this creates the effect of having a good orchestra seat that lets one be close to the stage action and see it at ground level, and at the same time see the action radiate toward the wings on either side. There are a number of times in which Toland fits two whole-bodied actors within the same shot, while at the same time capturing the physical environment around them. In one particular moment, Smitty, after his humiliation below deck, stands in dark silhouette downstage and Olson appears slightly above him upstage. The shot frames both actors in their entirety. Whereas in the theater such a shot might emphasize the distance between the figures and the space around them, such a cinematic shot has an opposite effect: the figures fill up the screen. The entire film creates a claustrophobic sense of space as Ford fills up his shots with figures that often appear to be on top of one another. Oddly, for a movie that takes place mostly at sea, very few shots show the expansive ocean surrounding the ship. Instead, the camera emphasizes the cramped conditions under which the men lead their lives. In John Orlandello's *O'Neill on Film,* Peter Bogdanovich quotes John Ford: "We purposely kept it in confined space—that was what the story called for. Life on a ship *is* claustrophobic, but you get accustomed to it" (qtd. in Orlandello 100). The viewer gets accustomed as well to the experience that the camera creates.

The claustrophobic sense that the film develops deserves special comment because it is counterintuitive and contrary to the popular assumption of how films "open up" plays. My earlier discussion of the cutting between land and sea in the opening sequence of *The Long Voyage Home,* moving between shots of the women on the island and the men aboard ship, describes an unusual expansiveness. But that sequence of shots also emphasizes the distance between the men and women and the isolation of their lives. Ford could have depicted the vast spaces of ocean travel. O'Neill often conveys very romantic notions about the sea and what it represents as a kind of escape from life on land.[5] The essential claustrophobia of the movie is, itself, another important irony. The sea is often referred to as representing a kind of freedom, but in the film it is anything but that. In the film, Ford chose to shoot at close quarters to depict lives of confinement. The cramped conditions that Ford creates in his film are not possible on the stage.

While the film director and photographer decide how to break up space in accord with a vision of the picture, the playwright and director enjoy no such plasticity in a theatrical space. Whereas the film director works on a new canvas with each shot, the playwright and director must use one canvas for the entire play. O'Neill spreads the stage both visually and aurally in his sea plays. The number of distinct voices, dialects, and nationalities gives the director the chance to develop an interesting sound to the play and establish a rhythm akin to a musical score. Among the sailors are a Swede, a Russian, a Norwegian, an American, Englishmen with several different dialects, an Irishman, and a Scot. Speaking from various points on a stage creates a sonorous effect. Distinct voices divert attention in the theater to each respective position on the stage. In the film, of course, this is not possible, because all of the sound comes from a few speakers. Visually, O'Neill's stage spaces constantly balance groups of community with individuals in isolation or solitude. Whereas the film must cut from one part of a scene to another, the stage space accommodates both pictures simultaneously.

The first part of *Bound East for Cardiff* introduces the men of the ship, who are either returning to their bunks after a shift on deck or preparing for their next shift. Only after the men settle does Yank, the sailor who has had an accident, groan from an upstage berth. Having already shown some of the men immediately "fall asleep" in their bunks, the initial sequence establishes the link between sleeping and dying as normal human processes. The stage space telescopes once Driscoll kneels by his friend's bunk to stay with him until the end. The continual comings and goings of the crew as they go about the very necessary business of the ship counter the intimacy of this exchange. Yank's dying speeches border on the highly melodramatic, but the relative disinterest among the crew gives notice to the fact that while one life ends, the life of the ship must keep to a routine. The ship's bells, which signal changes in post, further remind an audience that the cyclical pattern of daily toil is ongoing. As he lies dying, Yank sees fog and then "a pretty lady in black." Both of these visions are rather formulaic tropes for death, but the visual reminder that life goes on elsewhere gives the scene poignancy. Yank's last muffled gasps are masked by the indifferent snores of men resting before the next bells will revive them for several more hours of work. The insignificance of Yank's death, the fact that he will not be missed dearly by anyone other than Driscoll, lends unusual dignity to the final moments of the play.

Similarly, both *In the Zone* and the play *The Long Voyage Home* present simultaneous scenes in which the loneliness and isolation of one character balance against the community building of a larger group. Smitty is the outcast in the former play and identified as such primarily because of his dialect. Educated with the "King's English," his speech, combined with his loner sensibility and perceived arrogance, separates him from his fellow shipmates. At the start of the one-act, he surreptitiously takes out a metal box from hiding and checks its contents. Unfortunately, another member of the crew sees him at it, and when Smitty steps out of the forecastle to stand alone on deck, the remaining shipmates begin to discuss his behavior. Because they don't like him, they run wild with an imaginative story that he might be a German spy. One man is assigned to watch Smitty through the doorway. O'Neill doesn't indicate whether or not Smitty is visible to the audience, but a contemporary production would do well to show him sitting quietly on deck alone with his own thoughts while his shipmates concoct a fantastic, though almost logical, story against him. Once Smitty returns to the forecastle, they bind and gag him and, fearful of finding a bomb, open his precious box. They discover, to their surprise, only personal letters from his fiancée. As described above, the film effectively cuts between a shot of the group reading the letter and a close-up of Smitty's face. Obviously, the close-up is not possible in the theater. Instead, in O'Neill's dramaturgy, the audience sees Smitty's complete, full-bodied physical reaction simultaneously with the words that are spoken. Once it becomes clear to the crew that Smitty is not guilty of espionage, they feel completely ashamed by the nature of the personal disclosures and slink away wordlessly to their bunks and finally turn off all lights at the very end of the play. The last image reveals Smitty alone with his grief, surrounded by the feigned sleeping rituals of the *Glencairn* crew.

Ostensibly, *The Long Voyage Home* begins as a farewell celebration for Olson before he boards another ship for his family farm in Stockholm. Olson's refusal to drink, out of fear that he will lose his resolve under the influence, makes him an outcast. While his friends abandon him, first at the bar and then in the adjoining party room, Olson sits on the side where he is joined by the prostitute

Freda. Olson's attempt to separate himself from his comrades is ultimately successful, albeit ironically so, and the unscrupulous plotters at Fat Joe's Bar drug his ginger beer, knock him out, and send him off with two roughs to the *Amindra,* a ship with a terrible reputation that is destined to sail below Cape Horn at the tip of South America. The visual separation of Olson from his friends shows dramatically the cost of his attempt to leave the sailor life. It explains as well, without saying so, why Olson has failed in every previous attempt to leave the sailor life behind. Visually, the stage picture makes clear his sense of unease and longing to be part of the group. The fact that he falls victim to outsiders, and not to his own lack of moral resolve, makes events in this short play more ironic.

Smitty, once again, is the lonely figure in the last of the *Glencairn* plays, *The Moon of the Caribbees.* There's really no plot at all in this short play, but it is the best of the bunch. Smitty continually holds himself aloof from the singing, dancing, drinking, and cavorting that happen on other parts of the stage. He remains lost in memories of the past, memories that are never fully articulated but clearly have to do with a woman. The Donkeyman is his only confidant, though his rather brutal suggestions about how to solve "woman problems" further alienate Smitty's refined sensibilities. The sound of singing and rhythmic chanting from the distant island adds yet another element of anxiety to the scene. Smitty finally says, to no avail, "I wish they'd stop that song. It makes you think of—well—things you ought to forget" (*Complete Plays* 1:530). As an atmospheric piece filled with moonlight, singing, music, dancing, and drinking, the play creates a space for reflection—certainly for Smitty, but by extension for the audience as well. The whirl of activity—dancing and drinking and celebrating—offers a means of escape that Smitty simply can't embrace. As the Donkeyman observes, Smitty is tied to memories of the land. Moments of stillness, when the ship is anchored and at liberty, allow private thoughts to creep aboard. When the Donkeyman sees another sailor and one of the native women moving off evidently for some privacy, he observes, "There's love at first sight for you—an' plenty more o' the same in the fo'c's'tle. No mem'ries jined with that" (539). The action of the play presents the sailor life as an escape from life left behind on land. Reflection, looking back, a product of deep feeling, the necessary exacted price for living in the world, causes heartache and despair.

Recurring patterns in O'Neill's sea plays raise questions about their authenticity as autobiographical works. O'Neill scholars commonly assume that the playwright wrote about what he knew from personal experience. Indeed, the number of fine biographies on the playwright all chronicle his adventures as a seaman and the pride he took in achieving "Able Bodied" rank.[6] The most colorful character in the *Glencairn* series, Driscoll, named after a sailor whom O'Neill befriended and who later killed himself, became the model for Yank in *The Hairy*

Ape. And the *Glencairn* plays were certainly not the only early plays drawn from O'Neill's life at sea. His first volume of published plays contained three one-acts staged in a sea environment. The Ahabish *Ile* (1917) concerns a captain's determined hunt for whales. *Beyond the Horizon* (1918), O'Neill's first Broadway success, takes place entirely on land, but the image of the unseen sea lifts the play from moribund realism. *Chris Christophersen* (1919) and the revised version that became *"Anna Christie"* both feature a land and sea division that casts "dat ole davil" sea as a kind of fate. In his later, more mature plays, such as *Mourning Becomes Electra* (1931) and *Long Day's Journey into Night* (1941), sailing and the sea represent an attempt to escape the fate of one's family, even as the characters remain rooted on land in their New England homes.

O'Neill's novel subject matter certainly challenged audiences to accept a muscular rawness on the stage that had not been seen previously. The visual dynamics of *The Hairy Ape,* for example, explored new realms of adventure as the ghostly Mildred, tired of life on the main deck with her wealthy crowd sunning themselves on deck chairs, determines to go below to the bowels of the ship to see "how the other half lives." Like the audience who watches her descent, Mildred is giddy with excitement about the prospect of a new experience, perhaps one she can record in her diary that evening before she pulls up her satin sheets. She wants to glimpse something new, and "the lower depths" serve as her amusement park. Fittingly, Yank crawls into the cage with the gorilla at the zoo at the end of the play because he has learned to see himself as a curiosity to be viewed from a distance. Just so, *The Hairy Ape* serves as something fresh for an audience constantly in search of filling its entertainment appetite. With all his sea plays, O'Neill provides representations of the mostly unseen and often ignored. His plays often fulfilled in the early part of the last century the politics of representation that have become so much more visible in our world today. After seeing *"Anna Christie"* in 1922, David Bone, who served in the British merchant marines, wrote to the *New York Times:* "I have seen Eugene O'Neill's play and I am greatly rejoiced that one has come who can show sailormen as we stand and the sea as something more than, than—a dressing room to the wings." Much like Yank, such men swelled with pride to see themselves at last onstage.

In fact, Ford's movie makes much more of this issue of representation than O'Neill's plays. After the titles at the beginning of the picture, a paragraph of text which Nichols wrote especially for the screenplay scrolls up the screen: "Men who live on the sea never change—for they live in a lonely world apart as they drift from one rusty tramp steamer to the next, forging the life-lines of nations." Given the representations of the seamen, the social statement is clear: the workers are being exploited, and while the conditions under which they work are inhuman, their toil makes riches possible. In the war effort depicted in the 1940 film, these simple and unheralded men perform truly heroic actions. That the film should highlight the heroism of ordinary men is perfectly fitting for the filmmaker who would next complete *The Grapes of Wrath* in the same year.

While the film begins with a social statement about the role of the unsung worker in a capitalist society and a paean to the workingman in aid of the war effort, the end of the film hints at a more existential note in keeping with O'Neill's visions in the plays. Once again, text scrolls to end the film:

> So men like Ole come and go
> and the Driscolls live and die
> and the Yanks and Smittys leave their memories—
> but for the others the long voyage home never ends.

The film actually does very little to explain why the long voyage "home" never ends. Ford's film does an excellent job of showing the sailors in their social situations, but those situations don't really lend themselves to the existential problem that O'Neill exploits in the stage plays. O'Neill is not particularly concerned with who forges the "life-lines of nations," but he is preoccupied with the individual's sense of worth, fate, and destiny. The film, quite brilliant in its own way, is ultimately interested in something quite different from what concerned O'Neill. Both Ford and O'Neill exploit their particular medium toward radically different ends. Ford makes a social statement with his film; O'Neill makes an existential one.

Here, the critics' preoccupation with O'Neill as an autobiographical artist leads to trouble. Instead of looking at the plays as a direct reflection of the writer's experience, it is important to turn that question around and determine what the chosen subject matter does for the dramatic message. What is the dramatic usefulness of the sea environment for O'Neill, such that he returns to it again and again in his plays? The sea plays allow him to articulate a vision of humanity that trumps any auxiliary social statement. Ford is surely right when he asserts that life on a ship is claustrophobic. Why, then, don't O'Neill's plays set aboard the *Glencairn* at sea produce a claustrophobic effect? Perhaps because that is not at all what interests him. For him, the ship does not produce a realistic image but serves a metaphorical purpose, one that is consistent with images perfected in his final great masterpieces. It's not, then, that O'Neill wrote what he knew, so much as the plays set at sea gave him an opportunity to write a certain kind of play to reflect his artistic vision. The same kind of argument could be said about Chekhov. Surely the great Russian dramatist knew more than life as it existed on dull, country estates. That estate, however, provided him with a means to express perfectly his dramatic landscape of life in the subjunctive mood ("If only I were in Moscow . . .").

The story surrounding the original production of *Bound East for Cardiff* spawned one of the great foundation myths in the American theater. It didn't hurt that Susan Glaspell, an outstanding writer and playwright herself, chronicled O'Neill's introduction to the American theater. Her book *The Road to the Temple* satisfyingly describes the opening-night performance of O'Neill's sea play. The Wharf Theatre, a shed really, at the end of a dock at Provincetown, provided the perfect environment for O'Neill's little play. The sound of the sea and water running underneath the floorboards augmented the performance. Edna Kenton, one of the founding members of the Provincetown Players, also described the natural beauty of the converted theater on the wharf:

> Old fish houses must have been constructed originally with some idea of a native theatre in mind—they are so native themselves to shore and sea. The whole seaward side of this one consisted of a great sliding door through which in the old days the fishermen's catch was thrown. Rolled back, it gave for backdrop Nature herself—the living sea. Through the holes in the floor—they were never mended—the lucky spectators watching the play at high tide could see and hear and smell and feel and almost taste the sea. In afternoons the passing boats moved in panoramic planes across it; at night their multi-colored lights drifted like slow fireflies between the audience and Long Point Light at the tip of Cape Cod. (Kenton 20)

All the above sounds lovely, but the pictures of the theater and the production photographs once it "transferred" to The Playwrights' Theatre on MacDougal Street in Greenwich Village convey none of the same romance. The famous picture of the Players rigging scenery for *Bound East for Cardiff,* including O'Neill on a ladder and George Cram (Jig) Cook holding a pole, is, however posed, a study in amateurism. Indeed, Cook's idea for a theater was always in the best spirit of amateurism. There is every reason to believe that the now-celebrated first production of an O'Neill play was pretty awful. O'Neill, by his own acknowledgment a terrible actor who suffered terribly from stage fright, played the part of the second mate. If that initial production could be seen with fresh eyes, opinion might pull it down from its lofty position in theater history. For good reason, O'Neill bolted from such a theater once he got an opportunity to do so.[7]

The difference between the nostalgic images of a legendary theater and the reality that must have existed is analogous to the expansive vision of O'Neill's early sea plays and the restrictions of their locales and the limitations of the characters within them. While the actual execution in performance in some of O'Neill's early plays may have been lacking, the vision for what they could be was not. This same tension is evident in the text of the plays themselves. O'Neill's first produced play was originally called *Children of the Sea.* He later changed it to a much better title that resonates with the pun on "bound." Certainly in *Bound East for Cardiff* the *Glencairn* is bound for port in Wales. Significantly, the ship is in transit, between one stop and another, moving, neither here nor there. O'Neill creates an image of a ship on a transatlantic voyage in the middle of the ocean, in play, between one stop and the next. Furthermore, once the ship does arrive in port, it will quickly reverse course and head back. So, in fact, there can be no final destination. But O'Neill also gets a second meaning from "bound," in the sense that the sailors are not free. They are confined to the ship and must go wherever it sails. The dying Yank utters his final lament: "This sailor life ain't much to cry about leavin'—just one ship after another, hard work, small pay, and bum grub; and when we git into port, just a drunk endin' up in a fight, and all your money gone, and then ship away again. Never meetin' no nice people; never gittin' outa sailor town, hardly, in any port; travelin' all over the world and never seein' none of it; without no one to care whether you're alive or dead" (*Complete Plays* 1:195).[8] To and fro, the cycle turns over endlessly. In the fog at sea, the *Glencairn* is a tiny ship in a vast ocean that dwarfs the human scale of existence. The ocean fosters the illusion of freedom, but the fog blankets the men and imprisons them as well.

O'Neill's characters try to escape from land and memories associated with events that happened in the past. In *The Moon of the Caribbees,* Smitty says to a companion, "We're poor little lambs who have lost our way, eh, Donk? Damned from here to eternity, what? God have mercy on such as we!" (1:538). The continual back-and-forth voyages of the ship, from port on one side of the world and then back to the other, are the means to escape memories of what has been left behind. When the ship anchors, the sailors have time for thought about such memories that the movement of the ship would otherwise cancel. The sea offers an escape from living life. It offers activity, but no purpose. This becomes clear in the only one of the plays that is set on land, *The Long Voyage Home.* Olson, the Swedish sailor, faces a Chekhovian predicament. He says that he wants to leave the sailor life behind and return to his family farm outside Stockholm, yet every time he gets drunk and spends all his available travel money, and must then return to the ship for yet another voyage. Chekhov's three sisters don't go to Moscow because they don't want to go; Madame Ranevskaya loses her orchard because she doesn't care for it. Olson, too, doesn't go home because he feels more comfortable saying he wants to go home than actually doing it. He prefers, actually, to get drunk and enjoy the sodden camaraderie of his shipmates.

The *Glencairn* thus functions similarly to Harry Hope's Last Chance Saloon in *The Iceman Cometh*. O'Neill fills that play, set entirely on land in a bar, with sea and water imagery. Larry Slade, the most articulate of the bar's patrons, describes the environment there to newcomer Don Parritt as "the Bottom of the Sea Rathskeller." He elaborates further, "Don't you notice the beautiful calm in the atmosphere? That's because it's the last harbor. No one here has to worry about where they're going next, because there is no farther they can go" (*Complete Plays* 3:577–78). The bar, like the ship, is a safe zone in which the men are completely free—free from worry, free from responsibility, free from family, free from friends, free from commitment, free from love, free from all pain, and thus free from all things that might make life worth living. The denizens of Harry Hope's each have their pipe dreams that someday they'll do the things they say they want to do and return to productive lives and intimate relationships. But, of course, those pipe dreams are smoky. The sailors, too, have the prospect of getting off the ship at each port and not returning to the sailor life. But, in most cases, they sign up for yet another tour of duty and the endless deferral of their own lives. In Ford's movie, one of the final setups is of the gangplank connecting dock to ship. One by one, the crew returns from leave, silent, downcast, somber, nursing hangovers, disheveled, perhaps disappointed that they must once again return to the *Glencairn,* having spent all their money, to sign up for another voyage just as the captain predicted they would before they left. This scene is quite similar to the start of the final act in *The Iceman Cometh,* in which the drunks return to Hope's bar, one by one, after having faced the fact that they do not have the courage to live outside the safety of the bar and the company it affords. Hickey, of course, was the one who set them on such a course for self-knowledge, arguing that they would find peace once they recognized and accepted their own wretchedness. At the end of act 1, Hickey, echoing Slade, advises them to "[l]et yourself sink down to the bottom of the sea. Rest in peace. There's no farther you have to go" (3:613). Hickey is wrong. The folks in the bar need their pipe dreams to give themselves the illusion of freedom, of choice, of a better life tomorrow. The sailors of the *Glencairn,* too, always have another port in the distance at which they can disembark and make a home. They instinctively know that they cannot stop, reflect upon their lives, and thus sink down to the bottom of the sea with self-knowledge. Their only choice is to get off or keep going. And so they sail the seas in repeated cycles, back and forth, back and forth, with hope in the distance, more frightening as it looms larger on the horizon.

These primitive little sea plays read as line drawings for the later masterpieces such as *The Iceman Cometh* and *Long Day's Journey into Night.* The imagery in them corresponds well to that found in the mature plays, and I greatly prefer these plays to the flashier ones of the 1920s, when O'Neill fully established himself as an experimental and, at the same time, highly successful dramatist. The sea plays don't rely upon expressionistic techniques, marionette figures, beating tom-toms, collapsing walls, historical figures, spotlights, masks, split personalities, choruses, interior monologues, big themes, or impressive technologies. They are simple plays, but it is their rudimentary nature that sets up the poetic stage beauty of an imagined world outside the theater. These simple one-acts play upon our emotions and perhaps ask us to look inside ourselves to that which we would otherwise keep hidden. They lack the pomp and theatrics of O'Neill's more experimental plays, and their simplicity is easy to dismiss, but these early plays provide the essence of the best O'Neill has to offer. Playwright Romulus Linney wrote recently about the neglect and derision O'Neill suffered at the hands of the New Critics in the 1950s, and countered their opinion with his own deep feelings about having acted in one of the sea plays. Looking back, Linney champions the adolescence in O'Neill's work, the very quality that filled his professors with scorn: "It was evidently impossible at Oberlin College to believe a genius also adolescent. But I really did like *The Long Voyage Home.* With everyone else deep in Jean-Paul Sartre and Albert Camus, it may have seemed clumsy and primitive. But I liked it. I respected it. I knew the hush it drew from its audiences, because I had stood on a stage and both heard that hush and felt the understanding that was behind it" ("O'Neill" 847). Even today, the academic world, preoccupied with theories and big ideas, blanches at the prospect of dealing directly with human emotions. Quite simply, that's where O'Neill lives and triumphs.

Scenes from another movie, Warren Beatty's *Reds* (1981), summarize everything I've tried to say in praise of the theater. The movie chronicles the life of John Reed, the journalist who is the only American buried in the Kremlin. Reed dabbled in the arts as well, and he, his wife Louise Bryant, and Eugene O'Neill were all at Provincetown when O'Neill's plays were first presented. The film depicts a rehearsal from another of O'Neill's sea plays, *Thirst,* which was the second O'Neill play performed after *Bound East for Cardiff.* Beatty as Reed, the director, and Jack Nicholson as O'Neill, the intense playwright, huddle together to watch Diane Keaton as Bryant deliver an important speech near the end of the play. The scene takes place on a lifeboat in the middle of the ocean with three surviving members of a shipwreck. O'Neill's stage directions describe the sun as "a great angry eye of God" (*Complete Plays* 1:51). He also specifies the fins of sharks circling around the boat ready to devour prey. A vast emptiness surrounds the little boat: "The sky above is pitilessly clear, of a steel blue color merging into black shadow on the horizon's rim" (1:31). As it was in real life, the actual stage space for the performance in the film is pitifully small. There is room only for the rowboat. There are no sharks. The ceiling of the Wharf Theatre, that vast expanse of blue sky, is only about as tall as Keaton. A variety of drapes masks the windows immediately upstage to highlight the playing area. In a play about heat from the sun driving the characters to madness, and despite the presence of a bright spotlight that hangs above Keaton and intrudes upon the action, the film somewhat inexplicably changes the reference from the sun in the play to the moon. Nicholson turns to Beatty in conference to make one important direction: "Tell them not to stand behind the moon!" Keaton reads her lines woodenly as "The Dancer," moves stiffly, and appears incapable of avoiding what little exists in the way of scenery. The film deftly presents this hilarious little scene in all its extreme tawdriness.

Beatty undoubtedly chose to represent this scene in his film because, although Reed didn't actually direct the play, Louise Bryant did act in it, and O'Neill himself played the mostly silent part of the Negro Sailor, the target of The Dancer's address.[9] Creative license put Reed in the director's chair and placed the passionate playwright beside him to watch the actress perform. Bryant, too, became O'Neill's lover for a short time, and so the film packages their ménage à trois in theatrical terms. But despite the comic nature of the scene, which shows all the slovenly talent and impoverished conditions of the amateur theater, the words of *Thirst* warrant listening to them. The Dancer, desperately going mad from the tropical heat, reaches out to the mulatto: "Look! I am offering myself to you! I am kneeling before you—I who always had men kneel to me! I am offering my body to you—my body that men have called so beautiful" (1:48). Just as The Dancer offers herself to the sailor, just as Louise Bryant offered herself to the playwright, the little play offers itself to the public. Detached observation allows an audience—watching in the dark—to see clearly the cost not simply to live, but to love and to commit deeply to choices and responsibilities. The *Glencairn* sailors stand in for the audience and perform their cyclical voyage as a sacrifice, the true gift theater offers. God have mercy on them.

4

There's Something about Mary

All the things we knew about each other, all the things that accumulate
through a lifetime, or through ten years, sat quietly, waiting for us, while we
lived politely and tried, like most people, to push them out of sight. Polite and
blind, we lived.

—Lillian Hellman, *Days to Come*

Lillian Hellman's *The Children's Hour* (1934) combines a highly melodramatic
plot, fueled by the malicious lies of an evil child, with sensational (for its time)
subject matter concerning an alleged lesbian relationship between two teachers at a private boarding school for girls. The playwright's biographer, Richard
Moody, registered no doubts about the root cause for the play's spectacular run
of 691 performances on Broadway: "And though audiences may have focused
on the evil machinations of the child as they watched the story unfold, it was
the advance gossip about unnatural love that drew them in" (38). While such illicit stuff may have been and may, curiously enough, continue to be the compelling interest of this play, I'm going to dig at the clunky dramaturgy, rather
than its subject matter, to discover hidden values. The limitations of the stage
cram all the action in a living room, and the loose talk there titillates the audience's imagination about what goes on elsewhere in more private spaces. The
play first incites and then indicts the audience as an obtrusive and prurient witness to the action. But, unlike in either subsequent film treatment of the drama,
what actually happens in these unseen places remains unclear. Whatever enduring strengths the play possesses lie within the undiscovered countries of doubt
and ambiguity.

William Wyler directed both film adaptations of the play that feature the
bad-seed child, Mary Tilford, but distort the relationship between Karen Wright
and Martha Dobie. Produced twenty-five years apart, the two films chronicle
the rise and fall of the Motion Picture Production Code (1930–66) as enforced
by the Hays office. Among its many moral duties, the Hays Code aimed to reduce sexual content in films. In his first effort to make a movie of Hellman's
play, Wyler could not even use the same title. *These Three* (1936) starred Merle
Oberon, Miriam Hopkins, and Joel McCrea and lesbian love transfigured into a
heterosexual triangle with the two women competing for Dr. Joe Cardin's affec-
tions. In this version, Mary accuses Martha of subjecting the students to sexual

situations in Martha's bedroom. In the end, Martha admits her feelings for Joe but sacrifices her love so that Karen can reunite with him at his favorite cake shop in Vienna. The Hollywood ending dissolves with a big kiss between a man and the woman who loves him. Twenty-five years later, Wyler produced and directed a second version in an attempt to be more faithful to the original material. The Hays Code, about to be replaced by the familiar ratings system, had weakened significantly by then and grown lax during the intervening years. *The Children's Hour* (1961) starred Audrey Hepburn and Shirley MacLaine and restored Martha's confessional speech to Karen and her subsequent suicide at the end. Martha names the exact charge leveled against them, propagated first by a not altogether comprehending Mary, as "sinful sexual knowledge of each other." Analyzing the later film, Joan Mellen declares, "*The Children's Hour* is most interesting from a sociological point of view, in showing the intolerance of a puritanical, self-righteous community which would drive a woman to death for her sexual preferences" (98). This critic, like most others, discards the film's container, form, and dives quickly into its meaty contents.

Despite the apparent differences between the two film treatments of the same material, remarkable similarities persist as well. Mary, the engine behind the plot, tells a different lie in each version, but it is a lie nonetheless and it produces the same effect. Doris Falk, taking Hellman's point of view, describes the play as "the ruin of two women by the spreading of a malicious lie" (29). For critics such as Falk, the question of whether Martha is or is not a lesbian is irrelevant. The fact that what Mary says may contain the seeds of truth is also irrelevant. It may not even be significant that Mary lies at all. As Joe says in the play, "Look: everybody lies all the time. Sometimes they have to, sometimes they don't. I've lied myself for a lot of different reasons, but there was never a time when, if I'd been given a second chance, I wouldn't have taken back the lie and told the truth. You're lucky if you ever get that chance" (52). What remains significant is the motivation behind the child's lie and Mary's adherence to her lie even after she has an opportunity to confess. Even more important is the powerful and influential adults' decision to believe the lie. The action asks the audience to consider under what conditions and circumstances a lie can become the truth. In defense of her interpretation of the play as being about a lie, Falk refers to a subsequent production: "In the 1952 revival Hellman directed the play herself, to point up the analogy between the destructive forces in *The Children's Hour* and those represented by McCarthy and the House Un-American Activities Committee" (42). Responding to that same production, quite unfavorably and without the political analogy, Eric Bentley boils the play down as either a story about heterosexual teachers accused as lesbians, in which case the enemy is a society who punishes the innocent, or a story of two lesbians accused of being lesbians, in which case the enemy is a society who punishes lesbians ("Lillian Hellman's Indiscretion" 74). He argues that Hellman couldn't play it both ways.

More than fifty years later, I'm convinced that the answers are not as easy as Bentley and probably most people presume and that the demand for a clear choice may be impossible and unknowable. Mandated, perhaps, by the times in which Hellman wrote it, the play's refusal to out itself highlights a fascinating aspect of this conventionally melodramatic play in comparison to the later film versions. Stanley Cavell, who greatly prefers *These Three* to the later, more "authentic" version, calls both films "studies of explicitness" in which the truth inevitably becomes clear and palpable (53). Whereas the films juxtapose the past with the present through edited flashbacks and move effortlessly from place to place from one shot to the next, the stage play confines the action to one setting in each of three separate acts. The films verify much of what remains offstage and purely speculative in the play version and piece the story together in a far more complex way than the stage can offer. Paradoxically, in this case, the sophistication of cinematic narrative makes a complex story far more palatable and digestible (in Bentley's terms). Everything is solved; no mysteries remain. Things don't come to light in the same way in the play, which remains untidy, unresolved, and uneasy. Whether the play is about lesbians, or heterosexuals, or the effects of a lie, the primitive stage implicates the viewer as a subject and improves the telling of the story by leaving a lot to the imagination.

Hellman's stage play offers neither the shifting scenes from bedroom to living room, interior to exterior, nor the juxtaposed action in remote locales that the films provide. The variety of tracking and point-of-view shots as well as close-up and long shots that the camera makes possible is completely foreign to the theater. The films are able to cut quickly from scene to scene, alternate temporal chronology, and pack in needed exposition. By contrast, the stage play is a crude piece of work. Hellman's play, very typical of its era in form, might still be considered as a kind of Platonic model for what many people think of when they conjure the idea of a play.[1] The audience sits in a fixed position and watches the condensed action of the story unfold before it. The three-act drama introduces the problem in the first act and sets up the action; it reaches a crescendo at the end of act 2 and resolves at the end of the final act. A living room is the essential setting for almost all of Hellman's plays: *Days to Come, The Little Foxes, Watch on the Rhine, Another Part of the Forest, The Autumn Garden*. Richard Moody regards "an elegant room" as Hellman's favorite setting (47). Act 1 of *The Children's Hour* takes place in the living room of the Wright-Dobie School, act 2 shifts to the living room at Mrs. Tilford's house, and act 3 returns, several months later in the fall, to the school again.

What does this pervasive setting allow Hellman to do? Not to overlook the obvious, a living room is generally a big room, one that can easily fill the entire width of a proscenium opening and provide many seating options (couch or sofa, maybe two; love seat; window seat; reading chair; straight chair; settee) and opportunities for people to talk. A play, of course, unlike a film, relies upon dialogue in which characters voice their problems and usually solve them at the end. Not only does the living room facilitate dialogue, but this room in a house is a public space that encourages free and open conversation. It does not seem unnatural, then, for the audience to "overhear" the remarks that are made in such a room. Finally, as an open, public space in the house, the living room contains access to other rooms in the house as well as to the outside. A "stage" living room generally sports at least three entrances to the room and thus supplies a logical means for scenes to change from moment to moment. Dramaturgy revolves around entrances and exits, and so a production puts a great deal of care into determining the precise location of and timing for various entrances. Typically, a box-set drama has at least one entrance at stage left and right, and a third upstage. Characters make entrances to the living room from the "outside" through the offstage "foyer," as well as from other rooms in the house (upstairs, other parts of the house, bedrooms, an outside veranda, the kitchen). The audience watches characters come and go to discuss their problems and fully expects a resolution to those problems at the end of two hours or three acts, whichever comes first. Hellman does nothing to upset such an expectation.

Hellman's preference for "an elegant room" provides a helpful clue about how to read *The Children's Hour.* Act 2, set at Mrs. Tilford's house, is the only scene that presents such a room. Mrs. Tilford wields power and authority as the moral conscience of the community. Karen Wright and Martha Dobie, on the other hand, are young outsiders who have transformed an old, dilapidated farmhouse (a not too elegant living room) into a vibrant school, the fulfillment of their dream and the product of intense hard work. As Joe tells Mrs. Tilford, "They've worked eight long years to save enough money to buy that farm, to start that school. They did without everything that young people ought to have. You wouldn't know about that. That school meant things to them: self-respect, and bread and butter, and honest work. Do you know what it is to try so hard for anything? Well, now it's gone" (49–50). The state of the living room, as described in the stage directions in the final act, reflects Mrs. Tilford's aggression against the two women: "It is not dirty, but it is dull and dark and uncared for" (58). The progression of scenes goes from the farmhouse school in full swing, to Mrs. Tilford's house, then back to the deserted main room of the school, and marks the powerful against the powerless, the haves against the have-nots. Dramatizing the elegant living room as the seat of power, Hellman portrays how the inhabitants of such a space came by such power and the means that they use to hold onto it and perpetuate it.

The play's plodding movement from one living room to another reflects the dispersal of energy and interest among the primary characters. This makes the play's message difficult to locate. Mary, for example, incites the action in the play, dominates the first two acts, and flaunts an impressive range of bad behaviors: she gets the featured entrance in the opening scene when she arrives late for class, she lies outrageously, she flies into hysterics and faints, she receives punishment from her teachers and vows revenge to her roommates, she blackmails one of them to help her, she beguiles her grandmother and concocts a story on the fly to escape from the school permanently. For a young actress, it's very good to be the bad girl. But after catalyzing all the catastrophic events in the play, Mary disappears from the action and does not appear in the final act. The old movie, at least, metes deserved justice. Margaret Hamilton, the Wicked Witch from Oz, plays the part of Mrs. Tilford's maid, Agatha, in *These Three* and finally silences Mary's indignant protests by slapping her hard across the face. Such retribution is unthinkable today in our time of enlightened ideas about corporal punishment, but it is a satisfying and well-earned moment in the film.

Mary hands off the baton driving the play to Mrs. Tilford once she whispers in her grandmother's ear about what's been happening at the school. After she has run her leg of the race, gotten things started, Mary drops out to allow an adult to take over and finish the job. Mrs. Tilford makes the fateful decision to believe what she has heard, and she calls all the parents to tell them about the school and advise them to remove their children from such a perverse environment. The future of the school hangs in the balance until, halfway through the play, at the end of act 2, scene 1, Mrs. Tilford picks up the phone and begins to dial her friends: "This is Amelia Tilford. I have something to tell you— something very shocking . . ." (40). Curtain.

Finally, Martha and Karen, the victims in the play, dominate the final act. Karen breaks up with Joe and Martha confesses her love for Karen, but these scenes merely react to preceding events. In the previous act, the three of them storm the gates of Mrs. Tilford and demand answers with indignant protestations. The problem with the third act's "big scenes" is that the audience has seen nothing of Karen and Martha's relationship to judge what's at stake. By contrast, *These Three* begins with the women on college graduation day and shows them together throughout the first several scenes in that movie. Ironically, the movie version that had to present the women in a heterosexual love triangle shows them as a viable and loving lesbian couple much more effectively than both the stage play or the more "authentic" 1961 film.[2] In the play's final act, Martha tells Karen that she's always loved her, but there has been no previous scene exploring the nature of that relationship. Even Martha's suicide takes on a passive role. She says that she feels dirty, and then she kills herself. Again, *These Three* shows Martha actively exposing the lie against them and willfully sacrificing herself for her best friend whom she loves. Certainly, the Hollywood happy ending in the 1936 film is somewhat nauseating and contrived, but it is also quite pleasing in terms of its dramaturgy, whereas Martha's suicide in the serious play seems made up and depressing to boot.

Despite Judge Brack's curtain line in *Hedda Gabler* that "People don't *do* such things!" male and female characters have killed themselves at the end of plays throughout theater history, and particularly well and often at the end of the nineteenth century and beginning of the twentieth. Even Chekhov, that master of irony and nonaction, had a hard time giving it up, finally choosing merely to parody gunplay in *Uncle Vanya*. Martha's suicide seems like a particularly tired dramatic cliché. Hedda, by contrast, gets to play with her father's pistols and prepare the audience for what she might do with them throughout the play. As for Martha, where does she get the gun? If I were the parent of one of the children at the Wright-Dobie School, I'd be much more worried about loaded firearms in the house than any supposedly sordid lesbian affair. At least the movie had the good sense to change her method from a gun to a hanging rope. The sequence of shots around Martha's death and the rise in the music are all deftly executed. The shadow of the rope, brilliantly filmed by Gregg Toland, creates a poignantly devastating moment. Still, I couldn't help wondering about Martha and her habit of keeping a good bit of hemp around. Judging by the knots in the rope, too, she'd learned well how to tie a hangman's rope (all this before the Internet!). In the end, I attribute my cold reactions to the fact that the melodramatic ending seems unmotivated and, I think, unnecessary according to the dictates of the plot.

The fatal gunshot would seem to end the play, yet a coda follows. Mrs. Tilford, having discovered the truth about Mary's lies, arrives at the door to set things right and make amends. She also unlocks the entire play as she emerges as its tragic character. Having made a terrible decision and wielded her authority to bring about the ruination of the women's lives and the destruction of the school, Mrs. Tilford realizes her error and returns as a completely remorseful woman: "I didn't come here to relieve myself. I swear to God I didn't. I came to try—to try anything. I knew there wasn't any relief for me, Karen, and that there never would be again. [. . .] Take whatever I can give you. Take it for yourself and use it for yourself. It won't bring me peace, if that's what's worrying you" (76). Regarding her granddaughter, Mrs. Tilford resolves not to send her away but to keep her close as part of her own unending punishment: "Whatever she does, it must be to me and no one else" (77). Mrs. Tilford suffers the most as the character most responsible for the disaster. The Fool says to Lear, "Thou should'st not have been old till thou hadst been wise" (*King Lear* 1.5.41–42). Powerful and very well respected within her community, Mrs. Tilford uses all her authority in service of a bad decision, and the results prove devastating. Joe tells Karen in *These Three*, "What she [Mrs. Tilford] says pretty much goes around here." Film critic Brett Elizabeth Westbrook astutely observes that the play is much more about issues of power than it is about whether or not the women are lesbians. According to Westbrook, the play is about "the ability of those in power to make a lie into the truth, to simply make it so because they have money and social standing." To claim Mrs. Tilford as a true Shakespearean tragic character obviously stretches the point beyond credulity. She's not King Lear, but a supporting character that upholds the point of view of the audience and serves as its surrogate. If the play is about power, it is ultimately about the audience's power as a witness to a dramatic event.

The play breaks open in the crucial second scene of act 2 in which Joe, Martha, and Karen interrogate Mary about what she says that she saw at the school. Under pressure, Mary lies that she spied on Karen and Martha through the keyhole in Martha's room. Triumphantly, Martha reports that there is no keyhole in her room and that therefore Mary could not have seen anything. By analogy, the audience sees the play through the keyhole of the proscenium arch and the missing fourth wall. Realism is a performance style that refuses or pretends not to recognize that an audience observes the event in silent darkness. Mary's lie amplifies the voyeuristic performance dynamic of this style. An earlier first-act quarrel between Martha and her aunt, Lily Mortar, provides yet another example of this type of play-within-a-play metatheatricality. During their argument they discover two students listening to their conversation outside the upstage center door. Martha opens the door to catch them in the act, a gesture that mirrors the position of the audience located directly opposite, downstage center. The actors pretend that a wall covers the downstage opening. In this scene, Martha exposes her "audience" by opening an actual door. Mortar, in her supercilious manner, instructs, "Eavesdropping is something nice young ladies just don't do" (20). Eavesdropping and spying through a "keyhole" are exactly what an audience does when it watches a realistic play.

Just as the girls strain to see something they should not see, the play promotes desire to see that which cannot be seen. Whereas the films show everything and expose Mary's lie before she even tells it, the stage play always refers to illicit things that happen somewhere else just out of view. Mary levels an accusation against Karen and Martha that she doesn't even understand herself; she merely follows the reactions of Mrs. Tilford and heads down the path that seems most likely to reward her efforts. Mary's lies against the two women are not part of a calculated plot, but rather an improvisational fabrication designed to catch the imagination of her doting grandmother. Bragging to her roommates in an earlier scene, Mary confides, "I'll think of something to tell her. I can always do it better on the spur of the moment" (28). Mary may not understand the frank sexual nature of her accusations, but Mrs. Tilford, the staunch figure of strong community values, the surrogate for the audience, certainly anticipates them. Mary finally whispers to Mrs. Tilford what the two women did together, but the audience "hears" only synesthetically what she says by seeing Mrs. Tilford's shocked reactions. Quite likely, whatever Mary says ignites the imagination of the audience into conceiving a multitude of sexual acts that surpass what Mary actually describes. Under later questioning, Mary says that she saw the women "kissing or something," but that statement surely only veils the acts that she implants suggestively in the mind of Mrs. Tilford and, by extension, the audience. Jill Dolan, in her critique of realism, views the performance dynamic between Mary, Mrs. Tilford, and the audience in exactly these terms: "Whispering her description of the alleged sexual crime into the older woman's ear, Mary doesn't even understand herself, but the spectator, directed by Mrs. Tilford's response, is voyeuristically invited to imagine the horrors of a lesbian encounter. The scene, which is never named aloud, is unraveled for their disapproval, and for their prurient interest. In a climate of sexual repression, imagination breeds pornography" (46).

While Dolan uses the passage above as evidence against realism as a bankrupt style, I believe that implicating the audience in the action through the role of Mrs. Tilford creates the true moral force in the drama and saves it from being just another tawdry tale for amusement and titillation. The "climate of sexual repression" to which Dolan refers does not belong to the world of the play nor to the time period in which Hellman wrote it, but rather to Dolan's own time (the essay was published in 1990). Times have changed somewhat since then, and definitely since the play was first produced, and society has become much more tolerant of "alternative lifestyles," but I'm skeptical about human nature changing very much; people enjoy the exertion of power and control. Since most people feel helpless to control their lives, the illusion of power to control other people and feel superior, the temptation to hold sway over events, prove irresistible.

In the play, reacting to the rapid evacuation of all the girls from the school, but before she even knows the exact charge against her, Martha proclaims that "[a]n insane asylum has been let loose" (47). The films go to great lengths to focus on Mary's expressions which reveal a completely villainous child. Why does Mrs. Tilford not see what everyone else plainly does see? Pointedly, even in the play, Agatha, Mrs. Tilford's maid, sees through Mary from the beginning, although she can't divine the intent or consequences of the little girl's actions. A voice of common sense, Agatha says to her very early in the play, "You might pull the wool over some people's eyes, but—I bet you've been up to something again" (32). She implies that Mary has always performed similar stunts and that her sneaking home from school represents only the latest scheme. Agatha theorizes to Mrs. Tilford that Mary came home only to enjoy the fudge cake that is always baked for that night. In short, Agatha treats Mary as a child and underestimates her capacity for evil. Her view of Mary, too, is exactly the one the audience sees. Later, in the second scene of act 2, even Mrs. Tilford expresses doubts about Mary's story and admits that she may have been grievously wrong to slander the women. "I don't know," she says. "I don't know, any more" (55). Why, then, does Mrs. Tilford ultimately take Mary's side?

It is surely not because Rosalie Wells, blackmailed by Mary, backs up Mary's story with a tearful corroboration that rings completely false. Rather, Mrs. Tilford (and the audience) wants to believe Mary in order to sustain her own illusion of power. Mrs. Tilford enjoys playing the role of the protector, undoubtedly to mask her own reservations about Mary as a problem child. She feels responsible, and she wants to do something about it. By exercising her authority, influence, and social position, she can convince herself that she is doing something good for the sake of not just Mary but all the children in the school. She justifies her actions to Joe by saying simply, "I have done what I had to do. What they [Martha and Karen] are may possibly be their own business. It becomes a great deal more than that when children are involved" (49). Mrs. Tilford acts from a position of righteousness, but she warns Martha, ironically as it turns out, that her dogged pursuit of a public lawsuit for libel would be foolish. "I am an old woman, Miss Dobie," Tilford begins, "and I have seen too many people, out of pride, act on that pride. In the end they punish themselves" (50). This is indeed exactly what happens to Mrs. Tilford in the course of the drama. Lear-like, this old woman who has been the most influential woman in her community makes one foolish decision that destroys all the good she has done. She gives in to her vanity and her most base instincts and destroys herself as well as the two women.[3]

Pride, that great "tragic flaw" drawn frequently from grammar-school textbooks, takes down Mrs. Tilford, the scapegoat of the community; but the same temptations that entice her to act impulsively also thrust the audience into a similarly vulnerable position. Martha, indignant, upbraids the older woman: "Try to understand this: you're not playing with paper dolls. We're human beings, see? It's our lives you're fooling with. *Our* lives. That's serious business for us. Can you understand that?" (48). The title resonates with this passage. It doesn't refer to Mary and her cohorts spreading their nastiness around the stage. Mary, remember, disappears from the action after act 2. The title refers to the adults, led by

Mrs. Tilford, who behave like children when they elect to treat other people as if they were paper dolls, inanimate playthings which they move about to suit their moods. Just so, the audience indulges its passion to view the dramatic characters as paper dolls in a pop-up playhouse in order to maintain a comfortable position of power, control, and uncontested superiority.

Events take Mrs. Tilford and, by extension, the audience to the brink of a new reckoning by play's end. The action dramatizes the limits of seeing and knowing and suggests that judgments, in light of limited knowledge, must be withheld. The films focus on Mary as an obvious little villain, complete with facial tics and clear motivations that make her a readable character. The clarity of that portrayal makes her a melodramatic character whose "badness" is clearly visible and exposed for all to view. In the films, it's a matter of convention that anyone believes Mary at all. She's obviously, based on her actions, a hideous child with almost no redeeming features. She is much more enigmatic in the stage play, in which no one can diagnose her problem. Early on, Martha says about Mary, "She's had more attention than any other three kids put together. And we still haven't the faintest idea what goes on inside her head" (14). After Karen adds, "She's a strange girl," Martha continues, "There's something the matter with the kid" (14). Reacting to Mary's charges against her and Martha, Karen says again to Mrs. Tilford in act 2, "Your Mary's a strange girl, a bad girl. There's something very awful the matter with her" (51). Mary does behave very badly, certainly, but the cause of her troubles (no mother and father? the product of too much privilege? not enough love?) is not known nor knowable from the text.

Ironically enough, the play includes even the suggestion, voiced by Martha herself, that Mary's lies contain a grain of truth. By the end of the play, after all the trouble and the public humiliation of the failed libel suit against Mrs. Tilford, Martha, in the midst of her "confession" speech to Karen, dismisses the evil intent of Mary entirely. She describes her personal crisis existentially: "There's something in you, and you don't know it and you don't do anything about it. Suddenly a child gets bored and lies—and there you are, seeing it for the first time" (72). There's "something" in Mary, there's "something" in Martha, but that something cannot be seen; it can only be felt. For Martha, that something is her sexual attraction to Karen that she claims she never realized until Mary put a name to it with, as far as she knew, false accusations. But in a play that might be about the power of making a lie the truth, Martha suggests that the lie might actually be the truth. Mary only named something accidentally that was actually there all along, waiting to be discovered. The action in *The Children's Hour* begins precisely at the moment in which characters can no longer turn a blind eye to what clearly exists and poses an obstacle for ongoing relationships.

This begs the further question, though, of the exact nature of Karen and

Martha's bond and friendship. *These Three* goes back in time to trace the two women together from the end of their college days. The play presents no such collegial depictions, only signs of stress and friction between two fast friends, markers for what Mortar labels their "unnatural relationship." Three scenes in the first act lay out a pretty good case for Martha's attraction to Karen. First, Martha registers disappointment that she and Karen won't be able to vacation together as they always have previously. Karen counters happily, "Of course we will. The three of us" (15). Clearly, Karen's prospective marriage to Joe and the impending date for that event upset Martha. Mortar observes that Martha is always in a bad mood when Joe is on the premises: "You don't like their being together. You were always like that even as a child. If you had a little girl friend, you always got mad when she liked anybody else. Well, you'd better get a beau of your own now—a woman of your age" (20). Joe, too, confronts Martha and notes that she always "winces" when the subject of the marriage comes up in conversation. Later, once Mary makes her accusations against Martha and Karen, the stage directions indicate that Martha responds with a "combination of disgust and interest" (53). She asks the girl, "Where did you learn so much in so little time?" This line suggests that Martha makes her startling realization about the true nature of her feelings right at this moment, but doesn't speak of them until the end of the play, immediately prior to her suicide.

Finally, there is the dubious truth of Martha's confession of love for Karen. Still preoccupied with her breakup with Joe, Karen doesn't really hear Martha at first, then emotionally blocks her friend completely. The last thing Karen tells her is that she'll feel better (differently?) after she lies down. Defending Karen's lack of compassion for Martha's pain at this point, Lorena Ross Holmin observes, "it is surprising that no hint of the fact [of Martha's attraction to Karen] has become apparent to either of them before" (24). Is it possible that Karen never had a second thought about the nature of her friendship with a woman who has "never loved a man"? Is it really possible that Martha never had sexual thoughts about Karen until a little girl put them in her mind by accident? Now, Martha may be a lesbian character and Karen might be one as well. That possibility exists. But the possibility also exists that one or neither of them is a lesbian. Martha's confession is not convincing on face value. It could well be that she seeks an endgame to relieve herself from emotional pain and torment and that suicide provides an ultimate remedy. Joe says to Karen in the preceding scene, "Everything I say to you is made to mean something else. We don't talk like people anymore" (66). In the light of a public trial, words have been said in public that deserved to remain private. Once they became public, once they belonged to the crowd, the same words between two people no longer serve them as they once did.

The major problem in the play, Karen's engagement and impending wedding to Joe, would still exist even without Mary's lies and manipulations. Sensing Martha's resistance to the wedding, Karen puts an end to their first-scene squabble by saying, "For God's sake, do you expect me to give up my marriage?" (16). That question goes unanswered as Joe arrives, and it goes unanswered throughout the rest of the play. Martha even seems to acquiesce to the normative demands of marriage at the end of the play when she tells Karen, simply and sincerely, "Oh, God, I wanted that for you so much" (70). Karen throughout the play is the entitled character who seems to have it all: best friend and supportive prospective husband. The play does not examine why it might not be a bad idea for Karen to "give up her marriage" in favor of a life with Martha. Karen might well want to marry Joe because she wants a "normal" life and all the social prerogatives and privileges that go with that. She does say that she wants to have children right away. Clearly she cannot anticipate (at the time of the play) children in a life spent with Martha. Karen denies that her marriage will change any aspect of her relationship with Martha, but Martha can view the situation only as her loss. She tells Karen, "I don't understand you. It's been so damned hard building this thing up, slaving and going without things to make ends meet—think of having a winter coat without holes in the lining again!—and now when we're getting on our feet, you're all ready to let it go to hell" (16). The play's triangle doesn't straighten out within the dramatized frame.[4] The action interrupts their problem before they get a chance to work it out for themselves. In the name of doing good—protecting innocent children—probing adults alter other lives by insinuating themselves into a private matter. Based on the text, it is impossible to know the true relationship among the three characters, and the action warns the audience about the dangers of meddling where it does not belong. The lesson in the school teaches the audience to mind its own business and not interfere with matters that are beyond understanding. As much as the audience wants to see what happens in the school, the play demonstrates the limits to such seeing and the moral imperative to keep judgments at bay.

The opening scene of the play takes place in the "elocution hour" led by Mrs. Mortar in which the students recite Portia's "The Quality of Mercy" speech from *The Merchant of Venice*. The students read badly and break up the speech many times with hesitant voices and faulty memories. Finally, Mrs. Mortar demonstrates proper acting techniques that she learned from Sir Henry [Irving]. A "ham" actress, Lily Mortar implores her charges to feel pity for the fictional characters in Shakespeare's comedy, but she shows none of that pity or empathy toward her own niece, Martha. One of the main reasons that the women lose their libel suit against Mrs. Tilford is that Lily Mortar refuses to return from her acting engagement to testify on Martha and Karen's behalf. She claims that because she had a moral obligation to the theater she couldn't get away and that it "couldn't have done any good for all of us to get mixed up in that unpleasant notoriety—" (63). The basis for good acting is to step inside someone else's shoes and experience life as someone else feels it. The human value of acting, what makes it worthy of study in a liberal arts school, promotes new perspectives of understanding and tolerance for foreign points of view. Mrs. Mortar is an awful actress, completely wrapped up in her own dramatic performance and the vanity of appearances. She pays no attention to what the words on the page actually mean, and her self-absorption prevents her from discerning anything going on around her.

Words, no matter how pretty, have no value once severed from their contexts. No one listens in Mrs. Mortar's elocution class. Portia's speech is beautiful not simply because of the lovely words strung together and the lovely sounds they make, but more for their passionate and compassionate intent:

> The quality of mercy is not strain'd,
> It droppeth as the gentle rain from heaven
> Upon the place beneath. It is twice blest:
> It blesseth him that gives and him that takes.
> 'Tis mightiest in the mightiest, it becomes
> The thronèd monarch better than his crown.
> His sceptre shows the force of temporal power,
> The attribute to awe and majesty,
> Wherein doth sit the dread and fear of kings,
> But mercy is above this sceptred sway,
> It is enthronèd in the hearts of kings,
> It is an attribute to God himself;
> And earthly power doth then show likest God's
> When mercy seasons justice. (4.1.184–97)

Mercy is mightiest in the mightiest: the Mrs. Tilfords of the world wield power but need mercy to match. The dramaturgy of *The Children's Hour* blocks and ultimately frustrates the desire to see and know everything and to determine all the motives for the characters. Eric Bentley wrongly labeled Hellman's play one of "indignation." Faced with a dearth of knowledge about a particular situation, the play demonstrates the need for tolerance. Restraint and withholding of judgments on the part of onlookers would allow the three injured parties (Martha, Karen, and Joe) to resolve their problems among themselves in due time. The theater is the perfect place to practice the quality of mercy.

5
Bedroom Ballet in the Delta

> But there are things that happen between a man and a woman in the dark—
> that sort of make everything else seem—unimportant.
> —Tennessee Williams, *A Streetcar Named Desire*

Lillian Hellman charges the action in *The Children's Hour* by setting the scene in a public space (a living room, a schoolroom) and stirring the imagination of the audience about what goes on in private parts unseen. The desire to see what cannot be seen concludes with Martha's despairing self-analysis regarding her latent attraction to Karen. The visibility of the relationship threatens Martha and prompts her suicide. Tennessee Williams's *Cat on a Hot Tin Roof* (1955)—rife, too, with homosexuality—takes a radically opposite tack to explore life-and-death terrain. All the action occurs in Brick and Maggie's upstairs bed-sitting room at Big Daddy Pollitt's old plantation home. One interior door and French doors leading to a balcony that runs around the entire perimeter of the second floor allow for constant spying and frequent intrusions into a private space. Instead of wondering about what goes on elsewhere in the great house, throughout the play the audience stares at a large double bed, which serves as a constant reminder of the play's meanings.

Despite the fact that the MGM trailer billed Elizabeth Taylor's title character as "a girl too hungry for love to care about how she goes about getting it," the 1958 film downplays sex, in comparison to the play, and features a rather small bed tucked into an alcove in the bedroom as just one element in the overall production scheme. The movie version creates quite a different experience for the viewer by moving out of the bedroom and into different rooms of the house and the surrounding grounds. The relative expansiveness of the film emphasizes the material possessions of the family and the idea that money can't buy love or everlasting life. In the stage play, on the other hand, the bed makes an explicit, if silent, comment about the commitment to love and the facts of life. It's not a thematic statement; it's a material presence, visible at every moment and vital to an understanding of the imminence and eminence of death, but also of the possibility for redemption and regeneration. The image of the large bed embraces both the living and the dead and captures the profound ambivalence and contradictions in what I think is Williams's finest play. The life-affirming aspects of the play, sparked by Maggie the Cat, offer a flip side of experience to Williams's great but certainly more depressing works, such as *The Glass Menagerie* and *A Streetcar Named Desire*.[1]

In the film, the bedroom shown is not even Brick and Maggie's, but just another guest room in the large house. Brick and Maggie live in New Orleans and have only come up to Mississippi to celebrate Big Daddy's birthday and to welcome him home from the cancer clinic up north. At one point, Brick packs a suitcase to return home; later he escapes to his car as if to drive away. The room, then, reflects nothing of the former occupants, the homosexual lovers Straw and Ochello, the two progenitors of the estate, and nothing of Maggie and Brick either. It suggests only a certain taste and wealth that might just as well belong to a hotel room. It reveals no blemish of history. Likewise, the heterosexual couples turn out wrinkle-free in the film's action as well. Father and son reconcile and help each other up the stairs arm in arm. Before making his final exit, Big Daddy invites Big Mama to survey his kingdom with him (in the play he goes alone and Big Mama runs after him). Brick ascends the stairs to the bedroom and calls down for Maggie to follow him. Their kiss ends the play as Brick tosses his pillow from the couch back to the bed, signaling that they will soon sleep together in the same bed. Even Gooper, the son who stands to lose everything to Brick and has lost his father's love to Brick ages ago, nods approval over all these final couplings and silences Mae's pecuniary objections with a final thundering admonition to "[s]hut up!" The final arrangements of the picture are decidedly happy in that traditional Hollywood ever-after sort of way.

Clearly the film takes things away from the play (for example, homosexual references and themes), but it also adds many things as well (such as the happy ending and the story of Big Daddy's daddy). The playwright, who liked many other film versions of his plays, and who liked and respected the director Richard Brooks very much, didn't care for the movie.[2] He confided in a 1973 *Playboy* interview, "Though *Glass Menagerie* may be my best play, *Cat on a Hot Tin Roof* is still my favorite. But I hated the movie. I don't think the movie had the *purity* of the play. It was jazzed up, hoked up a bit" (Jennings 244). I relate the "purity" that Williams talks about to the directness and simplicity of the mise-en-scène, which I'll discuss at length momentarily. As for "hoking up" the play, obviously Paul Newman and Elizabeth Taylor make very attractive main characters, but the movie regularly highlights the individual stars at the expense of the characters they play. In the opening, for example, the camera focuses at length upon Taylor changing out of her stockings and putting on a pair of new ones. The filmed scene is not included for Brick's benefit at all, but for presenting Liz Taylor's legs to the audience. They are quite beautiful legs, and the camera lovingly caresses them, but such moments are gratuitous.

Taken out of the bedroom, the movie dilutes the emphases and meanings of the play. The prologue at the high school athletic field, for example, shows that which is only alluded to in the play. Similarly, the film shows one of the No Neck Monsters hurling ice cream on Maggie's dress, an act that she merely describes in the play, and later Big Daddy, whose voracious eating habits are discussed but never depicted in the drama, hunching over his food at the dinner table. The film presents extensions of Big Daddy's empire as well. It includes a shot of his private airplane, emblazoned with "Pollitt Enterprises," pulling up at the airfield and a musical celebration performed by Mae and her No Neck Monsters in honor of his arrival. This scene reveals unequivocally Big Daddy's distaste for that brood as he brushes past them in order to ride home with Maggie. Before returning to the plantation home, they stop on the grounds and Big Daddy surveys his horse stock while leaning on a fence, proclaiming, "I'm alive." The statement, along with his obvious attraction to and appreciation of Maggie, together with the awesome virility of the horses, makes clear Big Daddy's own animal nature and proclivities.

The most significant change, however, involves the treatment of the confrontation scene between Big Daddy and Brick. In the play, the scene takes up almost the entire second act, after which very little is left to say or do, except for Maggie to step back into the picture and take control of the situation. In the film, though, this pivotal scene only begins in the second-floor bedroom; then unwinds down the stairs and through the house, outside to the carport in a severe thunderstorm, back inside, cutting between Gooper's plea to Big Mama for a plan of legal succession for Big Daddy's estate; and finishes in the cellar. The visual progression of the scene laid out by director Richard Brooks literally shows the two men working through the layers of lies and excuses until they get to the bottom of the situation. According to Gene D. Phillips, "He [Brooks] follows the action from Maggie and Brick's bed-sitting room upstairs down to the cellar where Brick and Big Daddy plumb the depths of their relationship" (148). At the midlevel, the living room, Big Daddy confronts Brick about Skipper and even asks Maggie to corroborate the evidence. Fleeing from these revelations, Brick hobbles to his car in the carport outside but, under constant pressure from his father, blurts out the truth about his father's cancer. Angry at himself, his father, and the whole situation, Brick tries to leave but his tire sticks in the mud, the spinning wheel a fitting image for his situation, and he inadvertently breaks his crutch in the car door such that Maggie has to help him back inside.

Instead of movement from high to low, going from the upstairs bedroom down to the cellar below, the drama capitalizes on the familiar unities of time, place, and action. Each act dovetails with the previous one to provide continuous action in a single space. Early in the play, Maggie laments to Brick, "I'm not living with you. We occupy the same cage" (35). They cannot escape, but at the same time others can peer in to watch them. They act under pressure of observation from other members of the household, particularly Mae and Gooper who inhabit the adjoining and unseen bedroom. Williams evokes the imagery of the cage in the preface to an earlier play, *The Rose Tattoo.* In "The Timeless World of a Play," Williams writes, "Fear and evasion are the two little beasts that chain each other's tails in the revolving wire-cage of our nervous world. They distract us from feeling too much about things. Time rushes toward us with its hospital tray of infinitely varied narcotics, even while it is preparing us for its inevitably fatal operation" (650).

Fear of death and fear of intimacy similarly drive the action of *Cat on a Hot Tin Roof.* The bedroom is not so much a realistic reflection of how a wealthy Southern planter lived in the 1950s, but a cosmic world in which to wage a struggle of life and death. The two major set pieces that Williams details define the two extremes of evasion and contact. The large double bed, the dual site of carnal pleasure and eventual death, occupies a central position which "staging should make a functional part of the set as often as suitable, the surface of which should be slightly raked to make figures on it seen more easily" (*Cat* 16). The other piece of furniture that Williams comments on is an enormous console combination stereo system, TV, and liquor cabinet, "a very complete and compact little shrine to virtually all the comforts and illusions behind which we hide from such things as the characters in the play are faced with" (16). The prominence of the bed emphasizes the draw of intimacy, raw emotion, and death, while the various pleasures found in the console cabinet inoculate, albeit only temporarily, against painful realities. Just as death is inevitable, the bed remains in view at all times and it is the object around which characters move throughout the action.

In his final "note" to the designer, Williams advises to "take as many pains to give the actors room to move about freely (to show their restlessness, their passion for breaking out) as if it were a set for a ballet" (16). Such direction indicates that the stage should not hold much more furniture than the pieces described above. The cage imagery exposes the vulnerability of the characters as they move to the edges, to the bars or wires of the cage at the extreme boundaries of their prison. One of Elia Kazan's directorial techniques for the 1955 production included breaking up the confidential nature of realistic acting scenes and having a character, particularly Big Daddy, speak directly to the audience. According to Brenda Murphy, author of *Tennessee Williams and Elia Kazan: A Col-*

laboration in the Theatre, one of the director's most significant contributions was "'opening the play out,' as if he were thinking about it as a film rather than a stage play" (120). The attempt to bring the actors downstage, directing the action outward instead of inward where the furniture sits, is the nearest the theater can come to creating a close-up. Kazan combined such presentational techniques with representational activities of the household in the background: black servants working; children playing; the sound of croquet coming from the grounds below; music filtering up. Frequent interruptions and intrusions into the room reinforce the one-way permeability of the cage that contains Brick, Maggie, and later Big Daddy. They must stop to shoo away the No Neck Monsters sent to spy on them as well as their mother, Mae, who lurks about the periphery to ferret out information as best she can. In contrast to all the swirling activity around the outside of the room, Brick remains hobbled with a broken ankle and largely anchored in the setting. He can't leave; Maggie refuses to leave him. The cage traps them alone together. Brick's attempt to dodge Maggie's advances orchestrates the first act, but it only takes a little while longer to understand what he's trying to avoid.

Death hangs over the entire play. The recent death of his best friend, Skipper, precipitates Brick's crisis. Two devoted lovers once inhabited the scene of the play, the bedroom, and when one man died the other "quit eatin' like a dog does when its master's dead, and died, too!" (119). Those events in the past serve to amplify the present, which ostensibly is a gathering at the Pollitt plantation to honor Big Daddy's sixty-fifth birthday. The eventual report, however, from the Ochsner Clinic up north from which he has only recently returned makes it clear that this will be his last birthday, what he later refers to as his "soft" birthday. Brick, goaded into a showdown with his father, finally decides to level him with the truth: "How about these birthday congratulations, these many, many happy returns of the day, when ev'rybody knows there won't be any except you!" (128). Including the audience, Big Daddy is the last to know that he's dying, and the entire play turns on the delivery of that terminal news. Before he discovers the truth, when he thinks he's beaten death, Big Daddy speaks with certainty: "Ignorance—of mortality—is a comfort. A man don't have that comfort, he's the only living thing that conceives of death, that knows what it is. The others go without knowing which is the way that anything living should go, go without knowing, without any knowledge of it, and yet a pig squeals, but a man sometimes, he can keep a tight mouth about it" (93). Maggie tells Brick in the very first scene that it is extremely hard to talk about dying because people don't wish to face the eventual and inevitable fact of death. She tells her husband, "Nobody says, 'You're dying.' You have to fool them. They have to fool *themselves.* . . .

Because human beings dream of life everlasting, that's the reason! But most of them want it on earth and not in heaven" (53).

Life is, as Blanche says in *A Streetcar Named Desire,* a "long parade to the graveyard!" And the final steps, too, are often not pleasant. At the end of the play, Big Daddy's "long drawn cry of agony and rage fills the house" from off-stage (170). "Sounds like the pain has struck," Gooper comments (171). Blanche, in the earlier play, reports that the actual funerals are pretty compared to the deaths:

> Funerals are quiet, but deaths—not always. Sometimes their breathing is hoarse, and sometimes it rattles, and sometimes they even cry out to you, 'Don't let me go!' Even the old, sometimes, say, 'Don't let me go.' As if you were able to stop them! But funerals are quiet, with pretty flowers. And, oh, what gorgeous boxes they pack them away in! Unless you were there at the bed when they cried out, 'Hold me!' you'd never suspect there was the struggle for breath and bleeding. (*Plays* 479)

The large bed in *Cat on a Hot Tin Roof* recalls the image of Blanche holding hands with her dead and dying. No matter how much the characters move away from the bed, or claw at their own wire cage, they will eventually have to lie down on the bed and make their final peace. With luck, they will have someone such as Blanche to attend their misery, hold them, cool them, mop their brow—an ultimate fate that Big Daddy tries to deny.

And, so, as Big Daddy says in an altogether different context, mendacity is the system under which humans live: "Hell, you *got* to live with it, there's nothing *else* to *live* with except mendacity, is there?" (111). Dr. Baugh, Gooper, and Mae first reported that Big Daddy got a clean bill of health from the Ochsner Clinic and that the only thing doctors found was something called a spastic colon, a relatively harmless condition. They hope to choose a better time to tell Big Daddy and Big Mama the truth, but that time never comes. The truth, which Big Daddy feels in his gut anyway because, after all, the cancer is inside him, finally leaches out in heated conversation. Nevertheless stunned by the news, Big Daddy's previous windbag eloquence deflates into angry stammering: "—ALL—LYING SONS OF—LYING BITCHES!" (130). Big Daddy prides himself on plain talking and honesty, and he accuses Brick of not being able to face the truth with Skipper. But, in the end, Big Daddy, too, cannot face his own mortality. He lashes out at others for lying to him (just as Brick does to Maggie), but the fact remains that he most of all lies to himself. He must lie in order to survive. Brick, who sees full well the corruption of the world, who has seen what he regarded as the one true thing in the world, his pure friendship with Skipper, destroyed, now views the entire world as false. Never having shared Big Daddy's quest for the truth, Brick drops out of the game of life. At the conclusion of act 2, he repeats Big Daddy's words back to the father, with heavy irony: "Mendacity is a system that we live in. Liquor is one way out an' death's the other. . . ." (129). His father accused him of drinking to dodge from life; Brick concurs: "I want to dodge away from it" (111).

Aside from alcohol, the only antidote for the fear of death is desire, a life-affirming gesture that also plays out right on the bed. Blanche labels this impulse as "brutal desire," but such a primitive and primal ferocity is necessary to match death's grip. Blanche admonishes her sister not to hang back with the brutes, but such characters as Stanley ("one hundred percent American" [*Plays* 539]) and Stella (pregnant with her first child) will inherit the Earth. Refined Blanche, plagued by death and dying, including her own guilt surrounding her husband's suicide, is "played out" (*Plays* 546) and no longer fit to survive in the modern world. Big Daddy, like Stanley Kowalski, is a survivor in the world, a man who became rich and powerful by planting things in the ground and watching them grow. He tells Brick near the start of their act-2 conversation, "Life is important. There's nothing else to hold onto" (86). Holding on to life is a commitment to life processes, especially the sexual act. Significantly, when Big Daddy believes, after a long period of anxiety, that he's been given a clean bill of health, he immediately seeks an outlet for his sexual (life-affirming) urges. He fantasizes to his son about indulging his senses with a new mistress: "I'll strip her naked and smother her in minks and choke her with diamonds! Ha ha! I'll strip her naked and choke her with diamonds and smother her with minks and hump her from hell to breakfast" (98–99). Big Daddy's descriptions of his pleasures with women are as coarse and brutal as anything in the play, but the exuberance of his sexuality, heightened by his exhilaration at having beaten death, responds directly to the morbid thoughts that forced him to shut down all life-affirming gestures. The violent sexual imagery answers in kind to the brooding fears of death. Even when he has digested the news of his terminal cancer, he defiantly returns in the final act to tell a dirty joke about the evolving profile of a sexually aroused male elephant. He adds that the mendacious smell in the room smells like death, and the joke stands as a grotesque rebuttal to death's encroachment.

Human desire revolves around the double bed in the center, a bed in which Brick no longer sleeps. Maggie desperately wants to reclaim her husband sexually and get him to join her in bed again. She reflects that they used to have an enjoyable and active sex life in the early years of their marriage: "You married me early that summer we graduated out of Ole Miss, and we were happy, weren't we, we were blissful, yes, hit heaven together ev'ry time that we loved!" (60).

For his part, Brick tells a different story to his father and says that "she and me never got any closer together than two people just get in bed, which is not much closer than two cats on a—fence humping . . ." (125). The dash halts Brick from blurting "two cats on a hot tin roof," a frequently repeated line associated with Maggie the Cat. The change in the line indicates Brick's discomfort with placing himself on that roof with her. Instead, he conceives of himself and Maggie as apart and never playing the same game. The image of two cats "humping" on a fence is a much more contorted and graphic image than the poetic one of a cat on a hot tin roof. Revealingly though, moments earlier Brick doesn't contradict Maggie's account of their satisfying sexual history. When Big Daddy asks, "How was Maggie in bed?" Brick answers, "Great! the greatest!" (124). For her part, she doesn't sugarcoat the present dire situation.

Big Mama, a less than impartial arbiter, sizes up their marital problems very simply. Having received from the spying daughter-in-law in the next bedroom the daily reports about Maggie's nightly entreaties to Brick and his regular refusals, Big Mama confronts Maggie with a direct question in the first act: "D'you make Brick happy in bed?" (48). She follows Maggie's equivocations with a firm statement while pointing to the bed: "When a marriage goes on the rocks, the rocks are *there,* right *there!*" (49). Maggie's desperation to reclaim Brick sexually drives the play, and she makes her passion and persistence abundantly clear to Brick by the end of the opening act: "You know, if I thought you would never, never, *never* make love to me again—I would go downstairs to the kitchen and pick out the longest and sharpest knife I could find and stick it straight into my heart, I swear that I would!" (30–31). While Big Daddy later voices regret for having slept with his wife faithfully for so many years and blusters crudely about sexual conquests he will never make—the empty boasts of a proud but hollow man—Maggie envisions a time when she will enjoy her former pleasures in bed with her husband. Her desire, along with Big Daddy's, fuels the entire play. Brick, on the other hand, prefers to mix cocktails at the liquor cabinet—positioned at the side, not the center, of the room—and observe the game of life from the sidelines.

Despite the tragedy of Brick's situation and his "state of spiritual disrepair," according to Williams's own description in his "Note of Explanation" (*Plays* 978), Maggie is the titular character and the protagonist in the play from a dramaturgical standpoint, as well as from an aesthetic and an ethical one. While Brick of "Three Players of a Summer Game" (1952), Williams's short story, is essentially the same character as the familiar one from the play, the playwright transforms and individuates Margaret anew in the play. Director Elia Kazan's suggestion to make her more likable in the play was, Williams notes, the only one that he embraced completely from the beginning. Williams allowed that Maggie the

Cat had "become steadily more charming to me as I worked on her character-ization" (978). Williams, of course, is famous for writing great female charac-ters, who are typically no match for the complexities of the modern world, and who long for a more gentle, polite, spiritual world (think of Amanda and Laura Wingfield, Alma Winemiller, Blanche DuBois). At the same time, male stud heroes in the Williams landscape include Val Xavier, Chance Wayne, John Bu-chanan, and even Stanley Kowalski. Maggie steals the sexual energy reserved for the male heroes of previous plays. She is not the same ball-busting faceless char-acter from the short story in which she first appeared. At the same time, Brick is a completely passive character, longing for the clarity of the past, possessing the "charm of the defeated" typical of the playwright's Southern heroines.[3]

Maggie personifies the saving grace and the redemptive life force in the play. To curry Big Daddy's favor in his will and provide an heir for the estate, she an-nounces in the final act that she is pregnant. In order to make good on that pledge, she then hides all Brick's liquor and promises not to give it back until he agrees to lie down and make love to her: "And so tonight we're going to make the lie true, and when that's done, I'll bring the liquor back here and we'll get drunk together, here, tonight, in this place that death has come into . . . —What do you say?" (*Cat* 173). Both her love for Brick and her compassion for the old man, whom she truly likes and admires, as well as her own greed and desire to beat out her sister-in-law for the estate, motivate Maggie's actions. Having grown up poor and impoverished, Maggie lies about her pregnancy as a desperate, last-ditch effort to get something for herself. Unlike Brick, she wasn't born with a silver spoon in her mouth, and she scraped for whatever she got. With the voice of experience, Maggie informs her somewhat naive husband, "You can be young without money, but you can't be old without it. You've got to be old *with* money because to be old without it is just too awful, you've got to be one or the other, either *young* or *with money,* you can't be old and *without* it.—That's the *truth,* Brick. . . ." (55). Big Daddy is dying; her husband is a drunkard; she is childless. She concocts a story to save herself and her husband as well. In another early Williams play, the short *Lady of Larkspur Lotion,* a character proclaims, "There are no lies but the lies that are stuffed in the mouth by the hard-knuckled hand of need, the cold iron fist of necessity" (*Plays* 334). Maggie does what she does in order to survive.

The biggest lie in a play about lies, and the need for lies, is one that might turn out to be true. But even if it's not true, it ought to be true. In this fashion, Maggie steals a line from Blanche in *Streetcar,* the character who puts paper lan-terns over naked lightbulbs to cast a spell over an otherwise dismal and dingy en-vironment and give herself the illusion of a younger, prettier self. Blanche doesn't even call her fabrications lies; to her they are simple transformations: "Magic!

Yes, yes, magic! I try to give that to people. I misrepresent things to them. I don't tell truth, I tell what *ought* to be truth. And if that is sinful, then let me be damned for it!—*Don't turn the light on!*" (*Plays* 545). The inspired plot Maggie springs at the end of *Cat on a Hot Tin Roof* is a kind of wish fulfillment for what, at least from her point of view, ought to happen. Big Daddy ought to go to his grave with the knowledge that he'll have a grandchild from his favorite son. He ought to have the illusion that his legacy will continue through generations. Brick's problems ought to be resolved, and he should learn to accept Maggie's love. The fact that the fairy-tale ending doesn't exactly happen, that it's not clear what the future of the characters might hold, except of course Big Daddy's death, strengthens the play. There's a big difference between what is and what might be, but allowing the possibility for a satisfying reconciliation between Brick and Maggie provides comfort. Maggie's hope for a future in a world of death and dying is something to cling to at the end. She pleads with her husband and tells him that she loves him, and he ends the play with a beautiful line: "Wouldn't it be funny if that was true?" It would be amazing if dreams and fairy tales came true, the line suggests. But the possibility can't be completely discounted, and therein lie the hope and dignity of the play and its message. It's hard to think that Maggie would love Brick without his money perhaps, but it's also not clear at all that she loves him *because* of his money and the prospects for more.

In the second act, the knock-down-drag-out father-son scene, the two men dance around the subject of Skipper's relationship to Brick and the possibility of homosexual attraction. Big Daddy will later speak of "tolerance," while his son reacts defensively and with ugly epithets at the mere suggestion that his relationship with Skipper was not "normal." In a rather lengthy stage direction, Williams hedges his bets about the true nature of those relations. Critics have taken the playwright to task for not being more forthright about homosexual themes in his work. Even when the play first came out (pun slightly intended), Eric Bentley attacked its reticence to erase the shadow of doubt: "*Cat on a Hot Tin Roof* was heralded by some as the play in which homosexuality was at last to be presented without evasion. But the miracle has still not happened" ("Tennessee Williams' New Play" 28). Writing much later, John Clum likened Williams's refusal to take his writing out of the closet to an actor who would pretend to be straight in order to keep getting parts in a commercial enterprise. "Williams was compelled to write about homosexuality [because he himself was homosexual?]," writes Clum, "but equally impelled to rely on the language of indirection and heterosexist discourse. Gaining the acceptance of that broad audience meant denying a crucial aspect of himself" (166).

This criticism doesn't seem quite fair. One reason for theater, one that we've gotten away from in this era of identity politics, is to pretend to be someone else, to imagine a different experience from the one inhabited every day. Williams does express "crucial aspect[s] of himself" all through the play, just not in the body or the characterization of one single character. Allowing for the possibility that Brick might not be homosexual makes for a much more interesting play. Williams avoids the trap of saying he is or he isn't. That's not a cop-out; it's simply a more accurate reflection of the way life truly is lived. Way back in 1955, Bentley asks that "[s]urely the author can't be assuming that a man is either 100 percent heterosexual or 100 percent homosexual?" ("Tennessee Williams' New Play" 28). Williams makes it clear in his lengthy stage direction that he wants to avoid making a definitive "he is" or "he isn't" statement:

> The bird that I hope to catch in the net of this play is not the solution of one man's psychological problem. I'm trying to catch the true quality of experience in a group of people, that cloudy, flickering, evanescent— fiercely charged!—interplay of live human beings in the thundercloud of a common crisis. Some mystery should be left in the revelation of character in a play, just as a great deal of mystery is always left in the revelation of character in life, even in one's own character to himself. This does not absolve the playwright of his duty to observe and probe as clearly and deeply as he legitimately can: but it should steer him away from "pat" conclusions, facile definitions which make a play just a play, not a snare for the truth of human experience. (116–17)

Inserted at a pivotal moment in the dialogue, the lengthy note serves as Williams's disclaimer of the importance of homosexuality in his play. Even so, more importantly the note—delivered at the major stress point in the play, the exact spot at which the play seems to break apart and reveal itself—helps to explain the play's many meanings.[4] It doesn't really matter whether Brick is or is not homosexual: the point is that Skipper did love him; Brick is complicit in his friend's death; his relationship with Skipper did not have the purity that Brick demanded of it; without that purity, he can't make sense of his world. Skipper's death forces Brick to take stock of an imperfect, corrupt, and human—all too human— world. The "common crisis" that the characters face is not Brick's sexual identity but the hard reality of death and the needed and too-often shrinking responses to desire and life.

The dominant and often-repeated titular image of a cat on a hot tin roof appears first in a purely sexual sense: Maggie desires her husband, but Brick refuses to sleep with her. "What is the victory of a cat on a hot tin roof?" Maggie first muses at the beginning of the play. "Just staying on it, I guess, as long as she can. . . ." (31). The resonance of the central image, embodied by Maggie, is the glory of the play. Maggie, allied with Big Daddy, recognizes that life is not pretty and that it demands sweaty struggle. The image of a cat on a hot tin roof is not pretty; it is not graceful. But the alternative is falling off. At the end of act 1, Maggie advises Brick that he must let go of an image of a perfectly Platonic relationship with Skipper in order to accept the world as it is lived. "My only point," she says, "the only point that I'm making, is life has got to be allowed to continue even after the *dream* of life is—all—over. . . ." (58). The play asks how to respond to a mendacious world in which the pristine image of life as it can be imagined is never what it turns out to be. Brick refuses to live in a compromised world, but this world of ideals is ultimately seen not as heroic but as immature. Both Big Daddy, screaming in pain with a devastating colon cancer, and Maggie, inventing a lie in order to inherit Big Daddy's estate, emerge as heroic figures because they said "yes" to life even after encountering life's many disappointments. Big Daddy's exit line reads, "Son, I'm goin' up on the roof, to the belvedere on th' roof to look over my kingdom before I give up my kingdom—twenty-eight thousand acres of th' richest land this side of the valley Nile!" (168). The epigraph that Williams chose for this play, a refrain from Dylan Thomas's "Do Not Go Gentle into That Good Night," perfectly accompanies and amplifies the title and the moral force of the play: "Rage, rage against the dying of the light!" Big Daddy carries that rage offstage with him, and his bellows of pain resonate long after he has left. Maggie the Cat embodies that same determination to bend life to her will and to get what she's after. She tells her husband early, "But one thing I don't have is the charm of the defeated, my hat is still in the ring, and I am determined to win!" (31). She embodies the life force in the play that still burns at its conclusion.

Maggie advances; Brick retreats. She advances again; he retreats farther. She wears a slip of ivory satin and lace; he wears silk pajamas. Both objects of desire, they perfectly fit each other. Maggie brings the heat of a cat on a hot tin roof, "consumed with envy an' eaten up with longing" (39). She admires her body in the mirror and touches herself to highlight admiration of her own physicality. She remarks that other men, including Big Daddy, still have a "lech" for her and that she thinks it's a healthy sign of respect that they do. In contrast to Maggie's heat, Brick is all cool detachment. As the play opens, he's taking a shower in the bathroom, an offstage room that features light blue tile, a cool color. Williams's stage directions dictate that the "fading, still warm, light from the gallery treats him gently" (20). Williams details, "He has the additional charm of that cool air of detachment that people have who have given up the struggle" (19). That struggle is the struggle of life. The air of detachment about him is not a new development, either, that has surfaced since the death of Skipper. Perhaps it has become more pronounced, but Brick's coolness is what has always made him so attractive to other people. He has never been engaged with life, and that is precisely what has attracted both Skipper and Maggie to him. Maggie describes the key to his wonderful ability as a lover as precisely his relative indifference to the act. His lack of engagement actually thrilled her: "Never had any anxiety about it, did it naturally, easily, slowly, with absolute confidence and perfect calm, more like opening a door for a lady or seating her at a table than giving expression to any longing for her. Your indifference made you wonderful at lovemaking—strange?—but true. . . ." (30). In the Broadway version of the play, Brick explains to his sister-in-law, "not everybody makes much noise about love. Oh, I know some people are huffers an' puffers, but others are silent lovers" (*Plays* 1003). Brick, clearly, fits into the latter category, and such detachment further increases the desire of those who love him.

Maggie confesses in act 1 that one reason she went to bed with Skipper was to feel closer to Brick: "Skipper and I made love, if love you could call it, because it made both of us feel a little bit closer to you. . . . And so we made love to each other to dream it was you, both of us! Yes, yes, yes! Truth, truth! What's so awful about it?" (56–57). Brick doesn't allow anything to get close to him, a way of being that only increases the palpable desire he generates in others. That dynamic raises the heat in the scenes in which he plays a part. Significantly, too, Brick is the only character that doesn't leave the stage for any length of time during the entire play. His coolness, his detachment, literally sets him off, and his silence suggests something valuable underneath for other characters—and the audience—to explore. There is nothing mysterious about Maggie. She harbors no secrets. Indeed, the first half of act 1 is a virtual monologue in which she never stops talking. Brick, on the other hand, remains laconic throughout the play, continuing to drink until he can get the peaceful "click" in his head, his alcoholic daze penetrated only by Big Daddy's accusations about his role in Skipper's death.

Just as Brick has never allowed Maggie to get close to him, the threat of Skipper's desire for him is equally shocking. Certainly the threat of homosexuality shocks his puritanical moral code, but it is desire itself that appears even more threatening to him. Brick doesn't admit passions into his world, doesn't allow anyone to get to him. Maggie calls him an "ass-aching Puritan" (23), and that fitting description captures the straitlaced, emotionally repressed, and oppressive world he inhabits. He played football as a means of never growing up and keeping his relationship with Skipper as pure as two athletes competing in a game and completing passes, quarterback to receiver, that "couldn't be intercepted except by time, the aerial attack that made us famous!" (124). Just as Maggie wants more from Brick, Skipper wanted more as well, but Brick refused to acknowledge his friend's desires. Speaking of that relationship, Maggie declares, "You two had something that had to be kept on ice, yes, incorruptible, yes!—and death was the only icebox where you could keep it. . . ." (59). Brick, himself, unwittingly describes the coldness of his friendship with Skipper even as he tries to defend the purity of two athletes and male companionship to his father in act 2: "It was too rare to be normal, any true thing between two people is too rare to be normal. Oh, once in a while he put his hand on my shoulder or I'd put mine on his, oh, maybe even, when we were touring the country in pro-football an' shared hotel-rooms we'd reach across the space between the two beds and shake hands to say goodnight, yeah, one or two times we—" (122–23). The image of two twin beds, separated by empty space in the middle, occasionally bridged by a manly handshake, speaks volumes about the loneliness that Skipper endured throughout his unrequited love affair with Brick. He died under the strain of that relationship about which nothing could be said. Brick would not listen and hear of it.

Maggie tells Brick earlier that Skipper is dead but that Maggie the Cat is alive! Maggie's persistence, her refusal to jump off the roof, gives Brick a second chance at love. Whether he can accept a love that is not necessarily pure is a question that goes beyond the action of the play. The erotics of the play dictate that Maggie and Brick have, in the words of Stanley Kowalski, "had this date with each other from the beginning!" (*Plays* 555). Maggie assumes the masculine role and blackmails Brick into bed by locking up his liquor. Yet, the possibility and the hope remain that Maggie's genuine love for Brick and his best interests motivates her actions and not simply her desire to produce an heir and inherit a big piece of land. The end of the play suggests that the world as it is lived and experienced is one that must embrace a panoply of motives and desires, most of which are not purely this or that. Brick and Maggie's tentative, compromised union, finally together on the bed that has beckoned them throughout the play, affirms the possibility that life, despite its corruption and many mendacities, might be worth living. It's possible to believe that Maggie just might hand Brick's life back to him by embracing him and allowing him to feel the heat of her passion for him. The large bed may be the final resting place in the parade to the graveyard, but lovemaking, huffing and puffing, defies death lying down.

6

Jungled Dreams

You get older, you want to feel that you . . . accomplished something. My only accomplishment is my son. I ain't brainy. That's all I accomplished.

—Arthur Miller, *All My Sons*

Would *Death of a Salesman* be regarded as a great play today if Arthur Miller had stuck with the original title of *The Inside of His Head?* Imagine not designer Jo Mielziner's skeletal frame of the Loman house dwarfed by a menacing urban landscape, but the playwright's initial visualization of the play: "an image of an enormous face the height of the proscenium arch which would appear and then open up and we would see the inside of a man's head. The play's eye was to revolve from within Willy's head, sweeping endlessly in all directions like a light on the sea" (qtd. in Gottfried 122). This iconic representation of the workings of a man's mind sought to give objective form to the subjective experiences of Willy Loman's last day on Earth. Literal depiction eventually gave way to descriptive irony, but before *Death of a Salesman* could open at the Morosco Theatre on 10 February 1949, producers tried to convince Miller to name his play either *Period of Grace* (referring to the grace period of Willy's life-insurance policy) or, even more emphatically, *Free and Clear* (a reference to Linda's last lines during the Requiem). Producers feared that a play with "death" in the title would scare audiences. Backed by his already-famous director, Elia Kazan, Miller held out, and his play opened to immediate acclaim and lasting success.

Anyone who grapples with this play today deals with the legacy of the original Mielziner design. The legacy persists not only because of the greatness of this particular designer, the champion of what became known as "selective realism," but also because the visual image that he created for the play connected deeply with the playwright's conception. The central image of the play is the man and his house, which he has practically built himself and which stands as an extension of his own being, surrounded by menacing apartment buildings. It remains a personal, family play, a domestic play, but one set within a social and political context. Furthermore, this visual statement gains power as it pervades the entire play. The single visual image dominates a theatrical representation, whereas film and television adaptations, through editing and the versatility of the camera, generally change and vary the visual field. The static resonance of the theatrical image in *Death of a Salesman,* which achieves some measure of plasticity through the wonders of stage lighting, creates a quite different aesthetic experience from the successful small-screen adaptations of Miller's great play.[1]

Miller's most famous play departs from the well-made formula and Ibsen model of *All My Sons* (1947), Miller's previous big commercial success, by breaking up time and space and intermingling past and present in various locations in and around New York and Boston. According to Matthew C. Roudané, "Miller wanted to formulate a dramatic structure that would allow the play textually and theatrically to capture the simultaneity of the human mind as that mind registers outer experience through its own inner subjectivity" (72). Centered on the Loman household, the action shifts to Howard's office and a restaurant, and it travels to the past with Willy's memories and recollections. Miller specified in his opening stage directions that in the "present," actors should act as though the "wall-lines" were really there. However, in scenes from the past, the actors could step through those same "lines" as an indication of a change in time. Lighting and music alterations, scenery shifts, movement to different areas of the stage further aid the audience in following the switch between past and present and give the action the fluidity of a dreamlike experience.

For all its novelties of style and performance demands, though, a familiar dramaturgical device drives the plot: the buried secret that comes to light! Biff discovered Willy with another woman in a Boston hotel room during his senior year in high school, and that revelation destroyed the young man's love for his father and ruined the boy's life. Prior to presenting the hotel scene, during which Willy's past adultery is discovered, Miller preps his audience to see the root cause of everything bad. "What happened in Boston, Willy?" Bernard, Biff's childhood friend and next-door neighbor, asks Willy fifteen years later. Willy's anger and immediate defensiveness indicate his guilt and suggest that more will come out later. The subsequent dialogue fully articulates the tragic situation in the play. Talking to Bernard, now a successful lawyer, Willy tries to find out what went wrong with Biff. Of course, he knows what happened in Boston; what he really wants from Bernard is a reason to rid himself of his pent-up guilt regarding the unfortunate events from the past. Nothing Bernard says can make him feel better; in fact, he hears everything as accusations against him, and the young man ends the conversation by trying to calm Willy down:

BERNARD: But sometimes, Willy, it's better for a man just to walk away.
WILLY: Walk away?
BERNARD: That's right.

WILLY: But if you can't walk away?

BERNARD (*after a slight pause*): I guess that's when it's tough. (73)

These mundane lines capture the tragic core of the play. Willy Loman, similar to classic heroes such as Oedipus, Hamlet, and Hedda Gabler, cannot "walk away" from the situation in which he finds himself, but must first make certain that Biff doesn't blame him and can make good in life. Willy's refusal to quit until he has secured his son's love and future gives the play an action to fulfill. Biff grants him an out by promising to leave home and not come back. The father cannot accept this scenario and remains determined to give something to his son. When Biff confesses his love on bended knees in one of the great acting scenes in American drama, Willy's determination to make a success of Biff grows even stronger. Biff's emotional breakdown attempts to stave off his father's suicidal impulses; ironically, his action emboldens Willy not to fail on his next try. The ironies of a play about a man who cannot "walk away" continue with the observation that, to fulfill his goal, Willy does walk away in the end, out of the house, into his car, and to death. He abandons his family and leaves his wife completely alone. The last lines of the Requiem belong to her as she voices her failure to understand Willy's action while still seeing the irony that the last mortgage payment has been paid and they're finally "free and clear."

Film and television productions typically try to open up a play to show scenes that cannot be presented on the stage. Given a play about a man who cannot walk away, two successful television productions wisely resisted the temptation to expand and alter Miller's dramatic text. Both of the television productions that I will discuss below also presented the play in a theatrical environment but filmed it in a studio to exploit best the television medium. The 1966 television version focuses on the acting at the expense of much visual interest. Preserved now as part of the Broadway Theatre Archive, the DVD documents Lee J. Cobb and Mildred Dunnock's original performances on a functional, if rudimentary, combination of a theatrical and television set. It's theatrical in the sense that you can see the wrinkles in the canvas "flats" and many of the walls are made from scrimlike material that enables them to appear transparent or opaque depending on the direction of light. Characters from the "past," such as Ben or The Woman, often first appear in the television picture behind a lighted scrim before walking into the scene. This technique allows the director to condense the stage picture such that a scene in the foreground, occurring in the "present," blends easily with characters from the "past" coming into focus behind a scrim in the background. The transition from the opening scene to Biff and Happy's bedroom operates similarly. Light behind the upstage wall illuminates their bedroom, and when that scene begins the camera perspective shifts 180 degrees so that the upstage area exists in the foreground of the picture and the dining room, where Willy was standing, blacks out in the background. On a stage, such scenes might spread over the entire width of the proscenium in a kind of "space" staging. That same effect is simply not possible in a television film. The director's only recourse is to cut from one locale to another, and that is precisely what Alex Segal does throughout the second half of the film (act 2) as locations change between the Loman house, Howard's office, Charley's office, Frank's Chop House, and the Boston hotel room.

The sets for all these scenes exist as independent units to promote a kind of realism that still lacks much detail, a fact typical of most television productions. Moreover, the sets, allowing the camera to move in, out, and about, resemble rooms in a dollhouse. A dining room—a space that is not mentioned in the dramatic text—serves as the main acting area. In the play, most of the interior scenes take place around a kitchen table permeable to the outside. And, of course, there are no walls to obstruct an audience's vision into this space. The actors merely pretend that the walls are there when they're performing in scenes happening in the "present," and they step through the walls when the scenes shift temporally to the "past." The camera work by contrast emphasizes the enclosed nature of the rooms by frequently shooting through the windows and pulling back to show the boxed-in characters. These shots occur at least three times in act 1: first, the camera frames Biff at close range as he talks to Hap at their bedroom window; second, as Willy sees the moon moving between the surrounding apartment buildings (which we don't see), the camera pulls back from a close-up on his face to the window through which he gazes, and further back to a position analogous to a window in an adjacent apartment; finally, the start of act 2 has a shot of Linda at the sink through the kitchen window. All these shots show the confines in which the Loman family lives.

The film's reliance upon the dining room, as opposed to the kitchen, serves both an aesthetic and a practical purpose. In the play, the kitchen, open to the surrounding outside, calls undue attention to the exterior space, which would look much more fake and artificial on television than the interior spaces. Most realistic plays don't call for exterior scenes. It's much easier to preserve the realism of a scene within the controlled space of interior walls. The exterior scenes in this television adaptation are among the least successful, partly because they claim, despite ocular proof to the contrary, to represent the observed world. The garden, for example, which Willy plants in the final act, is obviously an interior floor dressed up to look like dirt on the ground. The decision to present most of the action in the dining room confines that action within a small space that an audience can accept as "real." Although the lavender wallpaper grows increasingly difficult to tolerate as the action unfolds throughout the performance, the enclosed space helps to create a claustrophobic environment that is perfect for the television event viewed on a small screen in individual homes, compared to a proscenium opening in the theater.

The presence of walls, the shots through windows from the outside, and the confinement of most action within an interior dining room all help to promote the boxed-in feel that Willy vents early in the play when he walks outside and exclaims, "You can't see nothing out here! They boxed in the whole goddam neighborhood!" (101). In this television version of the play, the director chose to film the small, enclosed interior spaces of the Loman house at the expense of the surrounding apartment houses. When Willy goes outside, the audience can see a theatrical drop that represents the apartment houses surrounding the house. Again, though, the drop functions as a sign of that encroachment but does not emotionally impact the action in the play. Also taking into account the "boxed" nature of the television set, the medium through which an audience sees the picture, those same apartments have no sense of height. Seen from a distance and in the obvious two dimensions of flat scenery, the apartments pose no threat whatsoever to the Loman household. Throughout the piece, there is no sense of a world around the play. In general, then, the scenery gets in the way of enjoying the film. You have to make excuses for it in order to enjoy the artistry of the actors. That one can make such allowances testifies to the actors' skills, but given the available choices in this television film, performing without scenery in a large studio might have produced even more powerful results.

Volker Schlöndorff's 1985 film of the Broadway play from the preceding revival starring Dustin Hoffman is much more visually compelling than the previous television effort. While it uses the main cast from the stage revival, this film creatively adapts a stage play to the television medium. Schlöndorff's vision dispensed with any notion of surface realism. In a documentary film, *Private Conversations,* produced separately but released together with the film on DVD, the director explained his visual concept for the filming of the play: "Everything should be fake except the emotions; they will be true, and they'll be what we'll be moved by." In a very real sense, then, the visual field of his film begins with a bare stage or studio and builds around the actors. He justified the design choice by saying that "[i]f you have that much reality, you don't need that many words anymore." Realizing that he was filming a densely packed dramatic text, he figured that he could not have a thoroughly realistic setting as well because the effect would be too jarring. Instead, designer Tony Walton, also a veteran of the stage, created environments that linked thematically to the messages and meanings of the play. While the rooms have actual walls as in the 1966 version, they do not exactly fit together and gaps between them allow views outside the interior spaces. To create the effect of Willy feeling boxed in, the designer established a set-within-a-set motif.

Enormous redbrick apartment houses surround the dominant playing space of the Loman household. These weren't simple drops, but dimensional flats joined at right angles that literally boxed in the little house. Furthermore, the gaps in the household walls allow the audience to see the apartments during interior scenes in which they would not normally be visible. The camera also doesn't hide the fact that the action takes place on a set and not in a "real" room. It exploits the theatricality of the environment by creating images that would not be possible in a regular stage play or in a realistic movie. The camera accentuates the confined nature of Willy's existence by filming from above as Willy exclaims, "There's more people! That's what's ruining this country! Population is getting out of control. The competition is maddening! Smell the stink from that apartment house! And another one on the other side . . ." (7). Looking down at Willy from above, the image captures him within the four walls of his room and within the walls of the surrounding apartments as well. This production changed textual references to Willy as "fat" and a "walrus" to "short" and a "shrimp." The camera delighted in shots angled from above to make Willy appear even smaller than he would otherwise. In particular, the camera gazed down at him alone in his chair facing a much bigger Howard. After Howard rather awkwardly fires him and leaves, Willy stifles his own cry of despair as he shakes one clenched fist at the heavens, a gesture that captures in the instant the essence of the entire character. Near the end of the play, while Willy plants his garden, the camera shoots up at him from a low angle and frames him against the corner of the converging sides of the apartments. The immense size of such threatening shapes in the background mocks Willy's own claims that his "funeral will be massive." All of these extremely dramatic shots amplify the text at critical moments in the play.

The film portrays the idyllic home scenes from the past by a light filter change that makes the scenes both "whiter" and "lighter" in color. Without the presence of the apartments, which block out all the light, the scenes are much brighter. Instead of apartments on all sides, a drop shows the New York City skyline in the distance and a cemetery in the foreground. The paint job on the house, which makes everything seem crisp and new, further highlights the airiness and brightness of these earlier scenes. In the later scenes, the time of the "present," the house stands badly in need of repair with chipped and fading paint, as though regular household maintenance could not take place once the boys left home.

While the text doesn't comment on the house's need for paint, the changes in appearance portray not only the passing of time but also the psychological state of the entire household.

The film makes excellent use of color throughout the action and effectively juxtaposes chocolate brown, vivid red, and white. The front hallway leading to the door—always an important element in a theatrical design since exits and entrances determine focus—resonates with powerful images and meanings in this highly controlled film. The dark brown walls of the narrow hall lead to the front door which has opaque frosted glass until a figure stands right behind it to project a dark and enlarged silhouette. Willy's final exit is effectively dramatic on the small screen as he walks down the dark, narrow hallway and out the door. Ben precedes him, dressed in a white suit, and opens the door onto a white void. When Willy eventually follows, the door opens to the redbrick apartment houses and a dark landscape. Willy closes the door and pauses so that the silhouette of his head shows through the frosted glass. He turns in either direction, as if deciding upon a next move, before finally running off right. The music, composed by Alex North, who composed the music for the original stage production in 1949, swells to a crash as the entire picture whites out and cuts to the Requiem at Willy's graveside.

The film uses the color brown to signify anxiety and unease. At the start of act 2, in the morning after breakfast, a time when things look the most positive, Willy grabs Linda and they dance a little to express their affection and optimism about changing times and fortunes. The dark brown walls, a sure sign in this film of troubled times ahead, frame them in the shot. Indeed, the rest of the play spins downward toward death. Willy, in Dustin Hoffman's portrayal, frequently checks himself in the mirror to reflect his obsessions with his appearance and many crises of self-confidence. Looking in the mirror Willy sees The Woman, and this device cleverly slips past memories into the present. Later, when Willy combs his hair in the men's room at Frank's Chop House, which is also dark brown, The Woman appears again as he turns from the mirror and opens the door into the red hotel room, the same color as the interior of the restaurant. The pivotal scenes in act 2 take place first in the restaurant and then in the Boston hotel room, a memory from Willy's past. Both of these scenes portray acts of betrayal. Obviously, the hotel scene shows Willy's adultery, but in the restaurant scene the boys betray their father and leave him in the men's room. The film shoots both of these scenes in front of brilliant red walls to link them thematically. One more scene in red deserves special notice because it is as if the director stole the expressionistic moment right out of O'Neill's *The Hairy Ape*. After being fired in Howard's office, Willy wanders outside into the rain and along the New York streets. The building is once again redbrick, just like the apartment houses. As Willy walks in the rain, cursing his fate somewhat incoherently, passersby holding black umbrellas refuse to acknowledge him, just as the Fifth Avenue crowd did not pay Yank any attention in O'Neill's play of 1922. Umbrellas completely hide the faces of the crowd, and the black parabolic shapes moving horizontally in both directions against the dark red background show Willy cut up by inhuman and unkind forces. This transition scene, not in the text at all, bridges the scene from Howard's office to Charley's and demonstrates the fear and chaos raging within Willy's own mind.

Aside from the obvious advantages of close-ups and cutting, Schlöndorff's film creates a consistent visual picture that amplifies the text. He films realistic spaces, such as the hallway and front door, for aesthetic and metaphoric values in ways that would be impossible to see on the stage. There is no way, for example, to duplicate the precise feeling evoked by the hallway. In the film, the door fills the screen to an extent that would be impossible to achieve analogously within a proscenium arch. Similarly, the juxtaposed uses of red and brown would be impossible to control in a stage play. Quite originally and artfully, the director adapts a stage play into a film by taking aspects of theatrical scenery and technology and adapting them for cinematic use on the small screen. The camera intrudes inside the house to bring the viewers closer to the action than they could ever possibly be in the theater during a live performance. The meltdown scene between father and son, the last big scene, is brilliantly filmed as the camera moves around and cuts between Biff and Willy, fully capturing the tears, spittle, and sweat that mark this scene as a hallmark of domestic drama and a tour-de-force acting scene exemplary of a muscular, emotional style of acting.

The camera in this scene, and in the hallway scene I described above, is so close to the actors that the audience can't see where the scene takes place. The film gets inside the action, as it were, and distorts the viewer's perspective. Such intimacy to the emotional drama requires an establishing shot to indicate where in space the scene takes place. In the film, prior to the boys' return home, there's a shot of the front stoop, one of Linda inside mending her stockings (her habitual activity), and then one of Willy outside in the "garden," all three flashed in quick succession. The juxtaposition of the three shots indicates that the scene is back at the house, inside the Loman home, as the logical progression goes from outside to inside. Later, in this same scene, one very brief shot shows the entire "stage": Linda and Biff inside in the kitchen; Willy planting his garden outside the kitchen and driving stakes into the ground; the base of the apartment buildings upstage. Finally, the viewer can see the entire stage picture and the relationship of the various playing areas to each other, but only minutely so, and the shot has no impact, certainly not compared to the close-up views of the hallway for example. The shots document that the action takes place on a set. It's the kind of shot that would be taken from an orchestra seat near the back of the house. In order to fit the entire set within the viewfinder, the camera pulls back from the action.

The stage picture in a theater offers the cinematic equivalent of the establishing shot at all times. Unlike such a shot fitted to a small screen, however, the establishing shot in the theater fills the width and height of the proscenium arch. The theater, unlike the film, relies upon a single dominant image to convey meanings that are present throughout the entire performance or at least during the scene in which they are presented. The play onstage creates a different experience through the constant and omnipresent imagery of the design encompassing the performance. Miller's opening stage directions read, "Before us is the Salesman's house. We are aware of towering, angular shapes behind it, surrounding it on all sides. [. . .] As more light appears, we see a solid vault of apartment houses around the small, fragile-seeming home. An air of the dream clings to the place, a dream rising out of reality" (1). This single image dominates the entire performance. I noted above how in the 1985 film the director left gaps in the wall in order to remind an audience that the apartments lurk just outside. Several times the director creates powerful images by including shots of the background apartments. Still, the apartments only selectively and intermittently come into play. It's reasonable to imagine that a television audience would quickly tire of seeing a repeated perspective on the small screen. In a play, however, the single dominant image hovers over the entire play and works into an audience's consciousness as the stage action develops. The dialogue from the play interacts with the design such that new meanings and resonant passages stick in the mind and the eye as the action unfolds. Even though the scenery remains static, it continues to surprise the viewer as the play progresses. As Robert Edmond Jones said long ago, "When the curtain rises, it is the scenery that sets the key of the play. A stage setting is not a background; it is an environment. Players act in a setting, not against it" (24–25). Originally, Arthur Miller determined that the setting of the play should have only three raised platforms on an otherwise rather bare stage. Jo Mielziner's famous design solved the visual problems of the play brilliantly and economically. Surrounded by the urban landscape of modern living, the little Loman house, nearly transparent, floated on the stage as the personification of Willy Loman: "a little boat looking for a harbor" (*Death* 56). The playing areas around the house let the action spill out from a realistic context, and the projected images of apartment buildings on scrim fabric allowed lights to change swiftly from the dark of the present to the lighter shades of the past and to change from the menacing building shapes to the warm sunlight and trees from earlier, happier remembered years.

The central image of the play consistently reinforces the tragedy of a man who can't "walk away." Spatial elements have a temporal element, and temporal elements also carry a spatial dimension in this play. The apartments are the product of time; they weren't there when Willy first bought his house twenty-five years ago. When he talks in the opening scene about how he was dreaming and almost swerved off the road, he's actually recalling earlier days when he drove a red Chevrolet and opened the windshield to let in the air: "But it's so beautiful up there, Linda, the trees are so thick, and the sun is warm" (3). A bit later he recalls the floral abundance of earlier years: "This time of year it was lilac and wisteria. And then the peonies would come out, and the daffodils. What fragrance in this room!" (7). Here, where he stands now in his house, time has changed his view perceptibly over the years with the influx of more and more people, the growth of cities, and the prosperity of postwar America. Such progress, however, has been unkind to Willy: "The street is lined with cars. There's not a breath of fresh air in the neighborhood. The grass don't grow any more, you can't raise a carrot in the back yard" (6). An expanding city has replaced the open spaces in Brooklyn over the years. "The way they boxed us in here," he remarks. "Bricks and windows, windows and bricks" (6). The hulking apartments threaten to swallow the Loman house and feed the drive for progress and material consumption.

Against this onslaught of urban encroachment, Willy refuses to surrender. Always good with his hands, he can put up a ceiling, repair the stoop, fix the roof, or perform any of the sundry tasks that it takes to maintain a house over years of ownership. He says, with deserved pride, "All the cement, the lumber, the reconstruction I put in this house! There ain't a crack to be found in it any more" (54). Despite his best efforts to shore up his home, though, "the woods are burning" around him and his world is continually collapsing. Referring to his career as a salesman, Willy declares to Ben in one of the memory scenes in act 2, "I am building something with this firm, Ben, and if a man is building something he must be on the right track, mustn't he?" (65). "Where is it?" Ben inquires. A salesman's personality, contacts, and buyers are hardly the same as South African diamonds or Alaskan timber. Even Willy admits to Ben in an earlier scene in act 1, "I still feel—kind of temporary about myself" (36). Willy counts on building a future for his son and having something to give him. Just as Joe Keller in *All My Sons* built his business to give to his son, Willy Loman believes he is working hard in order to pass something along to Biff. This myth of building for the future is the bedrock of the American Dream upon which the power of the play grows.

The notion of building something to last for the future is an idea that Linda casually dispenses with when talking to her husband. Life, she says, is a continual casting off. Willy calls it a race with the junkyard. In this respect the temporal aspects of the play receive a spatial dimension. Willy laments with some bitterness that "[o]nce in my life I would like to own something outright before it's broken!" (54). Ironically, Willy himself is broken at precisely the moment at which he finally owns his house. Even before the end, though, at the very beginning of the play, Willy observes the curious labor of making the monthly mortgage payment: "Figure it out. Work a lifetime to pay off a house. You finally own it, and there's nobody to live in it" (4). Linda tells Biff emphatically later in the act, "You've got to get it into your head now that one day you'll knock on this door and there'll be strange people here—" (39). Even more matter of factly, Willy adds early in act 2, "Some stranger'll come along, move in, and that's that." Yet in an abrupt change of mood, he quickly inserts optimistically, "If only Biff would take this house, and raise a family . . ." (54). The idea of giving something to his elder son, leaving something behind, never escapes Willy's consciousness for long. The fact that neither son is settled ensures the home will eventually be a loss. Willy loses his job, too, along the way of thirty-four years of service and loyalty to one company.[2] With the passing of time, Willy simply doesn't know anyone anymore in the business, and nobody knows him. In a moment of rage, Willy yells at his boss about the injustice of a system in which business is business: "I put thirty-four years into this firm, Howard, and now I can't pay my insurance! You can't eat the orange and throw the peel away—a man is not a piece of fruit!" (61–62). Willy has even lost the love of the son who once adored him. Admonishing Biff and Happy, Linda notes that "he put his whole life into you and you've turned your backs on him" (43). Brother Ben promised Willy the chance to make millions, but Willy chose to remain where he was: "We'll do it here, Ben! You hear me? We're gonna do it here!" (66). Willy stays to build something in Brooklyn, and in the passing of time he loses everything.

Death of a Salesman is an extremely dark play in the literal sense that the apartments block out light for the little house. In act 1, Willy comments that you "gotta break your neck to see a star in this yard" (37). Willy tells Linda at the beginning of the second act that he'd like to stop and get some seeds for the garden. This is the most optimistic moment in the play: it's morning, and Willy slept well; he's going to see Howard about getting a New York job that would keep him off the road; and his son has gone to see Bill Oliver in the city about a stake to start a sporting-goods enterprise. Commenting on Willy's desire to buy seeds, Linda warns, "That'd be wonderful. But not enough sun gets back there. Nothing'll grow any more" (52). Surprisingly, Willy counters, "You wait, kid, before it's all over we're gonna get a little place out in the country" (53). This is the only time in the entire play that Willy suggests moving away from the city to the idyllic and ideal peace of the quiet rural environs. When he returns to the subject of seeds for the garden a short bit later, Linda, although laughing, warns again, "But you've tried so many times" (55). Later, after having been abandoned by his sons at the restaurant, and tormented by the memory of his adulterous betrayal with a woman at a Boston hotel, Willy staggers away, muttering, "I've got to get some seeds, right away. Nothing's planted. I don't have a thing in the ground" (96). And so, in the shadow of the looming apartments and by the light of the moon, Willy plants his garden, struggling to shed his "temporary feelings" and get something rooted for the future to take shape.

From first to last, that bright future assumes the form of his elder son, Biff, who is described—no pun intended—as the brightest star of all, the sun. Willy recalls the golden years of Biff's high school stardom and the "greatest day of his life" when Biff played for a city championship team at Ebbets Field. Willy's description of him that day shines through the bleak and dark shadows of the present household situation: "Like a young god. Hercules—something like that. And the sun, the sun all around him. [. . .] God Almighty, he'll be great yet. A star like that, magnificent, can never really fade away!" (51). For Willy, Biff's confession at the end of the play recaptures the glory days from his past. Stunned by the outburst, Willy proclaims, "That boy—that boy is going to be magnificent!" (106). Willy convinces himself, obviously mistakenly, that his insurance policy will buy Biff's love back and guarantee also his son's future successes in business.

Against Willy's decision to stay in the city and build something there, Biff voices an alternative move that suggests liberation from the capitalist/materialist chokehold leveraged against Willy and his second son, Happy. Biff longs to live in the country, work in the wide-open spaces of the mid- and far West with his shirt off and his muscles flexed. In a play that portrays the erasure of the natural world and all its beauty, Biff's epiphany charts a new direction in which to move. Running down flights of stairs after stealing Bill Oliver's fountain pen, Biff finally recognizes what he's been missing in his life: "I stopped in the middle of that building and I saw—the sky. I saw the things that I love in this world. The work and the food and time to sit and smoke" (105). Biff finally recognizes that he is not a leader of men and that he, like his father, is simply a dime a dozen. Finally, he divides even that claim to identity and blurts, "I'm nothing!" (106). In the Requiem, against Happy's competing desire to stay in the city and uphold Willy's legacy, Biff asserts that he knows who he is and remains at peace with that self-discovery. The play thus ends with the potential of happiness for Biff as a product of self-knowledge and a validation of the American worker and the common man.

Unfortunately, as nice as this all sounds, it's a lot of rot. The depths of Biff's self-actualization cannot be taken at face value. Biff harbored a deep grudge against Willy for the adulterous affair in Boston, after which he burned his tennis shoes with "University of Virginia" blazoned on them. Willy argues that Biff spitefully threw away his life on account of that incident, and the logic of the play determines that Willy is right about this accusation. It's therefore impossible to believe Biff when he says that he's not a leader of men. In the memory scenes—verified scenes and not the fancies of Willy's mind—Biff directs his friends to follow him and to clean out the basement furnace! He's the captain and quarterback of the championship football team. Three universities compete for his athletic services in the form of full-ride college scholarships. Most of all, his boyhood friend Bernard, whom he taunts and picks on endlessly and who would grow up to be a lawyer and argue cases before the Supreme Court of the United States, idolizes and loves him. To give all that up because of discovering Willy's affair in Boston represents the essence of spitefulness and profound immaturity.[3]

The drama reduces to a single defining moment what would have inevitably occurred without such a dramatic and scarring episode. In the normal process of growing up and in the passing of time, Biff and Hap would eventually discover the truth that their father is not the great salesman they worshipped as boys. All of his aphorisms about being liked, well liked, and whatever else would be uncovered as rather benign half-truths. Even if Biff never discovered his father in a hotel room with another woman, he would still inevitably have to face the fact that his father is not the great man he imagined him to be. Perhaps the novel form would treat this gradual discovery more delicately and beautifully. This discovery, though, is not a justifiable excuse to throw one's life away. Charley asks Willy the question midway through the play: When are you going to grow up? Biff says of himself that he's still a boy. Even Linda says of Biff, "You're such a boy!" (39). The fact is that neither father nor son has grown up. In *Cat on a Hot Tin Roof,* Maggie says to Brick, "life has got to be allowed to continue even after the *dream* of life is—all—over. . . ." (58). Neither Biff nor Willy can walk away from their dreams of what they thought life was supposed to be. If Biff could get past thinking of his father as a fake, if Willy could stop expecting Biff to bring home prizes for him, perhaps the two of them would see what they've missed and the years they've squandered building enmity between them. They might find love, support, and companionship. The final scene is a wish-fulfillment fantasy for all the silent fathers and sons in the audience who long to cry, "I love you, dad." "I love you, too, son. Forgive me."

7
Getting the Guests

There's . . . so much . . . over the dam, so many . . . disappointments, evasions,
I guess, lies maybe . . . so much we remember we wanted, once . . . so little
that we've . . . settled for . . . we talk, sometimes, but mostly . . . no.
—Edward Albee, *A Delicate Balance*

Midway through the first act of *Who's Afraid of Virginia Woolf?* (1962), winding up the first round of "Humiliate the Host," Martha describes boxing George
into a huckleberry bush. In Mike Nichols's 1966 film version of the play, George
exits during Martha's story and the camera follows him "offstage" into the back
hall. While Martha continues to speak in the living room, the camera closes on
George's facial reactions to her derisive tale. The handheld camera stays with
George as he walks down the hall and opens the door to a back closet and turns
on the light; then it looks down on him from an angle just above his head, as if it
were on the top shelf of the closet, as he locates a bundle and carefully unwraps
a rifle. A single incandescent lightbulb swinging in the foreground heightens the
murderous look on his face. The camera then assumes George's point of view as
he returns to the living room and stalks his prey (Martha) from behind. Seeing
the victim from the killer's point of view is standard suspense stuff. The camera
follows the gun sight down the barrel to the back of Martha's head, then cuts to
close-ups of Honey's and Nick's horrified reactions, and then a shot of Martha's
turn toward the gun, and a zoom-lens close-up of her startled eyes. Suddenly,
the point of view reverses to an objective position on the other side of Martha,
and the camera faces the rifle as George pulls the trigger and a colorful Japanese
parasol pops out to the shock, startled relief, and subsequent laughter of all.

The camera shot that ends the sequence above is the only one that captures
the reactions of all the players from the point of view of a theatrical audience.
While the film follows the same text as Albee's play, that scene onstage is more
primitive and at the same time much more inscrutable than its film counterpart.
A theatrical audience can't follow George offstage and thus can't see his reactions to Martha's story. He simply leaves and the story continues with no cutting
between what is said in the living room and George's reactions to those words
in the back hall. A theatrical audience, too, can't see the scene from George's
point of view. When he returns a short time later, he conceals a short-barreled

shotgun behind his back, so the audience doesn't suspect that he is hiding anything and never even sees the gun until George raises it to Martha's head. When he attempts to shoot her onstage, Nick and Honey react in concert with the audience in the theater.

Who's Afraid of Virginia Woolf? plays a very different game onstage with an audience than does the film version of the same drama. By using all the conventions of the suspense thriller, the film tricks the audience into believing that George really might murder Martha. This is quite false. As played by Richard Burton, George appears intent *to kill Martha.* At least that is what the audience thinks. Obviously, though, the character himself knows that the gun is a toy; George procured it and put it away to save for a special occasion. The film encourages the audience to believe something that does not reflect George's true feelings, and the camera techniques and the editing reinforce an illusion/reality theme. Onstage, however, an audience can't see what runs through George's mind; it doesn't have access to his brooding face. The actor, then, can honestly play the intent, *to scare Martha,* when he enters the scene with the fake gun behind his back. George harbors no latent desire *to murder Martha;* he merely wishes to scare her and to win the game that he is playing at all costs. The honesty of the stage drama counters the misleading dazzle of the film and highlights the rules of engagement by which George and Martha do battle. Innately theatrical, the games spark their lives in a brutally dull world of heartbreaking disappointments.

A gross comparison reveals alterations between the screen adaptation and the stage play. The film, first of all, is much shorter than the play. While the movie is long by Hollywood standards at 131 minutes, the play is much longer still. Among the cuts, a large section from the end of act 2 and a large section of the "exorcism" scene are missing in the film, about which I'll have more to say a bit later. While most of the changes involve cuts, the film also offers additions, with none more obvious than the inclusion of a scene at a roadhouse where the two couples go dancing. This scene attempts to open up the stage play by shifting the locale. Many critics of the play have asked why the visiting couple, Nick and Honey, don't leave the house once things begin to turn nasty. In the film, they do decide to leave and George offers to drive them home, but they stop along the way to grant Honey's whim for dancing. After George plays his vicious game of "Get the Guests," Nick and Honey do walk away. Martha gets in the car, picks them up, and takes them back to the house for what in the play serves as the third and final act.

The play, of course, is a living-room drama, and all the action transpires within a single, claustrophobic space. The film, not limited to one locale, explores the environment of the entire house. After George and Martha first enter their house, they go to the kitchen and George sits down and begins to work a crossword puzzle from the newspaper; Martha opens the refrigerator door and chews a leftover chicken drumstick. A few moments later, after she announces that company will arrive shortly, they walk upstairs to their bedroom and Martha comically tidies up by hiding clothes and dishes in drawers and under covers. George later refers to an abstract painting in their living room as "a pictorial representation of the order of Martha's mind" (23). The accumulated clutter in the house reflects upon Martha as a housekeeper and the gender roles of the time, but also, with the details of the living space revealed, silently comments on a standard of living. George's mediocre academic career creates tension in the marriage. He is certainly not going to succeed Martha's father as the next president of the college. Martha makes a point of saying that they have to live on an associate professor's salary. Despite Honey's initial exclamation, "Oh, isn't this lovely!" which may be simply polite discourse and/or flattery (Nick is new on the faculty; Martha is the president's daughter), the house is not lovely at all. It's small and comfortable in a worn sort of way and places George and Martha securely as middle, middle class with no better prospects ahead.

Several exterior scenes in the movie further break up the confines of a one-room drama. The action spills out onto the porch, the front yard, and all the way down to a swing tied to a tree at the property's edge. Two scenes that are not in the play at all deserve additional comment. The opening credits show George and Martha leaving the president's house late at night and walking home along campus paths to their nearby home. Obviously, such a sequence would be impossible to put on the stage, and without any dialogue at all, before one sentence of text is even spoken, the film captures the world of the play completely. The exterior shots were all taken on location at Smith College in Northampton, Massachusetts. This first sequence captures the rustle of the fall leaves as the couple toddles along past various academic buildings and even the college greenhouse. This opening carries its own perverse sense of humor. First of all, the adults are drunk, not the students! Secondly, the scene is, literally, a walking tour of an idyllic liberal arts college campus. All college guidebooks and campus brochures show plenty of pictures of a diverse and pristine campus in full fall foliage. If one actually attends college in the Northeast, one spends the bulk of the academic year knee-deep in snow, yet the advertising materials always display robust fall colors. In Nichols's film treatment, not only does the "walking tour" take place at night, the entire film is shot in black and white. Instead of extending an invitation to attend a vibrant institution, the opening scene establishes a pervasive mood of loneliness and quiet fear. The camera follows the couple at a distance and from above, and thus they look small compared to the vast silence and dark space surrounding them. Yet they do walk together, however much in silence, and the opening shows them walking through the world as a team, a theme that is important to a reading of the play and is a direct contrast to another scene two-thirds into the action.

The film covers the interval between acts 2 and 3 with a scene in which Martha wanders through the front yard calling and searching for George. As in the opening sequence, the shot is taken from above, as though from the second floor of the house, perhaps even from the window of the bedroom, where Martha has just seduced Nick. Now, in the desolate afterglow of that encounter, she looks for her husband. Like in the opening, this long shot shows the human figure against the vast black surroundings of the early-morning darkness. The viewer can see Martha flailing about, groping to turn off the blinkers of the hastily parked station wagon, staggering about the yard, braying her husband's name. Unlike the credit sequence, though, Martha staggers alone this time. While the same loneliness and sense of isolation loom throughout the opening walk, at least Martha and George face it together. The later scene shows Martha ominously alone and desperate to find her partner. The film cuts down much of Martha's opening third-act monologue but visually fills the dramatic moment with compelling images of her groping her way in the dark.

Having covered all of these differences, the film remains remarkably faithful to Edward Albee's play, although the playwright did voice reservations about the movie. Understandably, he objected to the roadhouse scene, which wasn't in his play at all. Overall, he felt that the film oversimplified his play. Director Mike Nichols has conceded Albee's complaint that the film emphasizes emotional aspects of the play, but Nichols pointed out that this was a consequence not of interpretation but of the particularities of the film medium. In his biography of the playwright, *Edward Albee: A Singular Journey,* Mel Gussow interviews Nichols about the film adaptation. Speaking first about the play, Nichols comments, "I always thought it was Shakespearean in that the two main characters compete in recruiting the audience to their side in a manner not dissimilar to *The Taming of the Shrew*" (235). It's irresistible to note that Elizabeth Taylor and Richard Burton also played opposite each other as Kate and Petruchio in the film version of that Shakespearean comedy (1967) soon after *Virginia Woolf.* Coincidentally, too, Albee's play parodies *Shrew* in the third act when George baits Martha by telling her that the moon went down and then came back up again; the film, in fact, shows the moon going down.[1] The problems and challenges of transferring a Shakespearean drama to the screen are analogous to the challenges of adapting Albee's play to the film medium as well. In the play version, the actors compete for stage focus and force the audience to choose whom to follow at any given moment. George and Martha play directly to the audience or to each other or to Nick and Honey. With the two main actors playing one off of the other or addressing all three at the same time, the bounce between the stage and the seated audience gives the language buoyancy and drives the action. The back-and-forth movement onstage, then, turns the pivoting heads of the collective audience.

Even though *Who's Afraid of Virginia Woolf?* was his first feature film, Nichols, a veteran stage director and performer, wisely understood that he could not duplicate the stage dynamic in a film. About that, he told Gussow,

> Claustrophobia did not seem to me to be so much an element. I also realized that the recruiting of the audience as a participant in the battle was no longer possible. Therefore the movie would be far more emotional than the play. In the play to a great extent emotion and tension are discharged in laughter, and although there are big laughs in the movie, it's not the same thing. It's frozen. That prizefight element of the play was gone, which left me with the emotional heart of it. (136)

The movie gets to the "emotional heart" through a series of close-ups that reveal what the characters feel about what has just happened in a way that a stage performance can never do. This structural device penetrates the exterior of the characters' defenses to reveal the essence of what they're thinking and feeling. The camera movement from distance to close-up enacts a recurring pattern in the film. Whereas the audience always remains at the same distance to the performer in a stage play and sees all the performers simultaneously, the film allows the audience to get closer to the action by focusing on the effects of the torrential words. One character says something; the next shot moves up close to catch the reaction of another character to what was just said. Viewers interpret what they see by relating one shot to the next. The relationship between these close-ups and the shots that come immediately before or after them determines the interpretation. As the action proceeds, this shift produces the illusion of penetrating the surface of the action to discover its "deep" mysteries.

Numerous examples of this technique abound in the film. After Honey exits with Martha to "powder her nose," George probes Nick on several subjects including how many children he hopes to have. After George notes, "Your wife is slim-hipped" (a repeated phrase in the film as well as the play), the film cuts to a close-up of Honey on the stairs, listening to the men. Obviously, such a transition is impossible in the theater, and this moment is not present in the play. The close-up of Honey's reaction to the men's conversation reveals her anxiety about the subject of children and childbirth. In David Mamet's parlance, such a shot is a "tell," a moment that punctures the cool exterior of a character to reveal for a brief moment what lies beneath. The film produces such a moment to tell the audience to pay attention to this sore subject and to foreshadow future revelations in the action. Honey, at this early point in the film, recovers her "public" face by the time she actually enters the scene. Shortly after her descent from upstairs, she innocently remarks to George, "I didn't know you had a son." The camera cuts to a close-up of George's reaction to this question, and his steely response gives away the fact that he's angry that Martha has spoken about such a previously agreed-upon taboo subject. Later, when the two men are alone again, Nick refers to Honey and admits that he married her because she was pregnant, after which the camera focuses on George's reaction. The obvious reading of this is that George is surprised by the news since Nick previously said that he and Honey don't have any children. The moment also displays George's significantly keen interest in the subject of children and perhaps his jealousy of Nick's procreative powers. The film doesn't fully disclose the nature of George's reaction, but similar to Honey's in the first example, his concern loads the plot for future revelations.

As the couples ride in the car on the way to take Nick and Honey home, Martha stings George by saying that he used to drink "bergin," a reference to the story that George told Nick earlier about an alleged third party. The shot quickly cuts to George's reaction, then to his foot slamming the brakes, and then to the car veering into the roadhouse parking lot for more drinking and dancing. Far more than in the play, this visual sequence shows the effects of Martha's barb against George and his emotional reaction to it. What it actually means remains entirely ambiguous. It's not clear that George did drink "bergin" at one time or that he was the boy in the story he told to Nick. That he might be that boy and that Nick—and by extension the audience—might think him that boy are enough to alarm George and provoke a violent reaction. During the vocal shouting match between George and Martha in the parking lot outside the roadhouse, George confesses that he can't stand her attacks anymore, a charge Martha refutes by saying that indeed George married her just for those same attacks. The text comes virtually straight from the play, but the film shifts to a close-up of George's face in profile and with his chin at his chest. That image connotes that once again Martha's words have worked their way home to the "emotional heart" of George, and that her retort is not entirely false. If it were, George would show much less pain than the image on screen portrays. After Martha races past George on the highway, the camera zooms in on George's face before dissolving into a transition back to the house. The portrait of his chagrin acknowledges that he knows what's going to happen back at his house, that it hurts him, and that he's helpless to stop it.

Albee initially wanted to call his play *Exorcism* but settled on using that title for the third and final act. The action moves from night to first light, a reversal of another classic American domestic drama, O'Neill's *Long Day's Journey into Night,* in which enveloping fog covers the clearness of the morning light and later pitch night surrounds the famous single burning electric bulb. By the end of that play nothing is as it seems to be, while Albee's play, which appeared to toil in absurdity, tidies up all its loose ends. Nick, speaking for the audience, repeats, "I think I understand this" (236). The secrets come out, one at the end of the second act and another at the end of the play: Honey doesn't want any children; George and Martha can't have any. All the action of the play pushes forward to disclose these private secrets, the "emotional heart" of the play as revealed in the film, the innermost secrets that motivated all the strange behaviors on display. Before the final game, George explains to Honey the purpose of the games they've been playing: "When you get down to bone, you haven't got all the way, yet. There's something inside the bone . . . the marrow . . . and that's what you gotta get at" (213). This reference to the body and to games describes the dramatic action of the play and viscerally parallels Nichols's statement about the film and his attempts to get to the "emotional heart" of it. The physical references indicate that the action penetrates the body and grabs hold of its essential parts (the marrow, the heart). The camera work, moving to and from close-up positions, further replicates the "going deep" model of this dramaturgy. The camera zooms in on the face to show the damaging effects of words and dredges up the secrets that more distance would effectively hide.

While the film, through its regular use of close-ups, reveals the secrets of the two couples, the play, through its sequence of games, never gets past the surface. According to Stephen J. Bottoms, the play is "fundamentally, *all about* performance and performativity" (*Albee* 5). Speaking in private to Nick, George allows that "[i]t isn't the prettiest spectacle . . . seeing a couple of middle-age types hacking away at each other, all red in the face and winded, missing half the time" (92). George remarks that, instead of penetrating the body and getting to the meat of the matter, the blows between Martha and him rarely, if ever, cleave the surface. Everything is visible and out in the open. The subtle joke, from George's point of view, is that their blows draw no blood and that the sight of two fifty-something people flailing at one another produces a comic effect. George introduces this image by calling their routine a "spectacle," which implies that someone is watching and that the entire action is a performance within a performance. Game playing between George and Martha thus offers an alternative dramatic structure to the surface/depth model produced by the film. *Who's Afraid of Virginia Woolf?* reigns as a spectator sport in which the audience can cheer for both sides.

Albee's stage directions indicate that the two main performers square off against each other as boxers or wrestlers. Even near the end of the play, George motivates Martha not only as her adversary but also as a kind of fight coach hovering over her in her corner of the ring. Before the final game, he urges, "I want you on your feet and slugging, sweetheart, because I'm going to knock you around, and I want you up for it" (208). The audience does not witness a psychological drama so much as a boxing match. Each character wants to knock the other out. The action does not go deeper but it does go longer in a succession of rounds, and the spectacle, a prizefight, requires onlookers. Nick and Honey arrive to provide the necessary audience for George and Martha's act. Obviously, a drama requires an audience, but *Virginia Woolf* magnifies that dynamic by bringing the audience onstage in the form of Nick and Honey, bland characters who function as stand-ins for the audience to witness the blood sport between George and Martha.[2] By standing in for the audience, they give the lead actors someone to play to, thus bringing the audience "closer" to the action. At the same time, Nick and Honey's role as an audience gives George and Martha license to theatricalize their behavior in pursuit of the ultimate objective of winning their game. Nick and Honey are absolutely indispensable for the life of the play: the action doesn't really begin until they arrive; when they leave, the play is over. Martha and George's games have no point without Nick and Honey present; there is no play without at least one person to witness the event.

Martha's opening gambit, "We've got guests," surprises George completely and throws down the gauntlet: "Do you want to play?" George responds with a challenge of his own. As they prepare to greet their visitors, George warns, "Just don't start on the bit, that's all" (18). Coming out of the blue as it does, this is a strange statement for George to make. It's hard to motivate this line on a naturalistic or psychological level precisely because talk about the child in front of other people is strictly forbidden and has never been done. Why, then, does George choose this particular moment to remind Martha about a taboo subject that has never been broached before in public? On a playwriting level, this line is like a dramaturgical revolver found in an Ibsen drama that the audience fully realizes will fire before the final curtain. George repeats his warning to Martha not to talk about the "kid." At this point, the audience knows that this is a contentious issue and that the rest of the play will culminate in a talk about the child. George refers to the subject of the child as a "bit"—in theatrical parlance, a physical or verbal routine that is generally comic, a sort of game. George's admonition to Martha, then, returns and raises the stakes of the game they play. By bringing up the topic and warning Martha not to speak of it, George lays down the rules and dares Martha to cross the line. She answers the challenge, talks about the son in her first private conversation with Honey, and moves the game further along while raising the stakes in the process.[3]

While the games begin practically with the opening line, only four "official" ones play out in the following order: "Humiliate the Host," "Get the Guests," "Hump the Hostess," and "Bringing up Baby." In terms of winners and losers, the last becomes the first in a reversal of fortune as the play unfolds. George is knocked down in all three rounds of "Humiliate the Host": his boxing match with Martha; his career as an academic "flop"; the story of his first novel, undoubtedly fictitious (he's a historian, not a fiction writer), which Martha's father forbade him from publishing. George turns the tables in act 2 with a rousing game of "Get the Guests," using an improvised story of his second novel to rise from the mat and destroy Nick and Honey with the facts and circumstances of their marriage. This further prepares the way for George's final triumph over Martha in the ultimate game, "Bringing up Baby." The man who appears weakest actually is the strongest at the end and he delivers the knockout punch.

Winning truly isn't everything, though, for this play, far more than the film, shows the human cost of playing games. "Hump the Hostess," for example, does not appear in the film, but it is a spectacularly theatrical scene in the play. Martha seduces Nick, although he thinks that he's seducing her, in front of George in order to make George mad. The visual picture of two playing for the benefit of a third reinforces the playing dynamic of an audience onstage mirroring the one in the house for a heightened effect. George, however, frustrates Martha by pretending that he doesn't care what she does. He acts as if nothing is wrong and pulls up a chair to read a book as if this is his customary 4:00 p.m. study time instead of twelve hours later (or earlier). He turns his chair away from the two "lovers" and positions himself near the door facing downstage. George refuses to serve as audience for Martha and Nick, and because of his withdrawal from the scene Martha must choose between admitting defeat in her game with George or carrying out her tease with Nick and actually taking him to bed. She tries to engage George and get him to stop her, but he refuses to act as if he cares at all what she does. His victory over her is a strange and hollow one, though, as his stiff posture and refusal to compromise push his wife into Nick's strong but uncomprehending embrace.

Once Martha and Nick leave, however reluctantly on Martha's part, George, alone, reads aloud a passage from his book: "And the west, encumbered by crippling alliances, and burdened with a morality too rigid to accommodate itself to the swing of events, must . . . eventually . . . fall" (174). It's impossible not to link this quotation with the preceding events. "Crippling alliances" may refer to George and Martha's marriage, which seems to bring out the worst in both of them and may drag them both down as the years go by; or, more to the point, it may refer to the offstage liaison taking place at that moment between Martha and Nick, a union that threatens everyone's future. George, the historian, the man of the past, gives way to the young man, blond and good looking, a scientist, a biologist, the wave of future generations. The future doesn't look very bright in such hands. George could have prevented his wife from sleeping with Nick by simply asking, begging her not to go with him. She practically begs him to beg her not to do it. He doesn't bend, and she goes off with another man. The game is not over at this point, but it is out of control and neither participant is willing or able to stop playing.

Adherence to the game becomes, in the words of the book George is reading, "too rigid" a morality "to accommodate itself to the swing of events." George recognizes the absurdity of his situation, but he does nothing to change it. However much this metaphorical passage amplifies the meanings and themes of the play, the full-bodied gesture that follows reveals even more important information. George responds violently to what he has just read by hurling the book at the chimes against the wall and creating a cacophony of sound that precipitates Honey's return to the stage, George's further revenge plot, and the end of the act.[4] This outburst cracks open George's complacency and, like a movie close-up, indicates an emotional reaction to events. The isolated character onstage is about the only means the theater has of creating an analogous situation to the close-up. While the camera moves in to catch the interior thoughts of a character, the theatrical audience responds to violent and explosive physical moves, which can be read from a significant distance, as signs of psychological states. Despite the fact that he's won the game of "Hump the Hostess," George's violent response signals that he sees himself as the big loser, a condition that spurs his next and final idea to get Martha.

"Bringing up Baby," the final game, is much more extensive in the stage drama than in the film. The film presents Martha remembering her son as if he were a real person. The play script, which is much longer, produces quite a different effect. Conditioned by the creative stories and games that have been played thus far, the theatrical audience regards all narratives as fictitious and probably suspects at this point that there is no son. This bit of foreknowledge helps in the final reading of the play and puts the audience in position to appreciate the storytelling adventures of Martha's improvisational narrative, gently supplemented by George's encouragement and a few corrections, which turn into a dynamic duet as they trade insults. The scene builds to a crescendo of simultaneous speech, Martha protesting that her son's purity is the one light in her marriage, George reciting the requiem mass in Latin. In the film, the camera mostly closes in on Martha's face with George present only as a voice-over. On the stage, though, the two combatants vie equally for attention, each trying to outdo the other. In the printed text, the simultaneous speeches are laid out side by side. Nick and Honey, the audience for the scene, say almost nothing during its entirety. Their function is to watch. Finally, George delivers his "telegram" announcing the death of the boy and disclosing the car accident that killed him in remarkably identical circumstances to the ones that killed the "bergin-drinking" boy long ago. Martha thinks she catches George in his lie by asking him to produce the telegram announcing the boy's death. George barely represses his pent-up laughter as he replies that he ate it. There is no evidence to corroborate the accident. Martha's anger comes not so much from acknowledging the end of her illusion of having a son, as from losing the game. Stephen J. Bottoms argues persuasively that "Martha is reduced to despair by George's announcement of the death of their imaginary son ('I have killed him'), not because she actually believes in this as a physical murder (she is not insane), but because she knows that George's performative decree has had the effect of taking them across a line which cannot be re-crossed" (*Albee* 6). The game has literally and figuratively gone too far. The play ends in a kind of no-man's-land in which all the former rules and boundaries of conduct have been erased and will have to be redrawn and renegotiated in the future.

Albee's play flirts with a form not totally dissimilar from one Ibsen employed almost one hundred years earlier, but he subverts the well-made-play use of inciting moments, arriving guests, and buried secrets with a unique turn. Rather than plumb the hidden recesses of the past and the private motivational/psychological drives of individual characters, Albee's play shimmers on the surface of witty dialogue and game structure along a horizontal, as opposed to vertical, axis. In her most confessional speech, Martha describes her relationship to George and discloses her fear that she will lose him someday. This description matches perfectly the physical action of the play and the to-and-fro movement of the games the two engage in:

> George who is out somewhere there in the dark. . . . George who is good to me, and whom I revile; who understands me, and whom I push off; who can make me laugh, and I choke it back in my throat; who can hold me, at night, so that it's warm, and whom I will bite so there's blood; who keeps learning the games we play as quickly as I can change the rules; who can make me happy and I do not wish to be happy, and yes I do wish to be happy. [. . .] whom I will not forgive for having come to rest; for having seen me and having said: yes, this will do; who has made the hideous, the hurting, the insulting mistake of loving me and must be punished for it. [. . .] who tolerates, which is intolerable; who is kind, which is cruel; who understands, which is beyond comprehension. [. . .] Some day . . . hah!

some *night* . . . some stupid, liquor-ridden night . . . I will go too far . . . and I'll either break the man's back . . . or push him off for good . . . which is what I deserve. (190–91)

More than anything else, Martha fears that the game will stop and that she will be left alone without her husband's comforting presence. As George sings "Who's afraid of Virginia Woolf?" he prods Martha gently to see if she still has the courage to continue the game. Having crossed the line of what she thought possible, Martha says no. Whether or not she will answer the challenge later goes beyond the scope of the play, but the audience sees and, more importantly, experiences the difficult challenges of playing and staying in the game onstage, a theatrical game that mirrors the game of life to which the audience returns when the play ends.

In a 1980 interview, Albee expressed succinctly the purpose of his work: "But all serious art, not just plays, is an attempt to modify and change people's perception of themselves, to bring them into larger contact with the fact of being alive" (De La Fuente 144). Compared to blond and bland Nick and his vapid wife, Honey, George and Martha are not a dysfunctional couple; they are desperately trying to sustain love by attempting to draw blood from each other in order to whet their appetites for living. At the very end of the film, after Nick and Honey have gone home, the camera closes on Martha's pained face, then pans slightly to her shoulder to capture her hand clasped in George's. They are still together at the end. The image next changes focus to the background, the window and beyond, the outside world, the dawn of a new day. The juxtaposition of these successive images of Martha's face, two hands held together, and breaking day suggests that the events of the night have not destroyed George and Martha and that they will resume their life together bowed, definitely, but not broken.

8

Lamebrains across Texas

One story's as good as another. It's all in the way you tell it. That's what counts.
That's what makes the difference.

—Sam Shepard, *Seduced*

The Broadway revival of *True West* in 2000 sparked renewed critical praise for
Sam Shepard's 1980 play. Jack Kroll heralded the show as a pinnacle of theatrical form by saying that "you are forcibly reminded of the ineffable power
of theatre, despite all the noise made by the unlive arts—movies, TV, cyberia"
("Wild Wild West"). These words offer powerful praise indeed, but they shroud
the virtues of theater in general, and Shepard's play in particular, with gauzy
prose that doesn't really convey much substantive argument. To define "the ineffable power of theatre" by showing how Shepard's dramatic text translates into
a transcendent theatrical production, I will refrain from aggrandizing theater
as a "live" event, but instead probe stress points in the text, those cracks subject
to the pressure of inquiry which divulge ambivalence and ambiguity, and try to
fill the empty spaces with imaginative possibilities. Paradoxically, and wonderfully, these stress points in Shepard's well-built play reveal its enduring theatricality and artistic strength.

Written in California, *True West* premiered at San Francisco's tiny Magic Theatre before heading east for a now-infamous production at Joseph Papp's Public
Theatre in December 1980. Shepard and his director, Robert Woodruff, wanted
the West Coast actors to appear in the New York premiere as well, but Papp insisted upon Peter Boyle and Tommy Lee Jones. Woodruff later resigned in protest, Papp took over, and Shepard disavowed the entire production. Two years
later, two unknown actors made the play, their theater, and themselves famous.
The Steppenwolf Theatre's production of *True West* in 1982 launched John Malkovich as a major star and garnered great press for professional theater in Chicago. When that same production moved to Greenwich Village in New York,
director Gary Sinise stepped into the other leading role. Many people take this
ballyhooed revival for the original, but that mistake can be excused because the
production, revered in its own right, was also filmed for television at the Cherry
Lane Theatre and broadcast on PBS in 1984. This film version, which still

fetches a good price on eBay, more or less documents a live stage performance. Its shortcomings begin with an admission that it fails to adapt the play for cinematic purposes, a claim I'll return to later when I try to clinch my argument about the power of the play.

Casting also provided the novel attraction for the most recent commercial stage production in which the lead actors, Philip Seymour Hoffman and John C. Reilly, alternated playing the brothers, Austin and Lee. At one point in the play, Lee says to his brother, "I always wondered what'd be like to be you" (*Seven Plays* 26). Since role reversal is the dominant structural device in the play, the decision for the actors to switch roles reinforced what was already explicit in the text. Kroll insisted that the casting decision was no gimmick: "Swapping the roles unlocks the heart of Shepard's much-revived play, one of his sharpest, funniest examinations of his favorite theme, the divided nature of the American soul" ("Wild Wild West"). Among wildly positive reviews, two Johns (Lahr and Simon) cast dissenting opinions, the former with a backhanded compliment ("minor play brilliantly cast" [121]) and the latter with a dismissive pun ("nice production of a good Shepard" ["Switch-hitters"]). Unlike Lahr and Simon, who favored the production over the play, Ben Brantley, writing in the *New York Times,* felt that the casting decision of the production demonstrated the richness of the dramatic text: "this production makes a persuasive case for *True West* as a great American play, arguably Mr. Shepard's finest. The contrast of the two versions, which are similarly staged but quite different in tone, also shows the incredible variety that can be harvested from a work this fertile without betraying its essential nature" (1).

How does one conjoin "essential nature" and "incredible variety"? It would be tempting to view the essential nature of Shepard's play as a muddle that clever directors could shape any way they see fit to satisfy their individual imaginations. *True West* remains, though, Shepard's most well crafted, tightly structured, and traditional in form work. Diverse opinions regarding its artistic value all agree that the play marked a dramatic departure from Shepard's familiar playwriting style. Whereas previous Shepard plays featured opaque, often impenetrable imagery and dazzling monologues with unconventional narratives, critics viewed *True West* as transparently obvious and chided the playwright for such simplicity. Reviewing the 1980 New York premiere, Frank Rich observed, "*True West* slips only when Mr. Shepard, a master of ellipses, tries to fill in his blanks" ("Shepard's *True West*"). Rich suggested that Shepard's desire for clarity made his work much less interesting than some of his former efforts. Douglass Watt reached a similar conclusion with his review in the *New York Daily News:* "what we see before us in *True West* is a slicker Shepard, but one just going through familiar paces in a thin variation on the old theme" (366), that theme being the debunking of the American myth and sad disclosures of the empty American Dream. Clive Barnes evaluated Shepard's most accessible play as his worst to date: "Despite a few thunder flashes of vivid drama it is conceivably the least satisfactory Shepard play I have yet come across, and I have been one of the staunchest supporters of Shepard from the beginning of his career" (Rev. of *True West* 369).

True West is the third installment in what has become known retrospectively as Shepard's trilogy of family plays. *Buried Child* (1978) immediately preceded it, and perhaps its critical success as a Pulitzer Prize winner for best play in 1979 raised expectations and directed an intense spotlight on all the perceived shortcomings of the subsequent play. That aside, *True West* is a very different play from either *Buried Child* or the first play in the series, *Curse of the Starving Class* (1977). The mysteries in the early family plays resist explanation. Who is the buried child? Who is the father of the child? What does one make of the burgeoning crops sprouting from the fallow fields? What does all the reckless symbolism mean? Similarly, the family repeatedly insists in *Curse* that they're not starving. "How can you be hungry all the time?" asks the mother, Ella, of her son. "We're not poor. We're not rich but we're not poor" (*Seven Plays* 143). Who is starving? And how? Physically? Emotionally? Financially? All three plays deal with family issues and treat the subject matter somewhat realistically, but the first two remain much more enigmatic and puzzling works. By contrast, Shepard hones the mysteries in *True West* to a bare minimum.

In comparison to all his work prior to 1980, dating back to his salad days as a celebrated avant-garde writer in Greenwich Village, *True West* exerts a discipline anathema to the flamboyance of his youthful efforts. Critics have referred to his early one-acts as "disposable plays," and indeed Shepard claimed to have written his first play, *Cowboys,* on the back of Tootsie Roll wrappers. When those were lost or simply thrown away, Shepard rewrote the play we know today as *Cowboys #2.* In an introduction written in 1985 for a republished collection, *The Unseen Hand and Other Plays,* Shepard labels his early works as "[a] series of impulsive chronicles representing a chaotic, subjective world" (xi). The published form of these plays contradicts the immediacy and intimacy with which they were first produced in the emerging tiny performance spaces of the thriving off-off-Broadway theater movement: *The Rock Garden* at Theatre Genesis (1964), *Icarus's Mother* at Caffe Cino (1965), *Red Cross* at Judson Poets' Theatre (1966). Written and performed to address the moment in which they were conceived, none was built to last.

All of the early one-acts exude improvisational spontaneity, monologic excess, and imagistic wonders. Engulfed in existential angst and the fears of his girlfriend's impending move for a new job, Stu sits fully clothed in a bathtub for the entire duration of *Chicago* and enacts a series of make-believe vignettes.

In *Red Cross,* Carol delivers a highly graphic and emotionally detached account of her own death in a skiing accident. An overhead jet's vapor trail instills paranoia among the male characters in *Icarus's Mother,* while falling bookcases form a recurring motif in *Fourteen Hundred Thousand.* Shepard's first two-act plays, or "full-length" works, display similar imaginative extravagances. In *La Turista,* a couple named after popular cigarette brands, Kent and Salem, battle dysentery in a lively Mexican hotel. *Operation Sidewinder* (1970), which premiered at Lincoln Center, featured an enormous cast and a drug-addled plot in which militant black protesters attempt to drop acid into the water supply of Fort George. *The Tooth of Crime* (1972), a futuristic and violent rock-and-roll fantasy, mythologizes pop stars as killers. In *Angel City* (1976), a lizardlike movie mogul replete with rotting, molting skin seeks to create a real-life disaster in his newest film.

As early as 1978, critic Stanley Kauffmann exalted Shepard as the best practicing American playwright, but he simultaneously issued a significant caveat. While Shepard's work displayed genuine talent, it lacked discipline. Kauffmann, responding to Shepard's latest play at the time, *Curse of the Starving Class,* observed that while the playwright had been writing plays for fifteen years and had been the recipient of numerous awards and honors, his work was no better than when he first emerged on the off-off-Broadway scene. Kauffman concluded that Shepard and other writers from his generation had "rejected the constrictions and intents of the commercial theatre for the freedoms of off and off-off Broadway" (106). As a result, they failed to grow up as artists. In a 1974 interview granted while he was living abroad in England, Shepard seemed to anticipate Kauffmann's criticism when he outlined his future playwriting goals in an entirely new direction: "I'd like to try a whole different way of writing now, which is very stark and not so flashy and not full of a lot of mythic figures and everything, and try to scrape it down to the bone as much as possible" (Chubb et al. 208). The following year he wrote a piece in *The American Place Theatre Newsletter* and ended on a similar note addressing the aims of the playwright: "He knows a great deal about things like: timing, rhythm, shape, flow, character (?), form, structure, etc., but still nothing about the real meat and potatoes. So he begins again. He strips everything down to the bone and starts over. And in this is where he makes his true discoveries" ("Time" 211).

A consideration of all his plays after *True West* further strengthens an estimation of 1980 as the watershed mark in Shepard's playwriting career. With the exception of the abstract *States of Shock* (1991), which responds to the Gulf War, the remainder of Shepard's plays deal with family issues and relationships. Male bonding and brotherhood in *True West* turn to romantic love and a possible incestuous relationship between a man and a woman in *Fool for Love* (1983). As a coda to his family play trilogy, *A Lie of the Mind* (1985) tosses all of the previous plays together in one melting pot of a long play. *Simpatico* (1994) achieves a Pinteresque flavor, a further refinement of dialogue first observed in *True West,* as it develops the gradual role reversal of two friends who are quite similar to Lee and Austin. Finally, *The Late Henry Moss* (2001) further explores the competitive relationships between two brothers and father/son dynamics first staged memorably in the tale of "How the Old Man Lost His Teeth" in *True West.* While the story remains the same for Shepard's plays, he now takes much longer to compose his familiar tales. Plays that used to fire in rapid succession now take years to appear. Shepard wrote forty plays in sixteen years prior to *True West.* Since 1980, he's written comparatively few new plays.

True West seems to respond directly to Kauffmann's stinging indictments. Shepard claimed to have rewritten it thirteen times. Prior to its New York opening at the New York Shakespeare Festival, Shepard told interviewer Robert Coe, "I worked harder on this play than anything I've ever written. The play's down to the bone. It opens up new ground for me" (Coe 122). "Down to the bone," for Shepard, means adhering to Aristotelian principles. The loopiness of earlier plays gives way to straightforward action in *True West.* The plot boils down to two brothers who compete against each other to sell a movie idea to a major studio. At the outset, Lee, an enigmatic drifter from the desert, arrives at his mother's house forty miles east of Los Angeles to find his brother, Austin, holed up in the kitchen working on "a simple love story" (*Seven Plays* 31) in preparation for a big meeting with movie producer Saul Kimmer. Austin gives Lee the keys to his car in order to get some privacy, but Lee returns early sporting a stolen TV and begins to insinuate his own movie idea as he hustles a game of golf with Saul for the following morning. In the interim, Austin appeases Lee by typing his brother's story for a true-to-life Western. The action of the play turns when Lee returns from his golf match with Saul and discloses that the producer has elected to green-light his story, not Austin's. Austin gets drunk and wagers that, just as Lee has assumed an identity as a screenwriter, he can enter Lee's profession as a thief. When dawn arrives, Austin proudly displays his previous night's booty, a row of gleaming toasters. Lee, unable to concentrate on his screenplay, burns his manuscript and destroys the typewriter with a nine-iron club. Austin, popping toast, begs Lee to take him to the desert. The boys' mother returns from her trip to Alaska and finds a house she no longer recognizes as her home: a mess of utensils, smoldering pages, beer bottles, dying plants, and small appliances. The brothers fight violently; Mom vacates. Two men square off menacingly as the lights fade.

Lee and Austin, whose names evoke the gun manufacturer Smith & Wesson, are blood brothers and Cain and Abel archetypes in this staunchly two-character play. The mother appears briefly, albeit hilariously, in the final scene. Saul Kimmer, a thoroughly insipid but slick studio executive, fuels the plot in two scenes. Shepard initiated dynamics between male partners and competitors in earlier plays with Stu and Chet in *Cowboys #2* (1967), Kosmo and Yahoodi in *The Mad Dog Blues* (1971), Slim and Shadow in *Back Bog Beast Bait* (1971), and most famously Hoss and Crow in *The Tooth of Crime* (1972). Compared to these previous forays, Lee and Austin are well-developed and psychologically complex characters. Shepard created a dramatic situation that focused exclusively on the relationship between the two brothers who share genetic information but who appear unlike each other in almost every other respect. In Shepard's world, opposites attract but they also repel each other, and that to-and-fro movement dictates the rhythm of action in the play. Shepard informed Robert Coe that *True West* attempted to get rid of all extraneous elements and explore only the physical and psychic battle between two brothers: "I wanted to write a play about double nature, one that wouldn't be symbolic or metaphorical or any of that stuff. I just wanted to give a taste of what it feels like to be two-sided. It's a real thing, double nature. I think we're split in a much more devastating way than psychology can ever reveal. It's not so cute. Not some little thing we can get over. It's something we've got to live with" (Coe 122).

The play almost devotionally serves the neoclassical virtues of time, place, and action. Rather than a single day, the action occurs over a four-day period, but the nine scenes succeed one another in a linear pattern of night, morning, midday, night, morning, midday, etc., etc. Like classical plays, *True West* develops as a succession of scenes rather than acts. Although the play divides into two acts, it unfolds scene by scene, each beginning and ending crisply in order to punctuate the action. The entire play takes place in a single setting, the kitchen of the mother's Southern California home. Shepard specifies, too, that no attempts at stylization should be made to the setting that he describes in the opening stage directions of the published edition of the play: "The set should be constructed realistically with no attempt to distort its dimensions, shapes, objects, or colors. No objects should be introduced which might draw special attention to themselves other than the props demanded by the script. If a stylistic 'concept' is grafted onto the set design it will only serve to confuse the evolution of the characters' situation, which is the most important focus of the play" (*Seven Plays* 3). Again, Shepard seems to protect this play from the artistic freedoms granted to his earlier, more improvisational plays. The realistic environment represents essential ingredients for his story. As a style, realism for Shepard is transparent. A sink is only a sink; a kitchen is a kitchen; a plant is a plant. These visual details don't represent anything other than what they are. This strategy allows the playwright to maintain focus on the central relationship of the two brothers.

The composition of *True West*—stripped down, unadorned, unencumbered by the excesses of some of his more slapdash works—resembles a musical score. Given Shepard's own background as a drummer and his reliance upon rhythm, this analogy is a useful way to discuss the structure of Shepard's work. Shepard's explicit use of music in his plays crosses the borders of rock (*Cowboy Mouth, The Tooth of Crime*), jazz (*Angel City, Suicide in B-flat*), and country (*Fool for Love, A Lie of the Mind*). Shepard dedicated *A Lie of the Mind* to the Red Clay Ramblers who performed in the play and wrote original music for it. In the preface, Shepard encourages future producers of that play to incorporate live music into the performance. Shepard sees music as an essential element to the play. While notes for actual music are easy to detect in the plays, the texts themselves are musical, and none more so than *True West*. In *The Theatre of Sam Shepard: States of Crisis,* Stephen J. Bottoms addresses musicality: "Indeed, the brothers' 'themes' which start off at diametrically opposed extremes, are eventually blended and blurred to the point where they cross over completely, in a role reversal which is as much musical device as it is character development" (185). In an interview with Stewart McBride of the *Christian Science Monitor,* Shepard indicated that he "heard" the play in terms of characters speaking and wrote it in terms of sound instead of mere words. As McBride reports it, according to Shepard the relationship between writing and music is explicit: "'I see actors as musicians, playing to each other, using their voices instead of instruments,' he tells me during a workshop break. 'I'm always surprised by the similarities between music and writing: the inner structure, tonality, rhythm, harmony. *True West* felt like a total improvisation spinning off itself. The writing of the play started when I heard the voice of Lee speaking very clearly, and then I heard Austin's response. The more I listened, the more the voices came'" (B2).

The ping-pong dialogue in the text establishes a strong rhythm throughout the play. The musicality of the language is evident even in this short clip from the opening scene:

(*pause*)
AUSTIN: You going to be down here very long, Lee?
LEE: Might be. Depends on a few things.
AUSTIN: You got some friends down here?
LEE: (*laughs*) I know a few people. Yeah.
AUSTIN: Well, you can stay here as long as I'm here.
LEE: I don't need your permission do I?
AUSTIN: No.
LEE: I mean she's my mother too, right?
AUSTIN: Right.
LEE: She might've just as easily asked me to take care of her place as you.

AUSTIN: That's right.
LEE: I mean I know how to water plants.
(*long pause*) (*Seven Plays* 7)

The section above, one beat from the dialogue, shows Austin and Lee trading offensive darts with questions. Question/answer, question/answer, first initiated by one brother and then the other, creates a lilting musical rhythm as the dialogue alternates between long question, short response, long question, and short response, finalized by a statement that ends the section. A "pause" of different lengths frames the vocal attack and further develops a rhythm of sound and silence. In the background, too, Shepard lays in a soundtrack of yapping coyotes in the nearby hills and a steady volume of chirping crickets. Early in the play, after another long pause, Lee explodes, "Those are the most monotonous fuckin' crickets I ever heard in my life" (9). Given the fact that a tape loop undoubtedly produces the sound, Lee's reaction displays self-consciousness of the theatrical surroundings and mechanics. Later, in scene 7, Lee tells his brother, "Between you, the coyotes and the crickets a thought don't have much of a chance" (36). The crickets drive the rhythm of the entire play as a persistent, ticking metronome.

Monologues, the subject of so much early acclaim for Shepard as a playwright, are conspicuously absent in this play. Pauses, silences, and clipped dialogue surrounding short speeches in *True West* compress the orgasmic speech of previous plays into modest outcries. It is as though a larger speech were there but unable to break out in its entirety, an effect that adds dramatic tension in the play. Compare, for example, the long monologue by Miss Scoons in *Angel City* to a similar one by Austin. In the former play, the character speaks as if in a trance: "I look at the screen and I am the screen. I'm not me. I don't know who I am. I look at the movie and I am the movie. I am the star. I am the star in the movie. For days I am the star and I'm not me. I'm me being the star. I look at my life when I come down. I look and I hate my life when I come down. I hate my life not being in a movie. I hate my life not being a star. I hate being myself in my life which isn't a movie and never will be" (*Fool for Love* 77). She goes on and on in a similar vein. In scene 6 of *True West,* after Austin has lost his bid for a fat advance, he directs his venom at Saul: "What's he [Lee] know about what people wanna' see on the screen! I drive on the freeway every day. I swallow the smog. I watch the news in color. I shop in the Safeway. I'm the one who's in touch! Not him!" (*Seven Plays* 35). The exclamation points make Austin's speech much "hotter" than Miss Scoons's above, but because Austin—unlike Miss Scoons—directs his attack at another character, it becomes more dynamic as well. The economical, pent-up language in *True West* builds pressure in each successive scene and erupts in physical violence at the end. Short speeches instead of long monologues, short scenes instead of long acts, a small rather than large cast, and direct action rather than loose narrative literally create more white space on the printed page and leave more room for improvisation in performance.

Relentless progression from one scene to the next disguises the fact that the play turns on a mystery that never quite resolves. What happened on the golf course? Disparity between the straightforward plot and the elliptical nature of offstage events marks a stress point in the text and requires an imaginative answer to fill the blank hole of mystery. How does Lee convince Saul to do his script and not Austin's? Perhaps Saul really does gamble with Austin's material and lose with the comfort and confidence of knowing that it doesn't matter which story he decides to produce. For the producer of mass-entertainment commodities, stories are interchangeable raw material for assembly-line production. In the fight over who will sell a screenplay, it goes almost unnoticed that there is no story on paper, only an outline. Saul tells Austin that he has a great story but that he should do nothing more until they have secured a "sale to television" and a "major star," "somebody bankable." At most, he advises Austin to write a "brief synopsis." Saul further flatters Austin by telling him that he's "really managed to capture something this time" (15), a comment that implies past failures. It remains unclear, however, what exactly, if anything, Austin has captured. He tells Lee only that it's a "period piece" (13) and under pressure from Lee he confides that it is "a simple love story" (31).

Lee's story, on the other hand, is a contemporary Western that is chock-full of suspense, true-to-life stuff in which two men, one who's evidently been sleeping with the other's woman, chase each other across the desert on horseback. Enraged by Lee's easy success with Saul, Austin lambastes Lee's feeble attempt at screenwriting: "It's a bullshit story! It's idiotic. Two lamebrains chasing each other across Texas! Are you kidding? Who do you think's going to see a film like that?" (30). Defensively, Saul claims that Lee's story contains "the ring of truth," "[s]omething about the real West," "[s]omething about the land" (35). Saul enters scene 6 prepared to manage both projects, but he doesn't seem particularly perturbed when Austin refuses to go along. As dumb as Lee's story may be, it's no dumber than Lee's poignant description of the last really good Western he saw, *Lonely Are the Brave,* in which Kirk Douglas dies for the love of his horse. And, although Lee is much more comic than Austin, it isn't clear that his story is any worse than his brother's. Lee's movie, in fact, sounds like one that has been made, perhaps more than once.

Ambivalence regarding the relative worth of the two movie projects offsets the binary oppositions that organize much of the play. Austin is smart, is college educated, has a family, works at his profession as a writer; Lee is a loner, lives off his own chutzpah, holds no job, and scavenges as a petty thief. It's tempting to stretch this study of opposites too far and cast Austin as an artist and Lee as the parasite living off of him. It's also too pat to think of Austin as a dedicated craftsman, and Lee in possession of the raw imagination and creative power of the artist. Indeed, the interchangeability of Austin's and Lee's stories, the fact that Lee can enter the scene *in medias res* and hustle his little work past his brother's project, traps both men in a system and in a game they cannot win. They may be opposites, but they find themselves in the exact same desperate situation of hoping to make a buck or two, and they discover that they are the victims rather than the perpetrators of exploitation games. Both characters seem equally lost. One character appears at any given moment to hold the upper hand over the other, but this always proves to be a temporary illusion and the sibling struggle for superiority and dominance ultimately comes to a draw.

In the inimical words of Lee, "What is this bullshit with the toast anyway?" (48). Is it just another wild, evocative, and ultimately opaque gesture such as peeing on the 4-H charts in *Curse of the Starving Class,* dumping husks of corn on Dodge in *Buried Child,* delivering Lobster Man in *Cowboy Mouth,* oozing green slime in *Angel City,* or bursting through the walls in *La Turista,* or does the visual array of gleaming toasters which appears in scene 8 have a darker purpose? Certainly, the smell of burning toast stimulates a visceral response for a live audience conditioned by an assault on all its senses: the sounds of coyotes killing people's cocker spaniels, of prowling police helicopters, and a golf club splintering a typewriter; intense lighting to reflect desert heat; the smell of beer poured over sweaty bodies, of wilted and dying plants, and a burning manuscript in a trash can; the sight of every drawer pulled out and contents strewn over the kitchen. The smell of burning toast late in the play, something that can be effective only in a theatrical space, offers a whiff of what Austin calls salvation.

Salvation leads to paradise in the Shepard lexicon. In scene 2, Lee reports peering into "a sweet kinda' suburban silence" during his nocturnal tour of the neighborhood: "Like a paradise. Kinda' place that sorta' kills ya' inside. Warm yellow lights. Mexican tile all around. Copper pots hangin' over the stove. Ya' know like they got in the magazines. Blonde people movin' in and outa' the rooms, talkin' to each other. (*pause*) Kinda' place you wish you sorta' grew up in, ya' know" (12). In scene 7, in a drunken paean to thievery, Austin echoes Lee's earlier account: "The bushes. Orange blossoms. Dust in the driveways. Rain bird sprinklers. Lights in people's houses. You're right about the lights, Lee. Everybody else is livin' the life. Indoors. Safe. This is a Paradise down here. You know that? We're livin' in a Paradise. We've forgotten about that" (39). At the end of *Buried Child,* Halie, referring to the offstage cornfields out back, reports to her husband, "It's like a paradise out there, Dodge. You oughta' take a look.

A miracle. I've never seen it like this. Maybe the rain did something. Maybe it was the rain" (*Seven Plays* 132). And, near the end of *Curse of the Starving Class,* Weston glorifies the family homestead in Southern California to his son: "This is a paradise for a young person! There's kids your age who'd give their eyeteeth to have an environment like this to grow up in" (192).

References to paradise belie the stark landscape and desperate circumstances of the dramatic situation in *True West.* Paradise has been corrupted; weeds have spread throughout the Garden. Austin doesn't even recognize the area in which he grew up: "I keep finding myself getting off the freeway at familiar landmarks that turn out to be unfamiliar. On the way to appointments. Wandering down streets I thought I recognized that turn out to be replicas of streets I remember. Streets I misremember. Streets I can't tell if I lived on or saw in a postcard. Fields that don't even exist anymore" (49). Progress, Austin implies, has had devastating and unforeseen effects. When he quips to Lee early in the play that the area has been built up, Lee quickly retorts, "Built up? Wiped out is more like it. I don't even hardly recognize it" (11). Shepard's notes preceding the final scene state that "the stage is ravaged" and that "all the debris from the previous scene is now starkly visible," which produces an effect "like a desert junkyard at high noon" (50). The sheer presence of all this stuff, including the stolen TV and toasters, produces an image of paradise lost. Reminded by Austin that she's home now, Mom, who has just returned from her trip to Alaska (the "final frontier") and is about to leave again to check in to a motel, adds, "I don't recognize it at all" (59).

The last image from *Curse of the Starving Class* further clarifies the search for salvation in *True West* as the search for self. The story about the eagle and the cat, Weston's story retold by Ella and Wesley in the final lines, evokes imagery very similar to the struggle of Austin and Lee:

> ELLA: They fight like crazy in the middle of the sky. That cat's tearing his chest out, and the eagle's trying to drop him, but the cat won't let go because he knows if he falls he'll die.
> WESLEY: And the eagle's being torn apart in midair. The eagle's trying to free himself from the cat, and the cat won't let go.
> ELLA: And they come crashing down to the earth. Both of them come crashing down. Like one whole thing. (*Seven Plays* 200)

Lee tells his brother at one point that he's not a parasite living off of Austin. He's independent. In fact, the blood relationship between brothers is symbiotic, not parasitic. The path of violent destruction that these characters cut in search of salvation suggests an eternal struggle.

True West achieves a mythic level, not only because the two brothers represent archetypes dating back to Cain and Abel, but also because in a play in which they compete to sell a movie to Hollywood, they themselves play the parts of dueling gunslingers in a Western, which is itself filtered through a consciousness of television and film representations of that genre. Clichés from bad Westerns bracket the action. In the very first scene, Austin seeks to lay down the law: "Lee, look—I don't want any trouble, all right?" (8). Lee's pointed response draws attention to the scripted nature of the text: "That's a dumb line. That's a dumb fuckin' line. You git paid fer dreamin' up a line like that?" (8). The final scene contains another line that quotes cowboy rhetoric, Hollywood style, as Austin reads Lee's script aloud: "'I told ya' you were a fool to follow me in here. I know this prairie like the back a' my hand'" (51). Lee objects to the line and, pointedly, a definition of clichés follows, after which Austin inserts a new line. Lee praises the freshness of the revision: "'I'm on intimate terms with this prairie'" (52). Earlier, Austin called the characters in Lee's screenplay "illusions of characters" and "fantasies of a long lost boyhood" (40), "grown men acting like little boys" (35). Austin's descriptions of Lee's story, however, perfectly capture the action of *True West.* Metaphorically at least, despite the playwright's warnings against stylization in the initial stage directions, Austin and Lee function as two lamebrains chasing each other across the landscape of the play. The metaphor, too, amplifies the playing style of the actors and simultaneously resonates with the play's themes. At the end of scene 4, which is also the end of act 1 of the play, the halfway point of the action, Lee describes the high drama of his proposed movie:

> So they take off after each other straight into an endless black prairie. The sun is just comin' down and they can feel the night on their backs. What they don't know is that each one of 'em is afraid, see. Each one separately thinks that he's the only one that's afraid. And they keep ridin' like that straight into the night. Not knowing. And the one who's chasin' doesn't know where the other one is taking him. And the one who's being chased doesn't know where he's going. (27)

Lee tells his story and Austin faithfully follows along, tapping on his typewriter. Visually, the same image that he describes above is reproduced at the final tableau, in which the two brothers square off as if to duel each other like gunfighters on Main Street at high noon. Mom, who has returned to her home, tries to get the boys (she calls them boys) to fight outside, as if they were still small and squabbling over who gets to watch which TV show. Instead, they're grown men engaged in a death match. After Austin nearly strangles Lee with the telephone cord, Shepard's stage directions finish the play with a lasting image of two lame-brains which dramatizes the "literary" image that ended act 1: "They square off to each other, keeping a distance between them. Pause, a single coyote heard in distance, lights fade softly into moonlight, the figures of the brothers now appear to be caught in a vast desert-like landscape, they are very still but watchful of the next move, lights go slowly to black as the after-image of the brothers pulses in the dark, coyote fades" (59).

The final stage tableau pits both brothers against each other posing as desper-ate cowboys. The displaced contents of the ravaged kitchen critique the detritus of a materialist society. Heat from the bright stage lights combined with the dis-tant sound of the coyote transforms the modern interior into a desert landscape. Theater's ability to frame and freeze the two bodies in space produces simulta-neous images of the Old West, of the Hollywood West, of the contemporary sub-urban West, and of two actors playing their parts in each of those stories. The ability to see all these things at once, to take them in simultaneously within the same space, to process the simultaneity of layered images, produces a powerful theatrical image that is not possible in any other performance format.

A good film of Shepard's play has not been made yet.[1] The Showtime pro-duction for cable TV (August 2002) starring Bruce Willis, which was filmed at a small theater in Idaho, and the Malkovich/Sinise version taped twenty years earlier at the Cherry Lane Theatre made use of film editing, multiple camera angles, and close-ups, but neither could be called cinematic treatments of the play. When I saw the Malkovich film for the first time, I could not even con-clude that he was a good actor. Critics exalted his performance onstage, but to my eyes his acting seemed mannered, calculated, and all ham. I'm quite willing to agree with reviewers who called his stage performance legendary, but I simply can't reach that conclusion based on the film. It exists as a crude and slavish rec-ord of a theatrical performance, not much different in quality and intent than the first movies of the last century, but leaving distorted residue of a live event. Actor Bruce Willis acknowledged the difficulty of filming a stage play: "When-ever I see even the best plays on film, it's always like the duckbill platypus. It's not a movie. It's not a TV show. It's not like anything. It's difficult to try to place it as a form of entertainment" (Gates 5). The liminal nature of the filmed stage play, neither here nor there, suggests that drama cannot simply be reformatted as a film without a true and thorough interpretation, integration, and execution of cinematic imagination.

The films don't capture the essence of the play. Furthermore, the desire to re-main faithful to the play keeps them from achieving any cinematic distinction. Both recordings of the stage play constrain the play's expansiveness and pluck out its mysteries. The relative smallness of the television frame cuts down the size of the play, and the need to fit both actors within the frame of the screen further shrinks and diminishes the action. Alternatively, directorial decisions to zoom upon individual actors prevent the viewer from seeing both figures simultaneously and rob the stage picture of sufficient context. The single location in Mom's kitchen suffocates the imagery original to the play because the films give no space to let it breathe. In a theater, actors must fill the surrounding space with their voices. Oddly, the amplification of the film process tones down the language and mutes the voices. The figures cover the screen, and language no longer has a space to fill. *True West* stokes many evocative images: Lee's peeks into windows of other people's houses; Austin's struggle on the choked freeways; the Old Man's panhandling on the desert; orange blossoms and sprinkler heads. The beauty of Shepard's play, despite his protestations, is that the action is evocative and metaphorical. The problem with the video versions, which follow Shepard's directions to the letter, is that they never leave the domestic scene, and the language—like so many filmed Shakespearean productions—fails to resonate within the confines of the small screen. *True West* is definitely not kitchen-sink drama. The lamebrains need room to roam.

9
Cadillacs Are for Closers

You know what is free enterprise? [. . .] The freedom [. . .] Of the *Individual*
[. . .] To Embark on Any Fucking Course that he sees fit. [. . .] In order to
secure his honest chance to make a profit. [. . .] Without this we're just savage
shitheads in the wilderness. [. . .] Sitting around some vicious campfire.
—David Mamet, *American Buffalo*

David Mamet has parlayed his success as a dramatist into a lucrative and vibrant
career as a Hollywood screenwriter and film director. One of the best film versions of any of his plays, *Glengarry Glen Ross,* directed by James Foley with a
screenplay by the playwright, resulted in a collaborative effort quite independent of the stage play that engendered it. Among an all-star cast featuring Al
Pacino, Kevin Spacey, Alan Arkin, Ed Harris, Jonathan Pryce, and Alec Baldwin, Jack Lemmon delivers a brilliant performance in the 1992 film as down-
and-out real estate salesman Shelley "The Machine" Levene working hard at
Premiere Properties to save his job with a last big shot. That he and his associ-
ates try to sell worthless Florida swampland to unsuspecting buyers, eliding the
line between capitalism and criminality, in no way diminishes the empathy one
feels for Levene's sad plight. Despite Lemmon's portrayal of a petty, venal man,
an audience might well root for his character to triumph anyway. Lemmon's
great acting enriches the film but also dilutes the poison in it that packs a wallop.
Mamet's characters typically do not tug at the audience's emotions, but the filming of Lemmon's heartbreaking performance creates a qualitatively different experience than the stage play of essentially the same material.

A dishonest, manipulative, backbiting braggart, Shelley Levene is one of the
least appealing characters in the play. Apart from Aaronow, who's completely
self-abandoned, Levene is also the least successful and is off the mark for the
month's competitive do-or-die sales contest to determine who wins the Cadillac and who loses his job. Richard Roma, played by Pacino in the film, is the
most likable, but then he can afford to be: he sits atop the leaderboard. Still, in
the movie, Jack Lemmon, more than any of the other actors including Pacino,
draws the most focus. For one thing, Lemmon (1925–2001) played in the twi-
light of his long and illustrious career when he made *Glengarry,* and he brought
all of his other performances to bear on the plum role of Levene. I don't claim
Levene as one of his best performances; it may be, but when I evaluate his per-

formance as Levene I also see the star of *Mister Roberts, The Apartment,* and *Save the Tiger.* The most endearing aspects of his performance combine intense vulnerability and dogged indefatigability. He absorbs blow after blow yet somehow keeps pushing forward with a new sales pitch, confident that he can turn each "no" into a "yes" and reverse his relentless streak of bad luck. He keeps striving even in the face of professional humiliation and, finally, absolute guilt. He doesn't sag until his chief adversary, office manager Williamson (Kevin Spacey), explains his reason for turning him in to the police: "Because I don't like you." In spite of everything, I do like him, and it hurts to watch what happens to his character in the movie.

Far more than the play, the film version builds up Levene's part and provides information wholly lacking in the drama. The film opens with Levene talking on the telephone to his daughter, who is evidently in the hospital and in need of an expensive operation. A subsequent call implies that the procedure has been canceled due to lack of funds. This circumstance, which is barely alluded to in the play, adds pressure on Levene to earn his commission or to come up with the money by any means necessary. Unlike the play, too, the film shows Levene and his coworkers making several sales calls to customers. The losing propositions of each prospective sale heap added sympathies upon all the salesmen. In one scene in the film, the audience even sees Levene make a house call, a "sit" in salesman jargon, in which the goal is to get inside the house, establish rapport and trust with the customer, sit down for a discussion, and close the deal with a signature on the bottom line. In the movie, Levene visits Mr. Spannel, a young thirty- or forty-something married man who evidently has everything he needs and who has no intention of buying anything from Levene. He's polite yet firm. Levene plays every angle but he can't turn the trick, and ultimately the front door closes behind him and he treads back to his car on a rainy night.

The camera, too, highlights the pathos and vulnerability of Lemmon's performance. Notice the close-up on his face, for example, when Blake (Alec Baldwin) insults Levene's manhood. Lemmon captures the welling hatred his character feels at that moment for Blake, along with the fear that what Blake says might be true. When the camera closes on his phone conversation with his daughter, one can sense the cost he pays for the little lies he tells her as his mind scrambles to end the conversation and to plan how he'll raise the sufficient funds for her health care. At the other extreme, when the camera pulls back to take in Lemmon's full figure in a long shot, the smallness of the character in relation to his environment becomes immediately apparent. When Blake addresses him at the coffee station, Levene turns, still holding the pot, as if he were a berated night manager at Denny's. Similarly, at the Spannel "sit," the camera frames Levene sitting on the sofa with the bigger man standing with his back to the camera in the midground. The comparative size difference between the hulking homeowner and the bumbling little salesman creates the image of a loser completely out of his depth. With that shot as a defining image, it is impossible to conceive of Levene closing a deal with this client.

In one of the special features included in the tenth-anniversary DVD release of the film, director James Foley comments that he felt the film is a more authentic version of Mamet's vision than the play as it was performed on Broadway. At first, such a bold claim seems difficult to deny, given the cinematic virtuosity of the film, ideal casting, and Mamet's own screenplay to boot. Surprisingly, Foley goes on to say that the film tried to capture an image of "humans as animals, lab rats in their cage trying to find their way out." That kind of objective, clinical, and cerebral image is inconsistent with Lemmon's empathy-inspiring performance. Lemmon's Levene is not just a human specimen, typical of the breed, caught up in a capitalistic experiment that causes his death, but an individual whose story and plight become almost unbearable to witness. To a lesser extent, all the actors deliver performances that highlight pain and desperation. These are certainly the results of fine acting, but also the products of skillful filmmaking, which isolates the salesmen in close-ups or long shots. The quick editing of the film, driven by a lively jazz score, knots each scene together by cutting from one man to another and leaves surprisingly few two-shots to promote a sense of community. On a stage, however, the audience cannot readily see the facial expressions of an individual actor simultaneously with those of other performers. In Mamet's dramatic text, Levene does not stand out as the main character as he does in the film. Unlike the film, the dramatic text does not demand an empathetic performance from any of the characters and accordingly divulges very little information about them. For all these reasons, Foley's image of humans as lab rats would be much more possible and appropriate in the theater, in which the audience sits back at a remove and sees all the actors onstage at the same time in full-bodied performances.

Foley's metaphorical view of his film is actually perfect for a theatrical setting. To stage a play is to take an actual environment out of context and place it in a box. The audience enjoys the fact that the world in a play is always under construction, built for the moment, and set apart from the everyday world. Turning the familiar phrase around, all the stage is a world, and as such it serves as a potent metaphor. Even in realistic plays, the stage environment always serves a metaphorical purpose. It is impossible, for example, to see Don's Resale Shop in *American Buffalo,* with all the detritus of a consumer society splayed out in full view, and not to associate that environment with the state of American society. Everything visible onstage accrues meaning, and in a play such as *American Buffalo,* which has only one setting, anything onstage for an entire performance attracts attention. If the designer were to, say, hang twelve toilet seats in a row, that decision would make a strong statement about American society but it also might prove too obvious and attract too much attention. Accordingly, Mamet's written stage directions provide few details about the scenic spaces of his plays.

Film, by contrast, always requires a specific context. The dramatic text of *Glengarry Glen Ross* does not specify where the action takes place, but since the home office of Mitch and Murray is downtown, the real estate office out of which the salesmen work probably operates in a not particularly wealthy suburb. The one specific geographic reference in the play is to Des Plaines, a suburb of Chicago located immediately north of O'Hare airport. In the first scene, Levene asks for two "sits" in Des Plaines. This is one of Mamet's only hints about where the action takes place. Chicago is not part of the fabric of the play. Since all the scenes in the play occur in either a restaurant or an office interior, geographic specificity is not all that important. The split between urban and suburban is important; the sense that the clients whom the salesmen swindle are not wealthy is important. But, really, beyond that, the action could happen in any American city.

The film, however, with the inclusion of both interior and exterior scenes, requires an actual urban location in which to shoot. The production team selected New York City as the site, although the movie makes no references to that city. They placed the office in Sheepshead Bay, a Brooklyn community located far south of Manhattan near Brighton Beach and Coney Island, not far from JFK airport. Located next to an el train track—the link between the white, working-class community and the big city—images and sounds of the subway train frame the opening credits and first plant the relationship of suburb to urban environment. Later, when two of the salesmen cross the street to go from the Chinese restaurant to the office, they pass the el tracks above them and the expensive BMW parked below on the street that belongs to Blake, the man from Mitch and Murray who has come out to motivate the sales force. Still later, as Levene stands in a phone booth on the road and makes another call, the distant Manhattan skyline, including the phallic Empire State Building, can be seen in the background.[1] The train to the city, the Manhattan skyline, the expensive foreign luxury car represent things and places out of reach and beyond the realm of the salesmen.

The first half of the film, act 1 in the play, takes place during a torrential rainstorm that soaks the men every time they come and go, back and forth, across the street. In the play, everything occurs inside, and characters don't fight the elements and the audience doesn't see the outside world or perceive the relationship between the restaurant and the real estate office. In the film, the sheets of rain are visible always, from the interior shots of the office, which has windows on two sides, the coffee shop where Moss and Aaronow stop, the phone booth where Levene makes his calls, and the car in which Moss and Aaronow ride. To complement the rain, a jazz score accompanies the action in the film. Besides being uniquely American, this score establishes mood in the film that alternates between brooding and upbeat but, above all else, creates an atmosphere of striving. The music, too, which evokes the night and a world of dim morality, adds to the sense of loneliness and desperation as well as the competitive muscularity and sweaty, testosterone-driven behavior among the men.[2] The film of *Glengarry Glen Ross* ends with Roma's exit to the Chinese restaurant to the tune of Duke Ellington's "Blue Skies" as the credits roll. Set up by the rain, this tune shines a sunny beat that, given the preceding demise of Shelley Levene, plays as irony but that also reflects the lives of salesmen, who do, in the words of Miller's *Death of a Salesman,* go "way out there in the blue, riding on a smile and a shoe-shine" (111). The end of *Glengarry Glen Ross* acknowledges the relationship to another great work about salesmen but doesn't allow an audience to wallow in a pitying requiem for a lost little man. Instead, the upbeat ending suggests that Roma, the high man on the leaderboard, will set out on a new course for fresh sales and easy profits.

Much more than the play, the film establishes overt motivation for the robbery. While the play remains entirely dialogic, the film shows the difficulty of what the men do for a living by presenting them at work. It accomplishes this by exploiting the stage device of the telephone call. Modern plays, under the burden of dialogic pressure and dependent on conversation to carry the action, often look for excuses that allow characters to talk to themselves (and to the audience) with the same freedom that Renaissance heroes such as Hamlet formerly enjoyed when addressing theater patrons directly. Alcohol is an excuse playwrights use that allows characters to speak to themselves. The dramatic conceit (though I'm not convinced that it applies to actual observed behavior) holds that drunk people talk to themselves when no one else is onstage.[3] Another good excuse to talk to oneself onstage is the telephone conversation, a device of countless bad TV shows, movies, and plays which allows the speaking character to deliver a monologue straight to the audience.

Conveniently, the salesmen in Mamet's world make their living by talking on the phone! The film version of Mamet's play exploits this by showing the salesmen cold-calling unsuspecting customers. The number of calls placed by Levene, Moss, and Aaronow in the first part of the film gives the viewer a sense of what they do and how hard it is to do what they do. These vignettes build sympathy for them to the extent that robbing the office for better leads seems like a natural progression of events, given the "deadbeats" to whom they have to pitch their schemes. Craftily, the filmmaker loads his plot such that the viewer empathizes with these desperate situations and the measures taken in response.

This is no small accomplishment, given that most people regard the telemarketers who make such calls as nuisances at best. The film, then, makes evident from the beginning what the men do and how hard their task is, whereas in the play the nature of the men's job is not entirely clear until the end of the first act and the relationships between all the men do not become clear until the second act is under way. Drama, which consists only of dialogue, requires the viewer to piece together information based on what characters say. The last piece of the puzzle does not fall completely into place until the last line of the first act. The film, on the other hand, exploiting the monologic capabilities of the phone call, makes use of narrative structure to inform the viewer very early about relationships.

The introduction of a character that doesn't even exist in the play enhances the clarity of the salesmen's dire situation and the motivation for their subsequent burglary. Blake (Alec Baldwin), the friend of Mitch and Murray from downtown, incites the action in the film by announcing the new terms of the month's sales contest: first prize is a new Cadillac, second prize is a set of steak knives, third prize is "You're fired!" Blake addresses the sales force as a military commander addresses the troops or a football coach speaks to his players. He says terrible things and uses terrible language. He motivates them by insulting them. His monologue, a "set speech" within the film, raises the stakes of the action and jump-starts the film. Blake challenges them as salesmen, but he also attacks them as men. Are you good enough to take people's money? Can you force your will upon them? This narrative speech establishes the terms under which the rest of the drama will be played. Blake disappears from the film as soon as he finishes; his only purpose is to get the film going. In the play, however, no such scene exists; there is only an implied sense that such a scene occurred previous to the start of the play. Characters allude in conversation to a sales contest and the possibilities of losing their jobs. In the play, the sales contest is already under way at the outset, prior to the first lines of the drama. The fact that the contest has already begun adds to the urgency of Levene's pleas for premium leads. Drama is assumed to be more "immediate" than other forms. Here, though, the film actually borrows typical dramatic structure involving an inciting moment, a "sales contest," and supplies necessary exposition in the form of a series of phone calls. The play remains much more elliptical and demands that the viewer/reader pay close attention to clues in the performance/text that will explain the situation.

Finally, the capability of editing and rearranging material gives the film flexibility in terms of time and space that the play simply does not have. I've already outlined above how the film adds material not found in the play to load the plot, culminating with Blake's salty pep talk. These preliminary scenes take the viewer from phone booths at the back of a Chinese restaurant to the men's room, down the corridors of the restaurant to the foyer and to the bar, across the wet streets, up to Premiere Properties in an upstairs office. The Moss and Aaronow dialogue, scene 2 in the play, similarly moves from a back room in the office to Moss's car, to a house and a failed "sit," to a coffee shop, back to the car, to a location in front of the office, to a seat at the bar in the restaurant, and finally next to a jukebox in the restaurant. This scene, unlike the play, is not played straight through in its entirety. The scene between Levene and Williamson (scene 1 in the dramatic text) intervenes, as well as Levene's visit to the Spannels, his call in a phone both to the Nyborgs, and his second call back at the restaurant to the hospital concerning his daughter. Levene's scene with Williamson does not stay in one place either, as Levene tracks his superior from the office floor to the younger man's car and, finally, into the vehicle. These changes in sequence and spatial juggles are possible only in the film medium. The drama is more or less tied to a progressive sequence within a single and unchanging space.

After all the dynamic cutting between dramatic scenes in the film, then, it is surprising to see it stop completely halfway through. Scene 3 in the play (Roma/Lingk) is filmed in the same location specified by the dramatic text with almost no change to that text. Such adherence to the stage text is harbinger for things to come. The second half of the film (act 2) begins with an exterior establishing shot of Roma arriving at work the morning after the robbery and having to push through a cadre of police officers at a crime scene. The rest of the film takes place inside the office and completely follows the dramatic text. The one—and it is a major one—difference takes place at the very end. I've already described how the film ends with the trumpeting of "Blue Skies" as Roma exits. The dramatic text has a lot more bite than what an audience sees in the film. In the text, Roma delivers a final speech to Williamson in which, on the heels of having forged a partnership with Levene, he demands all of Levene's leads in addition to his own. "I GET HIS ACTION," he shouts to Williamson. "My stuff is *mine,* whatever *he* gets for himself, I'm talking half. [. . .] My stuff is mine, his stuff is ours" (107). The play ends on this note of utter rapaciousness. Unbeknownst to Roma, Levene will soon confess to the robbery and head off to prison, but Roma makes certain that in the dog-eat-dog world, nice guys do finish last and that every man, in the end, despite making claims for partnerships and forging of communities, is alone, not just because of the society in which he lives but by choice (or nature?) as well.

Unlike the dynamic interweaving of scenes in the first half of the film, act 1 in the play consists of three episodic scenes set in the Chinese restaurant. Although the mechanics of the stage dictate that the scenes occur in sequence, it is as if all three scenes take place at approximately the same time. These scenes, each between two characters, break down to reveal power relationships among an employee and his office manager (Levene and Williamson in the opening scene),

two peers (salesmen Aaronow and Moss), and a salesman and a potential customer (Roma and James Lingk). The interest in these scenes stems wholly from
the dialogue; there is no visual delight. All the men remain seated in booths. At
the end of the first scene, the two men get up; that's about the extent of the overt
visual movement. Unlike in the film, the play contains no exposition. The action picks up *in medias res* and forces an audience to listen attentively in order to
piece together what's happening. There are no hackneyed phrases such as "What
did you think of that sales meeting last night?" or "How long has it been since
'Mitch and Murray' visited from downtown?"[4] Instead, the audience has to pick
up clues dribbled out in the conversations of the first two scenes, approximately
forty pages in the published script. The sales contest, established prior to the time
when the play starts, animates all the salesmen, informs every action, and gives
energy and vitality to the initial superficially nondramatic, talky scenes. In the
film, the characters discover the news of the contest at the same time the audience does. In the play, however, the characters know of the sales contest and what
it means long before the audience. This knowledge adds urgency and desperation
to the opening scenes. The audience does not know why the men act as they do,
but it knows that something drives their behavior and it pieces together what the
clues mean as the action unfolds.

Only in the final lines of the third scene does Roma show his hand to the au-
dience as a consummate salesman. He pulls out a brochure and opens it to the
Glengarry Highlands in Florida and says to his mark, "This is a piece of land.
Listen to what I'm going to tell you now:" (51). That's the last line of the act.
The audience must imagine Roma's exact sales pitch. The colon cleverly punc-
tuates the halfway point and sets up suspense and anticipation for what's next in
the second act, but it also emphasizes what's come before as the setup for the sale.
Only at the very end of the first act is there an explicit pitch for a piece of land.
Only in the last moments is there an actual exchange over property. It's the only
time one sees directly what the men do for a living. Yet all the preparatory work
before the actual pitch is also a great part of the salesman's job. The sale actually
began even prior to Roma's first words in the scene. Roma's elliptical wander-
ings at the beginning do the spadework for his blunt transition at the end. The
second and third scenes, then, run parallel to each other. Just as Moss springs a
trap on George Aaronow, Roma launches into a pitch for Glengarry Highlands
once he has gained the trust of James Lingk and learned something about what
that man needs and wants.

Mamet reduces human contact in the world of *Glengarry Glen Ross* to a series of sales transactions. "Always Be Closing" is the practical sales maxim that
serves as an epigraph for the play, an explicit phrase in the film made famous by
Alec Baldwin as Blake. The three scenes in the first act each consist of dialogue

between only two characters, the essence of a dramatic scene. One character controls each scene by relentlessly pursuing an objective, closing the respective deal, and asserting dominance over the other character. Each of the first three scenes is an excellent acting scene for class study, as it teaches actors how to work together, how to lead, and how to react, as well as the importance of goals, tactics, and strategies to get what one wants. The fact that these scenes are "pure" acting scenes comes as no surprise given Mamet's thoughts about dramatic character and his reliance upon the Stanislavsky tradition of theater and the paramount significance of action.[5] This approach to acting requires, above all else, the identification of a goal or objective for the entire play (a super objective) and for each scene—indeed each moment within each scene. That goal is the action beyond which there is no interest in a scene. The purity of Mamet's pursuit of action is evident in the three scenes from the first act that I've outlined above. If all drama is action, Mamet demonstrates that character is pure action as well. In his book *On Directing Film,* published after *Glengarry Glen Ross* had been produced on the stage but before the film adaptation, Mamet has this to say about character:

> The truth is, you never have to establish the character. In the first place, there is no such thing as character other than the habitual action, as Mr. Aristotle told us two thousand years ago. It just doesn't exist. Here or in Hollywood or otherwise. They always talk about the character out there in Hollywood, and the fact is there is no such thing. It doesn't exist. The character is just habitual action. "Character" is exactly what the person literally does in pursuit of the superobjective, the objective of the scene. The rest doesn't count. (13)

In drama, of course, character is made up only of words. Critics have richly and deservedly praised Mamet for his words, the specific rhythms of speech that he captures, the lyrical street vernacular that he composes for poetic effect. Words, however, are never mere adornment. They work in service of the action of the piece. In this play about salesmen, the action is always very simple: "To sell." There is nothing else of any interest about the characters. Anything diverting attention away from the action would be extraneous and unnecessary. Levene states this principle simply in act 2 with an attack against Williamson: "A man's his job and you're *fucked* at yours" (75).[6] The job of the salesmen is to sell, and that's what they do and that reveals who they are. In Mamet's own words, the rest doesn't count. He reduces the world of the play to a series of sales transactions in which the man who succeeds—and it is a man's world—is the one who can successfully close the deal and exert his will upon a victim. In the play, one doesn't learn anything about the men other than their ability to do their job: to sell. How much money they make, what cars they drive, if they're married or not, where they live (other than Moss saying, as he exits for the final time, that he's going to Wisconsin), and how many kids they have remain a mystery. Levene alludes to a daughter twice in the play, in the first scene and at the very end, and these allusions illustrate Mamet's particular use of personal information. Speaking to Williamson both times, plaintively so, Levene says, "John: my *daughter* . . ." (26, 104). The movie places her in the hospital and provides a context for Levene to mention her in order to get sympathy from Williamson as a last resort. The dramatic text, however, provides no such information and context. That Levene even has a daughter is never verified. What's crucial is the context in which he "creates" or "invokes" her: a last-ditch effort, a final tactic, to get what he wants. In the first scene, he aims to get a shot at the premium leads; in the last scene, he struggles merely to keep his job. Williamson's response each time suggests that Levene has pulled out the "My *daughter*" routine before and that his act as the family provider has grown stale. Again, the crucial thing is not whether or not she exists, but the context in which Levene uses her name in the scenes. It is crucial for the actor to think of the daughter primarily as a tactic to employ in service of the ultimate goal of the scene. Mamet's dramaturgy displays this simplicity gloriously.

Mamet's play, then, gives civil life to the old cliché "It's a jungle out there." He portrays primal man dressed in a business suit who uses words as weapons in order to sell at any cost. Short shrift is extended to the true victims of the play, the customers who fall prey to the salesmen's schemes and scams. In a moment of black humor early in the conversation between Aaronow and Moss in scene 2, the two men lament the unfair labor practices at Mitch and Murray that have enslaved and degraded them as men. Almost as an afterthought, Aaronow adds, "And it's not right to the *customers*" (31). Of course it's not right! The salesmen swindle people out of their life's savings! Moss concurs with Aaronow by saying, "I know it's not. I'll tell you, you got, you know, you got . . . what did I learn as a kid on Western? Don't sell a guy one car. Sell him *five* cars over fifteen years" (31). Moss, by making the analogy between real estate and cars, suggests that the real problem with the current sales scheme is that its aggressiveness will eventually alert the customer about the company's devious tactics. With an innocent-sounding logic, Moss reasons that they should divest the customer of his money a little bit at a time over a long period rather than trying for the big score at once, which he equates with killing the golden goose (32). That he feels entitled to take these people's money is not in question. The real estate salesmen of the play live in a world in which human interaction is a sales pitch and the man who can close the deal and get the customer to sign on the bottom line is the winner and the better man. That's all that matters.

Act 2 "closes" this survival of the fittest in the real estate office across the street from the Chinese restaurant. Someone burglarized the office between the evening at the restaurant on the previous night and the following late morning and stole all the new premium sales leads. Dramaturgically, the robbery provides a reason for all the characters to congregate and interact during this second and final act. Obviously, without the pretext of a robbery and an ensuing investigation in which the salesmen must remain at the ready for the detective's questions, they would be out of the office in search of "sits." The desperation of the sales contest would drive them to their cars and the streets radiating in every direction. The robbery offers them a break in the action and a reason to talk to each other in lieu of any productive work that they can pursue. While the previous act introduces the characters two by two at the restaurant, the second act allows the audience to see them all at the same time. All the visible action occurs in the main part of the office where the men have their desks, while a police officer conducts an investigation and interrogation in Williamson's office upstage. As mentioned earlier, the film follows an almost identical script to the stage play from this point forward in the action. Primarily, the film relies upon cuts from one character to the next to register the impact of the action upon each actor's face. The stage play, on the other hand, presents all the actors simultaneously within the confines of the homogenous office space. In a game that really does determine the survival of the fittest, who wins and who loses, the play shows the combatants together in their cage.[7]

This structure also allows the play to develop in a fairly typical way, filled with Aristotelian moments of recognition and reversal. Roma charges in to start the act by demanding to know the status of his "close" with Lingk the night before, but the sale "kicks out" at the end of the act when Lingk makes an unexpected office visit. Levene arrives on the scene fresh from selling the Nyborgs eight units for eighty-two thousand dollars, but Williamson crushes him by informing him that the check is no good. The audience, set up by the expectations of the previous act, suspects that Aaronow has carried out the crime, but Levene's slip of the tongue to Williamson discloses his guilt and wraps up the plot. Finally, Roma, who appeared to be hale-fellow-well-met, turns out to be the most dispassionate and cunning salesman of all; not surprisingly, he walks out of the office at the end, oblivious to his friend Levene's fate, and heads for lunch as the play concludes.

C. W. E. Bigsby notes the advantages that the appearance of a regular plot adds to Mamet's play:

There is, to be sure, an element of the thriller [a descriptive term with which I disagree!] about the play. Those who had regretted the absence of narrative drive were rewarded by a drama in which the planning and unraveling of a crime provide some of the energy and compulsion of the work. But the real fascination remained with the individual moments, the tainted arias, the brilliantly corrupt performances of characters who have invested their lives rather than their money in the dreams they present to others. And that did not in essence depend upon conventionality of structure. (125–26)

In other words, the plot is an excuse for something to happen, an opportunity for the characters to rub against each other to determine who's the best: the best salesman and the best man.

Surprisingly, despite the robbery that took place the previous night, a crime investigation being conducted by a police detective in an adjacent office space, and the guilt of at least one of the salesmen, the crime—the plot, as it were—is not the characters' main concern.[8] Richard Roma indicates no concern at all for the robbery, and he maintains sole interest in whether or not the contracts he closed are safe and properly filed downtown. Similarly, Shelley Levene shows exclusive interest in his Nyborg sale; the other salesmen, in turn, respond to the news and details of that transaction with mixtures of green envy (Moss) and overtures of belated admiration (Roma). Beyond the self-interests at stake for each salesman regarding the news of Levene's big score, lies the thrill of the sell. Again, that thrill is the only thing that counts in the play, and that is the sign that the salesman has done his job well and has, in fact, become his job. The high point of the second act is Levene's description of his sale to Harriet Nyborg and her husband in which he narrates and reenacts the scene in front of Roma. Roma, who is no less jealous than Moss, elects to stay and bide his time in hopes of assimilating Levene to his side. Roma seems to promote an "if you can't beat 'em . . ." kind of strategy. While he outwardly supports Levene, he, according to the action in the text, simultaneously plots to use the older man to his advantage. The sale intoxicates Levene because it provides a sign of his worth as a human being and salesman. He describes the sale to Bruce and Harriet Nyborg in physical terms as a test of wills in which his persistence and endurance culminate in a satisfying victory: "It was like they wilted all at once. No *gesture* . . . nothing. Like together. They, I swear to God, they both kind of *imperceptibly slumped*" (74). Telling this story to Roma gives Levene a chance to reenact it and thus relive it for himself, perhaps embellishing parts of the story. The sale gives him a sense of power; indeed, the description of the couple that relents under his onslaught imparts a martial quality to the sale. That quality is not surprising since Williamson has referred to his own primary duties as "marshaling the leads" (18–19). By inducing them to sign a contract on the dotted line, Levene describes a great victory as a kind of one-on-one duel of wills in which he has prevailed.

Having listened to Levene's story, Roma gains the older man's confidence and when James Lingk appears in the office, Roma recognizes a problem immediately and quickly enlists Levene to help him out of a tight spot and save the commission he won from the previous night. The most theatrical scene in the play unfolds immediately after the story of Levene's kill, as Levene poses as a client of Roma's in order to prevent Lingk from interrupting and canceling his sale. Roma guesses (correctly) that Lingk has come to the office to get his money back. He asks Levene to pose as an executive from American Express in order to avoid dealing with Lingk and to delay a meeting with him until the following week, at which time the grace period to reconsider the contract will have elapsed and Lingk will be stuck with the bad purchase. In the previous scene, Levene tells the story of his triumph. The encounter with Lingk theatrically plays out as a scene within a scene, with Roma and Levene posing for Lingk, and all, in turn, performing for the theatrical audience. Roma gets increasingly audacious with his lies as the scene progresses, calling Levene the director of all European sales and services for AMEX, getting into an elaborate evasion about what constitutes three business days (the grace period for the contract), and claiming authorship of a fictitious statute that would, according to Roma, protect Lingk against unscrupulous real estate salesmen (such as Roma!). Ultimately, Williamson intervenes and tries to soothe Lingk, but unwittingly (perhaps) blows the shot by divulging that Lingk's check has already been cashed.

Before inadvertently exposing to Williamson his own culpability in the robbery, Levene upbraids the office manager for his failure to do right by Roma and help him with his deal. He delivers a powerful message—the theme of the play, however ironic—right to the younger man's face: "Your partner . . . a man who's your 'partner' *depends* on you . . . you have to go *with* him and *for* him . . . or you're shit, you're *shit,* you can't exist alone . . . " (98). Evidently moved by Levene's attempt to save him from the reneging Lingk, Roma spouts words of solidarity: "I swear . . . it's not a world of men . . . it's not a world of men, Machine . . . it's a world of clock watchers, bureaucrats, officeholders . . . what it is, it's a fucked-up world . . . there's no adventure *to* it. (*Pause.*) Dying breed. Yes it is. (*Pause.*) We are the members of a dying breed. That's . . . that's . . . that's why we have to stick together" (105). Roma speaks of bygone days and lost brotherhood and the possibility of renewed kinship and bonding between them as kindred spirits, but of course that's bullshit, too. Within the first couple of lines in the play, Levene attacks Roma as someone who's not a real "closer." At the end, Roma's kind words to the older man belie his intent to take leads from him. It's a world of sharks.

The play effectively distills all human contacts down to a series of sales transactions. "To sell" is all there is. Winning is everything, and winner takes all. In *Death of a Salesman,* Hap vows in the Requiem to redeem his father's career: "He had a good dream. It's the only dream you can have—to come out number-one man" (111). If one believes Biff, though, Willy Loman had the wrong dream and would have been much better off and happier had he pursued a trade as a builder rather than in the cutthroat world of sales. Miller's play presents the possibility of alternative paths, and the audience perhaps realizes that things could have turned out differently if Willy had not been blinded by the promise of the American Dream. Mamet's play, on the other hand, presents no such escape route from the excesses of capitalism. No sense of community is possible when each man must strive to be on top of the board. Losers go home. The winner gets the car; losers get the pink slip. A play in which dialogue is action offers no room for idle conversation and the exchange of warm feelings and brotherhood. Instead, the appearance of conversation masks intent to make a sale and close a deal with an unsuspecting victim. In the second scene of act 1, Aaronow wonders aloud how Moss's plot to rob the office ensnared him. "Because you listened," Moss replies at the very end of the scene (46). Dialogue with such salesmen is dangerous business.

While the drama projects the world of the play onto the stage, with a few characters trapped within a single space, the movie provides a context for this world to look more like the one in which we live. Levene's daughter, the presence of Blake, the rain outside, and the impossible customers fill up the screen with justifications for why the men act as they do. Presenting the salesmen as perpetrators and victims gives the film a more human dimension than the play. The Jack Lemmon character, Shelley Levene, is thoroughly Lomanized in the film. He's almost the same age as Willy; he looks as tired. He's infuriating yet capable of drawing an audience's tears at the same time. The play offers none of that, instead coldly enacting the moral vision of another film, Coppola's *The Godfather*. After his part in a conspiracy to assassinate Michael Corleone is exposed, before he's hauled off for his own execution, Tessio (Abe Vigoda) asks Tom Hagen (Robert Duvall) to tell Mike (Al Pacino) that he always liked him and that "[i]t's just business." Pursuing this business, Mamet's play abstracts human behavior and asks the viewer to substitute the world onstage as a representation of life as it is perceived and viewed. Mamet offers the audience an awful metaphor for the way the world operates: there is no fraternity, everyone tries to be number one, no kindness is considered without self-interest. There's no room to think about the customers or anybody else in the ruthless pursuit of business in *Glengarry Glen Ross*.

In his disquisitions upon the drama and film, Mamet reveals a classical bent and a strong bias toward Aristotle. Classically tragic characters are not interesting apart from what they do. It's useless to ask whether or not Oedipus loves his mother; his only objective is to save Thebes from the afflicting plague. In pursuit of that single objective, he discovers that he murdered his father and married his mother. He saves the city, but he destroys himself. His greatest strength, his relentless pursuit of the truth, proves to be his greatest weakness as well. David Mamet's *Glengarry Glen Ross* presents characters with similar single-mindedness. As in Greek tragedy, nothing about the characters is important except their pursuit of a single objective: in this case, to sell. Even a relativist must realize when comparing the two dramas, though, that an enormous difference exists between trying to save Thebes and trying to sell swampland. The nobility of the cause in the former justifies the negligence of all other considerations surrounding that one glorious objective. That the same zealous energy could be applied to Mamet's play in which the characters prey on unsuspecting and gullible buyers comes across as a cruel joke and a bit of black humor. While the tragic perspective perhaps lifts the audience up to gaze upon Olympus in the former work, the downward tilt into the mud of basic human struggle to survive in Mamet's play gives occasion to smile, even laugh perhaps, with the realization of how far modern humanity has slipped. It's too much to expect to save our city; the keys to the Cadillac, however, lie within reach.

10

Making Oneself Big

I would just look at you and wonder how you could be that big. I wanted to be like that. I would go to school and try to make myself feel big. But I never could. I told myself that's okay . . . when I get grown I'm gonna be big like that.

—August Wilson, *Jitney*

The Hallmark Hall of Fame presentation of August Wilson's *The Piano Lesson* (1995) represents a much more typical television adaptation of a play than either of the taped performances of *True West,* which took place before live audiences in theatrical settings. Hardly films at all, the Shepard productions footnote stage performances. Unlike the televised productions of *Death of a Salesman,* however, *The Piano Lesson* disguises the fact that it originated in the theater. Wilson's teleplay, like David Mamet's own screen adaptation of *Glengarry Glen Ross,* discussed in the preceding chapter, departs radically from its theatrical antecedent, much more significantly than either Mike Nichols and Emma Thompson's version of Margaret Edson's *Wit,* or even Tony Kushner's sprawling *Angels in America,* the subjects of the final two chapters. The television production of Wilson's play, although it includes many of the original Broadway cast members, photographs action in the natural environment as well as on the studio set, and features multiple location shots to expand the world of the play beyond the confines of the kitchen and parlor of Doaker Charles's Pittsburgh home. It depicts many scenes that the play only alludes to as previous or offstage events. Despite these additions, however, the film version struggles to capture the essential theatrical "bigness" of the stage drama.

The fable of *The Piano Lesson* is simple and straightforward. Prompted by the death of a slave-owning scion, a black family learns the value of a legacy. The conflict, the only question in the play, revolves around the question of what to do with the piano. Boy Willie's early-morning arrival at his uncle Doaker's house opens the action. He has traveled north from Mississippi with his friend Lymon in order to sell watermelons out of a truck to the city folk in Pittsburgh. His larger purpose is to sell the piano in Doaker's house that has belonged to his sister, Berniece, who lives upstairs in the house since her husband's death three years earlier. Boy Willie intends to take the money from the sale to buy land owned previously by the recently deceased Sutter. This is the same land that Boy

Willie and Berniece's father worked as a sharecropper. Their patriarch never had the resources to buy the land for himself. In the name of his father, Boy Willie wants to claim the piano for his inheritance and buy the land upon which he was raised. He sees the sale of the piano as a means to an end, the possibility for economic viability and a source of livelihood for the future. His sister, Berniece, on the other hand, treasures the piano as a reminder of the past and a way to preserve family history. Significantly, although she refuses to sit down and play the piano, she nevertheless refuses to give it up. In fact, she insists that her daughter, Maretha, take lessons and practice on it.

Carvings in the wood piano chronicle the Charles family's dissolution and bind it together forever in history at the same time. They show the bloody history of slavery and the continued ramifications of poverty, prejudice, and oppression in the Jim Crow South. As told by Doaker Charles in a drawn-out tale, Robert Sutter, Sutter's grandfather, owned the Charles family back in slavery times. He traded "one and a half niggers," Doaker's grandmother and father, to a neighbor for the piano as a present for his wife. Doaker's grandfather, a worker of wood, carved the portraits of the two slaves into the piano when the lady of the house began to miss her former attendants. This way, Doaker observes, "she had her piano and her niggers too" (44). His granddaddy didn't stop with the portraits of his wife and son, but carved a history of the whole family all over the piano, on its sides and legs as well as its front. His grandson Boy Charles, Boy Willie's father and Doaker's elder brother, stole the piano out of Sutter's house a generation later and hid it in the next county in order to keep the family history together. Some white men caught him escaping in a boxcar along with three hobos of the Yazoo Delta Railroad (the Yellow Dog) and burned them alive in retribution. A series of strange deaths ensued, with the white vigilantes falling down their own wells. Folks theorized that the Ghosts of the Yellow Dog killed those men.

Boy Willie arrives in Pittsburgh with the report that Sutter, Robert Sutter's grandson, became the latest victim of the Ghosts of the Yellow Dog. Berniece believes none of it, instead accusing her brother of murdering Sutter in order to acquire his land. For his part, Boy Willie pleads innocent and claims an alibi that he was in the next county when Sutter died. More emphatically, Boy Willie points out the grotesque improbability of his being able to push a 340-pound adult down a well. His description of how he would have had to lie in wait for Sutter to peer down his own well at the right moment approaches the absurd. And yet Lymon, his traveling buddy, asks Berniece, after she has first spied Sutter's ghost, "Did he have on a hat?" (14), as if that were what Sutter was wearing when he and Boy Willie last encountered him. It's not clear, then, under what circumstances Sutter died.

It is clear, though, that Sutter's ghost has returned to haunt the Charles household. Berniece sees it first; Maretha's screams of recognition end the first act. Doaker rather casually mentions at the start of the second act that he's seen it, too, sitting at the piano in the parlor. Doaker reports that he's seen the keys playing by themselves. Boy Willie denies the possibility of the ghost at first, saying that Sutter never left Marlin County in his whole life, but he later conveniently argues that Sutter's ghost has come to Pittsburgh to reclaim the family piano. Boy Willie figures that this is reason enough to allow him to sell the piano and take the money. While Boy Willie's story of the ghost's motives serves his self-interest, the reclamation and possession of the piano are critical for the Charleses' freedom and preservation. Boy Willie's explanation underscores the entire family's need to take ownership of the piano and all that it represents. His father took the piano out of Sutter's house because he felt that it rightfully belonged to his family. According to Doaker, he felt that "it was the story of our whole family and as long as Sutter had it . . . he had us. Say we was still in slavery" (45). The presence of Sutter's ghost in the Charles household reminds the family that they are not yet free and will need to fight for their freedom.

Unlike Sutter's ghost, the Ghosts of the Yellow Dog are not seen in the play, but they represent a more vital force for change and transformation because they challenge characters to stand up for themselves. One doesn't have to believe in ghosts to appreciate their function in the play; one only has to believe that there is such a thing as justice in the world—perhaps divine retribution, that what goes around does come around—and that a connection exists between the events of the past, their impact upon the present, and the implications of such events upon the future. Wining Boy, Doaker's third brother, tells his tale about visiting the Ghosts of the Yellow Dog by going down to the place where the Southern Railroad crosses the Yazoo Delta tracks and calling out their names there. Wining Boy doesn't say that he saw them or that they spoke to him directly, but he does describe a mystical experience that he encountered: "I can't say how they talked to nobody else. But to me it just filled me up in a strange sort of way to be standing there on that spot. I didn't want to leave. It felt like the longer I stood there the bigger I got. I seen the train coming and it seem like I was bigger than the train" (35). Wining Boy allows further that as a result of this experience he "had a stroke of luck that run on for three years" (35).

Toward the end of the play, Boy Willie asserts that there "[a]in't no mystery to life. You just got to go out and meet it square on" (92). Wining Boy's confrontation with the Ghosts of the Yellow Dog is a means of drawing strength and courage for that battle with everything that life offers. Later, Boy Willie lays his cards on the table regarding what he hopes to accomplish in life by admitting that "[t]hat's all I'm trying to do with that piano. Trying to put my mark on the road" (94). The imagery in Wining Boy's account of his meeting with the

Ghosts of the Yellow Dog suggests fullness and increased size, which is a way of inhabiting the world with more confidence. Like his daddy before him Boy Willie has big hands, and he wants to put them to use: "Got these big old hands capable of doing anything. I can take and build something with these hands. But where's the tools? All I got is these hands. Unless I go out here and kill me somebody and take what they got . . . it's a long row to hoe for me to get something of my own. So what I'm gonna do with these big old hands? What would you do?" (91). By asserting himself in the world, Boy Willie seeks to make himself and his actions visible.

At the end of the play, Berniece makes herself big, similar to the way Wining Boy has said he felt, and begins to put her mark on the world. She hasn't dared to play the piano, she says, "cause I don't want to wake them spirits" (70). As long as she won't use it, however, it is difficult to side with her desire to keep it against Boy Willie's need to turn a profit with it. Avery, her would-be preacher beau, even tells her that "[m]aybe if Boy Willie see you was doing something with it he'd see it different" (70). Boy Willie himself tells Berniece that if she were using the piano for lessons in order to pay her rent he wouldn't dream of selling it out from under her. Tempted once by Avery to banish Sutter's ghost with her playing, Berniece doesn't try again until the end of the play. Avery, the man of God, fails in his attempt to drive the spirit from the house. Boy Willie rushes up to take on the ghost by himself in a final scene described by the playwright as "a life-and-death struggle fraught with perils and faultless terror" (106). Faced with imminent death and destruction, Berniece finally goes to the piano and begins to play: "It is intended as an exorcism and a dressing for battle. A rustle of wind blowing across two continents" (106). As critic Harry Elam points out, Berniece calls out in song to the spirits of her African ancestors to rid the house of Sutter's ghost because Avery's Christian exorcism has failed to perform that task. According to Elam, "Berniece's invocation of the ancestors in conjunction with Boy Willie's call to battle exorcises the ghosts of the past that threaten the present. Her actions re-member the family and reaffirm the African in African American experience" (379). When she finally plays the piano she does so violently to shake off all the ghosts from the past: Sutter, Crawley (her dead husband), and the history of victimization that has drained the life out of her. She announces at the end that she is a player who will be heard in the world. In order to encourage and support this new development, Boy Willie gives up his claim to the piano, figuring that he can come up with some other means to secure the necessary money to buy land from the Sutter estate. He finally says, admiringly, "Hey Berniece . . . if you and Maretha don't keep playing on that piano . . . ain't no telling . . . me and Sutter both liable to be back" (108). Berniece will have to continue to impose her "bigness" upon the world in order to stave off all oppressors.

Making oneself "big" is the metaphysical conceit running through all of Wilson's works that signifies independence, courage, and the ability to will one's way through tough times. In *Fences,* Ruby describes Troy Maxson's power and stature to her son in terms of size: "When your daddy walked through the house he was so big he filled it up" (98). His name, which combines Homeric bravery and genetic strength, evokes a large presence within the play. In the best story of *Jitney,* Booster Becker remembers his father as a big man and recalls the time when his father couldn't pay the household rent and the white landlord stood on the porch and made his father seem small. "That's when I told myself," Booster says, "if I ever got big I wouldn't let nothing make me small" (57). Indeed, when his white girlfriend tells a lie and accuses him of rape, he shoots and kills her to uphold his honor. He wanted his father to be proud of him for "being a warrior" (57). Levee in *Ma Rainey's Black Bottom* and King Hedley in *Seven Guitars* are the two most violent characters in their respective plays. In the former, Levee asks, "Is you gonna be satisfied with a bone somebody done throwed you when you see them eating the whole hog?" (*Ma Rainey's Black Bottom* 93). Similarly, Hedley refuses to roll over in the face of white oppression: "You think you can throw a bone and I run after it. You think I fetch for you and wag my tail for you. The black man is not a dog!" (*Seven Guitars* 88). The other musicians in *Ma Rainey* skeptically view Levee as a troublemaker. Levee is not willing to play music in an old style the way it has always been done. He's progressive; he has his own ideas; and he wants to play music that is new, daring, and exciting. One of the heartbreaking aspects of the play is the authentic way in which Ma Rainey, too, censors Levee and prevents him from getting his due recognition and monetary reward. Hedley also is the outsider who says, "Everybody say Hedley crazy cause he black. Because he know the place of the black man is not at the foot of the white man's boot" (*Seven Guitars* 67). Hedley sees himself as equal (a sentiment voiced by Boy Willie in *The Piano Lesson*), in possession of his own soul, and with an expansive inner life and spirit. While others view him as crazy, Hedley clings to a healthy self-image. He continues: "Maybe it is not all right in my head sometimes. Because I don't like the world. I don't like what I see from the people. The people is too small. I always want to be a big man. Like Jesus Christ was a big man. He was the Son of the Father. I too. I am the son of my father. Maybe Hedley never going to be high like that. But for himself inside . . . that place where you live your own special life . . . I would be happy to be big there" (67–68). Being "big" amounts to walking tall and carrying oneself with dignity and self-respect, never bowing and scraping, looking at people straight in the eye, encountering the world "square on" as Boy Willie says.

Carriage, bearing, composure, and forthright honesty all relate directly to vision and light. Herald Loomis in *Joe Turner's Come and Gone* provides the best example of the metaphysical aspects of light and size in any of the plays, his magical name evoking the promise of a new day coming. Having endured seven years of forced labor and losing the song within himself that animates his spirit, he finds his wife at the end of the play, comes alive, and reconnects with the world. Bynum's description of him links luminosity with growing size and stature and the display of human power and potential:

> Got around that bend and it seem like all of a sudden we ain't in the same place. Turn around that bend and everything look like it was twice as big as it was. The trees and everything bigger than life! Sparrows big as eagles! I turned around to look at this fellow and he had this light coming out of him. I had to cover my eyes to keep from being blinded. He shining like new money with that light. He shined until all the light seemed like it seeped out of him and then he was gone and I was by myself in this strange place where everything was bigger than life. (9)

Rising up, standing against oppression, protesting prejudice and wrongdoing—these actions evolve over the course of Wilson's plays, and the dramatic confrontation with Sutter's ghost in *The Piano Lesson* occupies a central position in an elaborate ten-play cycle chronicling each decade of African American life in the twentieth century. *The Piano Lesson* (produced on Broadway in 1990, set in 1937) is the fourth installment in that project, following *Ma Rainey's Black Bottom* (1984, 1927), *Fences* (1987, 1957), *Joe Turner's Come and Gone* (1988, 1911), and succeeded by *Two Trains Running* (1992, 1969), *Seven Guitars* (1996, 1948), *Jitney* (2000, 1977), *King Hedley II* (2001, 1985), *Gem of the Ocean* (2004, 1904), and *Radio Golf* (2007, 1997). *The Piano Lesson* occupies a middle position in terms of both decade-by-decade chronological order and production sequence as well. The same themes recur and resonate throughout the canon. History haunts the characters in each of the plays and forces them to confront the past before looking forward to alternative scenarios in the future. Dramatizing ghosts is one way to make the past come alive and give visible shape to inscrutable forces that diminish the characters in a cultural history ripped asunder and scattered across two continents.

The glory of each play affirms how African Americans gather their disparate lives, described as leftovers in *Ma Rainey's Black Bottom,* into a cohesive whole and stake a claim in the world. Near the end of *Jitney,* the men at the station plan to stand up against the city's decision to tear down the neighborhood. In *Seven Guitars,* Floyd Barton steals money to travel to the recording studio in Chicago after his white backer welshes on his deal That he's killed before he can actually go does not diminish his will to make something happen and to pursue his dream of another hit recording. In fact, the crazed Hedley, who at long last finally holds the cash he's wanted all his life, kills him. The best representation of standing up and moving on, though, can be found in *Two Trains Running,* the play that immediately follows *The Piano Lesson.* The character called Hambone is the most important one in *Two Trains Running,* although he plays very much a supporting role and says almost nothing except "I want my ham. He gonna give me my ham." Clearly addled in the head and ignored by almost everyone, he's so named because he once painted a fence for the businessman across the street in exchange for a ham. Unsatisfied by the quality of his work, the proprietor offered Hambone only a chicken instead. Ever since that day, Hambone has shown up demanding the ham and refusing the chicken. A deal's a deal and what's fair is fair, his actions insist. What's crazy about that? The crazy men, the outsiders such as Levee, Hambone, and Hedley, have a lot to teach the sane black folk who have grown to accept that foul is fair and that exploitation and victimization are completely acceptable. Memphis Lee, the restaurant owner in *Two Trains Running,* faces, like the men in *Jitney,* losing his business to the city's wrecking ball. Everyone assures him that he'll never get more than fifteen thousand dollars for it, but Memphis, inspired in part by Hambone's example, holds out for twenty-five thousand. In the end and to his surprise, the city ponies up thirty-five thousand dollars for the property. Elated by this win, having held out for a fair price and for what he deserved, Memphis decides that he will return to his former home in Jackson, Mississippi, and claim the land that white people stole from him. Had he not first held his ground by standing up for himself and what he believed to be right and fair, he could never have resolved to take the next step and venture back down south to reclaim what he once owned but lost.

The painful subject throughout Wilson's work is slavery endured by African Americans that violently and abruptly transplanted them from one continent to another, and his plays try to nourish cultural developments that have been remembered from the mother countries but also that arose in the rural South. The conditions of slavery spawned all of them: music, food, singing, dancing—born from suffering and from everything that white people didn't want. One of Wilson's talents has been to highlight the lives of ordinary people. In 1995, Wilson wrote "A Note from the Playwright" in the published edition of *Seven Guitars,* in which he voices his credo as a creative artist: "I happen to think that the content of my mother's life—her myths, her superstitions, her prayers, the contents of her pantry, the smell of her kitchen, the song that escaped from her sometimes parched lips, her thoughtful repose and pregnant laughter—are all worthy of art." The cultural specifics and details of the African American experience don't alienate viewers who are unfamiliar with such a context. While the systemic practice of American slavery is unique, anyone can relate to the drama of enslavement: to drugs, ideas, ideologies, or passions. At different points in our lives, we try to eradicate ghosts from the past—people, thoughts, events that cling to us through the years and threaten continually to pull us back to the edge from which we've crawled. We may claim not to believe in ghosts, but our actions often belie faith that the past is dead and buried.

The task, Wilson's plays suggest, is to cultivate the past in order to seed future growth and prosperity. Characters long for freedom and strive to achieve it, but the summoning of strength and courage is often a dormant event that is difficult to see. The drama of enslavement breeds passivity and nonaction, pushing a dramatic turnaround to the very end of the play. Boy Willie wants to sell the piano, and Berniece finally sits down to play it at the end of *The Piano Lesson;* Levee aspires to his record contract in *Ma Rainey's Black Bottom;* Memphis plans to return south in *Two Trains Running;* Herald Loomis tries to pick up a normal life after the chain gang in *Joe Turner's Come and Gone;* Becker and his boys plan to buck city hall in *Jitney.* In all these cases, the only action occurs at the end, or near the end, of the play. Until then, very little happens. Levee assumes throughout the action of *Ma Rainey* that at the end of the recording session he'll sign a record contract of his own with Mr. Sturdivant. Not until the end does the white man turn the tables and disabuse Levee of such a notion. In *Two Trains Running,* Memphis Lee fears that he won't get his asking price for his restaurant from the city, and the eventual offer stuns him at the end when it far exceeds his expectations, an event that inspires him to further action. Likewise, the men in *Jitney* accept the station's demolition as a fait accompli until the conclusion of the play when Jim Becker, in light of his son's homecoming, recaptures his former bigness in his son's eyes by standing up to the bulldozers.

The television film adaptation of *The Piano Lesson* verifies the passivity of the dramatic action. Without losing any important parts, the film cuts an almost three-hour play (with intermission) to only 104 minutes, just enough time for commercials in a two-hour time block. The film, then, sheds nearly one-third of the play, yet it's very difficult to tell what's been excised from the dramatic text. The Hallmark production eliminated all references to "nigger" and "niggers" in the play. Certainly this omission comes at a price; in the play the black men appropriate the slur as a sign of fraternity and affection, and the frequent invocation of this dirty word, repeated over and over, slowly acclimates an audience to its use. This sets up Doaker's ironic and repeated use of the word when he quotes a white woman in the story, previously mentioned, about the Charles family history as slaves near the end of act 1 (40–46). With a trace of bitterness, the audience hears the full force of the family degradation. Still, cutting a single word, no matter how many times it is used in the play, doesn't much alter the running time of a performance. The deletion of entire passages does, though, and extraneous stories that do not relate to the dramatic action, Boy Willie's attempt to sell the piano, get tossed out in Wilson's screen adaptation. Two such stories are Doaker's tale about the railroad and Wining Boy's yarn about Lymon Jackson's daddy. Other characters chide these older men as windbags and long for quiet moments. Such stories add flavor to the play, but do little to advance the action. They serve as a kind of filler designed to bide time until something dramatic does happen much later.

Though it is significantly shorter than the play, the film version actually adds many scenes that are described in the dramatic dialogue but not presented on-stage. This strategy attempts to open up the play to show, during the opening credits, Lymon and Boy Willie traveling up U.S. Highway 61 from Mississippi to Pittsburgh. In the play, the men describe their difficult journey in the beat-up truck with worn-out brakes and a faulty radiator. In the film, Lymon pumps the brakes to no avail and Boy Willie jumps out of the cab onto the road's shoulder. Later, the truck breaks down and the two men walk down the road in search of water. More scenes occur outside the house once the men arrive in Pittsburgh, as they negotiate a deal to repair their vehicle, sell watermelons in a wealthy neighborhood, and later go to a movie theater downtown. The dialogue in the play describes all these transactions from within the Charleses' house. The film takes the viewer there, diverting focus from the house and the main issue inside it. None of these scenes drives the action of the play forward; they merely illustrate the dramatic text.

Far more important are two scenes that show Avery and Berniece at their respective jobs in Pittsburgh as an elevator operator and a cleaning woman. Again, the dramatic text refers to such scenes, but in this case, the visual representation of African Americans at work makes a strong thematic statement, with no comment necessary, to counterpoint the perspective of the visiting Southerners. Boy Willie and Lymon visit Avery to pry information from him, but what the dialogue reveals and what the camera shows remain separate things. Dressed in uniform as an elevator operator at a downtown skyscraper, Avery looks fairly ridiculous in his garish costume. Boy Willie, dressed in his plain planter's clothes, also looks distinctly out of place in such a setting, but he doesn't hesitate to jump in the elevator and stand among the Brooks Brothers suits as Avery takes them to the top. Antithetical to Avery, Boy Willie defies any sentiment that says he's not good enough to stand with the white men. Avery is proud that he receives a pension with his new job and even gets a turkey at Thanksgiving. For his part, Boy Willie says he can kill his own turkey, and he revels in his plan to be his own boss as a farmer once he buys Sutter's land. Boy Willie's pride, confidence, and self-reliance counterpoint Avery's servile attitudes. Similarly, two shots depict Berniece at work in a wealthy house, first scrubbing floors, then polishing glass from a chandelier. There's no dialogue in these shots that begin what would be act 2 in the play, spliced between Boy Willie selling watermelons and Doaker ironing his railroad uniform, mending a tear, and feeding the dog a bone. Such shots establish the activities of a new day, certainly, but they also demonstrate what's at stake in the story by questioning the migration of African Americans to the North and their restricted opportunities to lead self-directed lives.

Although Wilson has certainly focused his efforts on the African American experience and has been pretty adamant about black theater for black people,[1] his plays have achieved a kind of universal appeal. If one can define the American Dream as working hard and passing on a better life for the children of tomorrow, then Wilson's plays celebrate capitalism and the American way of life. The context of the plays may be African American experience, but the underlying ethos in them is very similar to the immigrant ideals of Ellis Island. American blacks may have entered this country through the back door under horrific circumstances, but the plays show characters buying into the very system that oppressed and killed their forebears. There is a definite sense of forward progress and increasing optimism in the plays, from first to last. Circumstances may have forced Troy Maxson to work as a garbage collector, but his son returns for his funeral in uniform as a U.S. Marine. Booster Becker may have served twenty years in prison for a murder, but he says he's proud to be Jim Becker's son. Before his prison detour, he was a brilliant student and dated a white girl, the daughter of a Gulf Oil vice president. The end of the play indicates that he will pick up where his father left off with the jitney station and find a way to carry on his father's legacy. Rena, Youngblood's girlfriend in *Jitney,* explains to him why she's settled down and changed her life since their baby was born: "Cause I'm not gonna be that irresponsible to my child. Cause he depend on me. I'm not going to be that irresponsible to my family. I ain't gonna be like that. Jesse gonna have a chance at life" (*Jitney* 33–34).

Berniece plans on Maretha being a schoolteacher in *The Piano Lesson.* She may start out at the "bottom of life," but, Berniece insists, "she ain't got to stay there" (92). Everything that Berniece does is for the benefit of the child. She moved away from the South after her husband's death in order to escape the cycle of violence that seemed to ensnare her entire family. She works hard in white people's houses in order to afford Maretha's tuition at a special school. Although she cannot even move into a place of her own and lives in an upstairs bedroom in her uncle's house, she insists upon Maretha taking piano lessons. She pays special attention to the girl's appearance and spends inordinate time combing, straightening, and grooming her girl's hair. She demands that Boy Willie not wake her up when he arrives in the early-morning hours before the sun comes up. What she does not do is tell her daughter about the history of the piano, where it came from and what it signifies. Boy Willie encourages Berniece to tell her daughter about it so that she might connect with her ancestors. "That way she know where she at in the world," Boy Willie says. "You got her going out here thinking she wrong in the world. Like there ain't no part of it belong to her" (91). As much as for any other reason, Berniece ultimately faces her ghosts from the past so she can secure a better future for her child. She takes possession of the piano and banishes Sutter's ghost in order to act responsibly toward her child's future happiness, to look forward instead of behind her, to make progress down the path ahead instead of retreading familiar territory that's dead and gone. Sutter's ghost represents unfinished business in Berniece's life. She saves herself and her child by opening the keyboard and awakening her heritage.

The dramatic high point of Wilson's text actually begins to build much earlier, revealing crucial differences between the stage and film treatments, with Doaker's telling of the family history dating back to slavery times. In the play, he tells this story while seated at the kitchen table. The film flashes back to those days and casts actors as slave owners, slaves, lawmen, and onlookers, to act out the story as Doaker narrates. The story culminates with shots of a smoldering boxcar and lots of people looking gravely at its remains, a sign of the vigilant vengeance carried out against Doaker's brother in 1911. Casting all these extras for such parts undoubtedly added to the expense of the film; certainly styling the scene for the nineteenth century cost a lot as well. What's the payoff? The sequence of shots that follows along with Doaker's story contains nothing visually exciting. The visual experience grossly copies the words in the text. The play, of course, requires an audience to imagine these events. But there's more to my objection to this scene than an obvious appeal to the wonders of the theatrical imagination. By filming the past in a flashback mode, the audience again loses sight of the main action in the kitchen. The impact of slavery upon the four men sitting in the kitchen decades after their emancipation is what the scene is really about, and by showing the past the audience loses the full impact of the family history upon the men in the present.

Immediately preceding this story, the men break out to sing communally "O Lord Berta Berta O Lord," a chain-gang song that they all know from various stints at Parchman Farm, the penitentiary in Mississippi. As slavery is the common African American heritage, incarceration and hard labor are the collective experience of all these men, young and old. And while they are sitting in a kitchen, reunited in the big industrial city of Pittsburgh, their shared experiences relate to homes deep in the rural South. The film fails to capture the thrill and the dynamics of the song because it has to treat each aspect that makes up the song separately and sequentially. The camera first finds a face and a voice that begins to sing, then focuses on a hand that begins to bang a fork against a glass, then shows a foot that begins to stomp on the floor. In a stage performance, these separate activities occur simultaneously. Seeing all four men onstage at the same time, it's hard to tell who starts the song and who does what to add accompaniment. The song comes out of nothing, the product of communal playing, and builds to an awesome crescendo of great power and emotion that tap the roots of African American experience. Unlike the slave narrative that Doaker next tells, this moment actually performs history in the present, and the audience witnesses the shared pain and communal bonds of the men. As the titular character explains in *Ma Rainey's Black Bottom,* you "sing to understand life" (82). This particular song doesn't tell a story so much as convey an experience and a mode of living in the world, an accommodation and response to events in the world. If the conditions that first created such a song were hot sun, leg irons, and a shotgun-toting boss, the fervor underlying the performance is an undying longing for freedom. The song in *The Piano Lesson* expresses a desire for freedom under the strain of captivity that reaches full pitch when Berniece finally begins to play and sing at the end of the play. Singing in this way resembles the Juba dance in the preceding play, *Joe Turner's Come and Gone,* in which Herald Loomis breaks into a frenetic dance as if under a strange spell. The theater excels at showing the full body in space and the desire to transcend the corporeal limitations that shackle it to the earth.

Cancer and the Classroom

I take it that the intent of science is to ease human existence.

—Bertolt Brecht, *Galileo*

Ernest Lehman, the producer of the film adaptation of *Who's Afraid of Virginia Woolf?* also took credit for the screenplay of Albee's play, although the playwright contended that the script was all his and that Lehman added only one line![1] Similarly, the HBO Films production of *Wit* (2001) gives director Mike Nichols and his star, Emma Thompson, a screenplay credit even though the film adheres closely to Margaret Edson's Pulitzer Prize–winning play. Claiming that the film is "based on the play by Margaret Edson" sounds a little absurd when the words belong almost entirely to the playwright. Still, using essentially the same text, the film does things quite differently than the stage play. Reviewing the play in New York at the ninety-nine-seat MCC Theatre in Chelsea, critic Peter Marks said, "it's as if we are sitting in Vivian's hospital room, sharing her trials rather than merely witnessing them." Marks's bias presumes that intimacy is better than distance, but a narrative lecture-hall presentation is the operating conceit in Edson's play, and highly theatrical techniques actually make a large space a preferable venue for performance. Her play keeps the viewer from getting too close to the action, and the spatial separation produces tension but also allows the drama room to breathe and resonate. If intimacy were the only virtue of *Wit,* then Mike Nichols's television adaptation would be far superior to any possible stage production. His film traipses on the borders of intimacy and invasiveness in ways that thematically distinguish the film from the play.

The story and subject matter of Edson's play might, at first glance, seem to relegate it to the intimacies of the small stage. An English professor of seventeenth-century literature, a not particularly pleasant woman, undergoes eight months of intensive chemotherapy to combat advanced metastatic ovarian cancer and dies, predictably and rather undramatically, at the end. All theaters big and small throughout the land initially rejected the play as too much of a "downer." Edson wrote her play in 1991, but it was not produced until South Coast Repertory staged it in California in early 1995. Who wants to see a play about cancer? Most AIDS plays (such as *The Normal Heart, As Is, The Baltimore Waltz,* even *Angels in America*) trade on hysteria, homophobia, moral outrage, discrimination, victimization, and protest. How young! How unfair! How tragic! Cancer carries none of that sexiness, and, interpolating from Susan Sontag's *Illness as Metaphor,* there's even a sense that cranky Professor Bearing, fifty, deserves the deadly disease she gets. At best she is, as she says early in the play, "an *unwitting* accomplice" (8), and that does not suggest compelling drama. Sontag contrasts the theatrical nature of TB with the prosaic insidiousness of cancer. The former disease manifests its symptoms externally through fever, flushed cheeks, and the telltale cough. Therefore this disease, like AIDS, lends itself readily to dramatic representations. There's no better death scene than Greta Garbo's in *Camille,* George Cukor's 1936 tearjerker adapted from *La Dame aux camélias,* a mid-nineteenth-century novel/play by Alexandre Dumas *fils,* when the heroine embraces her lover for the last time. No such death scene suits Professor Bearing in *Wit.* The disease destroys the internal organs and makes no explicit show. When Dr. Posner gives Professor Bearing a pelvic exam, the audience discovers the "size" of the problem by gauging the doctor's physical reactions upon discovering the mass of the tumor inside her. "Jesus" is all he says, and he *"tries for composure"* before leaving quickly, leading the audience to infer that the tumor is very large (27). Still, there's nothing for the actress to do to convey that she's extremely sick. Halfway through the play, she confides to the audience, "I just hold still and look cancerous. It requires less acting every time" (32). The irony, Professor Bearing recognizes, is that the treatment to combat her disease, an experimental concoction of hexaminaphosphacil mixed with vinplatin, is what makes her physically ill. The chemotherapeutic agents kill all her reproducing cells and therefore cause her to vomit and lose appetite and precipitate hair loss. The cure, not the cancer, causes her to look "sick."

Cancer is nothing spectacular, but seventeenth-century metaphysical poetry offers little to see either. John Donne's Holy Sonnets, Professor Bearing's specialty, demand close reading and intellectual rigor in order to be understood. The quietness, subtlety, and intensity of the work seem more appropriate for a library than for a theater. In an early scene that flashes back to her college days, Vivian visits Professor Ashford, a leading Donne scholar, during office hours. Ashford critiques Vivian's paper and attributes the mistakes in it to a faulty edition that used "hysterical punctuation." In a phrase of complete condemnation, Ashford adds, "If you go in for this sort of thing, I suggest you take up Shakespeare" (34). While this line gets a laugh, it touches an important point about the untheatrical nature of Donne's poetry and, by extension, Edson's play. *Wit* offers none of the pageantry, bombast, and battles of a good Shakespeare play. Only one character dominates a small cast played by as few as nine actors. To get the most out of the performance would seem to demand an audience sitting close to the stage in rapt attention of every word. In her graceful summation of Donne's "Death Be Not Proud," Ashford discusses the subtleties of punctuation and says that a comma in the final line—not the dramatic capitalizations, semicolons, and exclamation points in the inferior edition—secures the rich meanings of the poem: "Nothing but a breath—a comma—separates life from life everlasting. It is very simple really. With the original punctuation restored, death is no longer something to act out on a stage, with exclamation points. It's a comma, a pause" (14). And so, too, perhaps Donne's poem resonates with the meanings of Edson's play, which again suggests a small, quiet, contemplative affair.

Writing in *American Theatre*, Toby Zinman augments Peter Marks's assessment and concludes that *Wit* "is an intimate play, requiring the tiniest of theatres and the boldest of actors, but it is, paradoxically, a play that declines intimacy." I see no paradox at all in Edson's play. The play deserves a large stage in order to fulfill the dramatic trajectory of its own arc: from proud professor to a woman in the fetal position; from metaphysical poetry to *The Runaway Bunny;* from verbal swordplay to simplicity and, in Bearing's words, "kindness" (55). Death closes in, but in preparation for one dramatic and highly theatrical final image. If everything were "small" and "intimate" in the play, then the final moments of Bearing's death and her "resurrection" would have no dramatic impact. Zinman is clearly right, though, to say that Edson's play "declines intimacy," and this should be a cue to the producer and director about how to stage the play. A number of strategies in the play actually exploit the distance between the performer and the audience: humor, narration, metatheatricality, episodic structure, and an overall lack of suspense. The end of the play is never in question. It's not the destination, then, but the journey that bears investigation.

The sequence of images in the film produces a much more moving portrait of sickness and death than does the play's action. The flashback scenes, for example, immediately juxtapose youth and health with maturity and illness. In the film, the cuts between shots of Vivian and her teacher and mentor E. M. Ashford alternately show Vivian as she was thirty years ago—a young woman, somewhat awkward and sheepish in front of her professor and, significantly, with a full head of hair—and as she is at the current moment—bald, undergoing cancer treatment, present in the scene as if she were reliving a past event. No such similar technique is possible in the theater. Vivian is always bald and must "act" the part of her younger self. Typically, she unhooks herself from her IV pole in order to signify scenes from earlier moments in her life. Later, a scene shows Vivian's fascination with words and language as a young child. She reads Beatrix Potter's "The Tale of the Flopsy Bunnies" and asks her newspaper-reading father what the word "soporific" means. As in the previous scene, the scene alternates between showing Vivian as a young girl and as a bald cancer patient. To heighten the realism in the film, Emma Thompson no longer plays both roles; a child actor portrays her in her early years. The play calls for the parts of Dr. Kelekian and Mr. Bearing to be played by the same actor. In the film, Christopher Lloyd plays the doctor, while Harold Pinter, in a cameo appearance, plays Vivian's father. Onstage, the effect of a mature actress, bald at that, playing a little girl *presents* rather than *represents* events that took place.[2] Having the same actor play the part of both the doctor and Vivian's father—with no attempt to hide the fact, not a product of a low budget but a conscious device—makes the scene a demonstration as opposed to an engrossing scene in which cuts between images of now and then draw the audience into the action by dramatizing the passing of time.

Finally, two flashback scenes of Professor Bearing in the classroom, one in which she lectures, the other in which she calls out students to elucidate Donne's poetry, contrast times of healthy confidence and sickly despair. The latter scene further demonstrates her lack of compassion toward her students. The former is more interesting as she stands and delivers a presentation before her class with Donne's projected verses on the screen behind her. She works at the height of her powers in this moment and speaks without benefit of notes, a point that her former student Dr. Jason Posner emphasizes in another part of the play. Suddenly, another character intrudes into the lecture hall, Nurse Susie Monahan, and the shots begin to alternate between Vivian as a professor and as cancer patient. Susie intrudes upon the flashback to wheel Professor Bearing to another X-ray exam, and thus the present pushes into the past. Onstage, the actress playing Professor Bearing must "act" the part of good health while appearing in her "cancerous" garb (her hat and gown), as the film juxtaposes worlds of health and sickness rapidly in successive frames, then and now, to project a sense of Professor Bearing's physical and mental deterioration over time.

Performed without an intermission, the play runs about ninety minutes. The story time is eight months, the duration of the experimental chemotherapy treatment, and Professor Bearing dies shortly after completing the final dose of drugs. The film indicates the passage of time by showing her with and without hair and getting progressively sick and frail as a result of her treatment. The time off camera to enhance makeup helps this progression nicely, but there's certainly no time for that in the theater. Once the actress playing Professor Bearing comes out for her first lines in the play, she's never offstage; she's the focus of every scene, and she never exits. She must act sick without any technical assistance.

Time passes on the stage through narration and without visual aids. The story of the play is not very dramatic and contains little action. It is all a matter of routine. The eight-week cycle of treatment follows a repetitive pattern: one week in the hospital for treatment; one week at home for recovery; two weeks off;

then repeat. It's difficult to portray the loneliness of the clinical experience on-stage. Drama requires people onstage, dialogue, and scenes to act. Time spent in a hospital is incredibly lonely, filled with abundant free time when there is nothing to do and no one with whom to do anything. Halfway through the play, Professor Bearing conveys this experience through narration: "But as I am a *scholar* before . . . an impresario, I feel obliged to document what it is like here most of the time, between the dramatic climaxes. Between the spectacles" (30). She proceeds to describe the experience of waiting endlessly for something to happen or someone to enter her room. She says to the audience, "If I were writing this scene, it would last a full fifteen minutes. I would lie here, and you would sit there" (30). She describes, in fact, a drama, that cannot take place and concludes, "But if you think eight months of cancer treatment is tedious for the *audience,* consider how it feels to play my part" (30). Again, this bit of narration acknowledges the theatrical environment and, rather intellectually, and wittily, asks the audience to imagine a play that cannot be staged (one in which nothing happens). She apologizes to the audience with assurances that she will not continue in this vein much longer and, with a wink, adds, "Brevity is the soul of wit" (30). The film, however, not constrained to convey the passage of time through narration alone, presents the same sequence as a voice-over to a series of time-lapse images which show Professor Bearing shifting positions in bed over several hours and even days. Very effectively, then, and very economically, these images evoke the experience of loneliness, isolation, and idleness and stir empathy for Bearing as a patient. The shots of her alone in bed in the film present her as a sympathetic victim. In the play, she seems very much in control as the stage manager, producer, and star of her own show. As shown above, she even refers to herself as an "impresario."

The biggest difference between the film and the play is that the leading player forms a relationship with the camera in the former and the audience in the latter. Professor Bearing addresses the audience directly in the play. In the film, Emma Thompson speaks straight to the camera and, instead of addressing a collective group seated in a theater space, relates to a silent audience of one, the unblinking camera eye. This creates the effect of the actress speaking individually to each person who happens to be watching the film. The camera's ability to move in close to a subject produces an intimacy that is impossible to achieve on-stage. As a graphic example, the camera frames a close-up of Professor Bearing as she vomits into a yellow plastic pail and catches the last traces of spittle on her lips. The camera often gets too close to the action and thus enables the viewer to see more than is comfortable to see. The invasiveness of such camera work reinforces the invasiveness of the clinical procedures performed on Bearing's body and the lack of human feeling and respect by the health-care providers in whose care she trusts. The medical histories, lab tests, X rays, and MRIs rob Bearing of her dignity and integrity as a human being, and the camera intensifies each transaction by looming too close.

The very opening scene of the film establishes the pattern used throughout the movie. The film transposes the first two scenes in the play with the abrupt diagnosis by Dr. Kelekian: "You have cancer." The two-shot scene between doctor and patient cuts between extreme close-ups of each actor. Christopher Lloyd's face fills the entire screen, which makes his actual pronouncement much more hostile and aggressive than it would be otherwise. Instead of shooting the scene so that both actors appear simultaneously, the camera assumes an extreme position right in front of each actor's face. The camera is much too close to take in the action. The scene becomes a confrontation between two doctors—one of medicine, the other a PhD in English literature. Threatened by Professor Bearing's calm and resolve, the doctor unloads the full terminology and specificity of Bearing's disease. In turn, Bearing shows no sign of weakness upon hearing the full force of Kelekian's verdict. While she submits to the radical healing treatment that her doctor proposes, the visual picture, not simply the words themselves, indicate that such medicine might be extremely painful and might not help her at all. In the next scene, the opening of the play, Bearing narrates directly to the camera, but as she speaks the camera moves closer for a tighter and tighter close-up of her. As she gets increasingly ill, the camera catches her parched lips, pallid skin color, and gaunt complexion at much too close proximity to be comfortable for the viewer. As an offset, the film also frames moments of intimacy. After all the little indignities that Bearing suffers, her nurse takes the time toward the end to moisturize her hands with lotion, a gesture that certainly won't reverse the effects of cancer but establishes a human connection that has largely been missing from the action. The camera effectively captures the kindness of this gesture up close in a way that reads far better than any stage picture might allow.

The emphasis upon close-ups and proximity to the action certainly provides an incomparable view, but the camera also furnishes a variety of perspectives completely foreign to the stage experience. In particular, the film uses camera shots from directly above some scenes, so that the viewer looks straight down upon Professor Bearing. Nichols uses this shot on at least four different occasions spread throughout the film, but the first and last instances deserve particular mention. As part of the pelvic examination, Dr. Posner, the young fellow under Kelekian's tutelage, pulls out the stirrups from the table and asks Bearing to assume the gynecological position. Realizing that he must have a nurse present during the exam, he rushes out and leaves Bearing in a rather awkward yet maintained position. The shot switches to one directly above her and frames her body perfectly spread-eagled on the table. Again, the camera angle conveys the invasiveness of the procedure and complements the highly personal questions in the preceding medical history written down by Dr. Posner.

Similarly, at the end, after Bearing stops breathing, the Code Blue emergency team rushes in by mistake to revive her. They bring to bear the full power of medical technology, applying a respirator, defibrillator, and CPR pressure, while a loudspeaker continually barks more orders and announcements. During this process, the camera once again shifts to an overhead perspective. Looking straight down, the viewer sees the calm and peaceful repose of Bearing's body shaken and disturbed by the frantic hospital staff and technicians. Once again, the camera captures the violent, physical invasiveness of medical procedures performed on the human body. One of the few times that the film shows the entire body, this shot blends the quiet and peace that death brings with the frenetic noise of the hospital workers and sets up an ending that is quite different from the one found in the play. Lacking film's flexibility to see the actress from above, the stage requires a radical solution to the visibility problem of the final scene. Faced with the problem of a dying patient—the star of the play on the bed surrounded by a crowd of caregivers—the playwright opts to get the leading actor up and away from the crowd in order to establish the equivalent of a film close-up. Standing downstage in full-bodied vulnerability, the lone figure attracts the full attention of the audience.

This move at the end of the play, in comparison to the final image in the film, demonstrates a theatrical technique designed to give the play ample visibility on a large stage. This play has many such devices. The presentational style of delivery that casts Professor Bearing as the narrator for the play's action operates as a dominant conceit throughout the entire script. Since the play acknowledges that she is a strong-willed and self-possessed college professor, it is only natural that she lectures to the audience. At the beginning, Bearing enters while the houselights remain on, a device that allows both parties to recognize each other. This frank theatrical device signals, too, the metatheatrical nature of the play, as Bearing acknowledges that she plays a part in a play that she has only partly authored. The progression of the disease itself, cancer, structures the action in the play. Whereas the film creates a singular relationship between the actor and an individual viewer via the camera lens, the play creates the opportunity for the actress to build a relationship with an entire collective audience simultaneously. Such a challenge requires concentrated projection to every seat in the theater: front and back, side to side. This means that the playing style for the actress in the theater must necessarily be "bigger" than for the actress in the film role. The actress onstage, bald and wearing a baseball cap, pulling an IV pole alongside her, speaks as if to students in her seventeenth-century literature class. The audience sees the cancer patient but hears the oration of the self-confident, polished, and witty professor.

Wit siphons the melodrama of victimization and focuses the action in a clinical perspective. Moments after her first entrance, Bearing dispels any questions about the outcome of the play: "It is not my intention to give away the plot; but I think I die at the end" (8). Peter Marks, the New York Times reviewer, claimed it was a virtue to feel that he was experiencing the play rather than merely watching it, but these techniques actually distance the viewer from the action in order to let that viewer gain perspective on what is witnessed. Bearing narrates the final eight months of her battle with cancer and presents scenes from her life to the audience for it to analyze. She stages this presentation as she would a lecture for her class, recognizing that she must condense her life story into a suitable lecture format. She finishes her first long bit of narration by saying, "I've got less than two hours. Then: curtain" (8). The houselights dim and the first dramatic scene begins, but Bearing continues to narrate her story and monitor her declining health throughout the rest of the play. After undergoing another painful battery of tests, she remarks, "My next line is supposed to be something like this" (43). Before she lapses into a morphine-induced haze near the end of the play, she again declaims the situation for her audience: "These are my last coherent lines. I'll have to leave the action to the professionals. [. . .] Not even time for a proper conclusion" (57). The metatheatrical, presentational style of performance allows viewers to learn something as they witness the play. Just as Ashford's insistence that Donne's poetry resists "hysterical punctuation" in order to convey profound meaning, so too the action of Edson's play resists pulling on the heartstrings of audience members so that they might discover the meanings within the play.

Alternating between narratives delivered by the principal player and dramatic scenes, the plot is episodic rather than linear, a further theatrical device to prevent the audience from becoming swept up in the pathos of cancer's inevitable path. Bearing's narrations title each scene and drain any suspense about what will happen. Thus the scenes function as flashbacks to what has already been written. The narrative quality of the play puts everything in the past tense, a device that further cools the action and makes it more available for analytical digestion. Bearing introduces the first scene by saying, "I'll never forget the time I found out I had cancer" (8). Then she plays—or, rather, reviews—the scene in which Dr. Kelekian offers his informed diagnosis of her condition. Each scene follows this exact format. The conclusion of a narrative speech by Bearing always introduces the dramatic scene that follows. For example, she announces early in the play, "That is why I chose, while a student of the great E. M. Ashford, to study Donne" (13). The scene shows Bearing's infatuation with the poet and, even more so, with her teacher. Later in the play, Bearing introduces another scene similarly: "through a series of flashbacks, the senior scholar [Bearing] ruthlessly denied her simpering students the touch of human kindness she now seeks" (48). The dramatic scene on the heels of this narration proceeds to show the professor exhibiting contempt for her students.

In an interview with Jim Lehrer, Margaret Edson defined *Wit* as "a play about love and knowledge. And it's about a person who has built up a lot of skills during her life who finds herself in a new situation where those skills and those great capacities don't serve her very well. So she has to disarm, and then she has to become a student. She has to become someone who learns new things." In her battle with death and medical science, Bearing undergoes a role reversal. "Once I did the teaching; now I am taught," she observes (32). Formerly, she studied literary texts; now she herself is the text of study. In the highly theatrical scene to which I alluded earlier, Bearing lectures to her class in front of a screen upon which one of Donne's sonnets is projected. At one point, she moves directly in front of the screen so that the words of the text display upon her. The doctors study and probe her body just as she used to probe a text. She literally becomes a text to read in the course of her treatment. "Now I know how a poem feels," she says, her first concession to empathy and a sign that she is truly on the path to learning something.

The same resolve Bearing applied to her scholarship she now applies to her position as a cancer patient. Her insistence on self-reliance keeps others at bay, including the audience, and prevents an emotional response to her growing pain and suffering. She refuses to see herself as a victim and meets the disease head-on as if it were a difficult passage of metaphysical poetry. If she were more vulnerable and less strong and prickly, she would not be able to endure the intense experimental treatment she receives. "Give me the full dose," she says, "the full dose every time" (15). Her ability to tolerate and withstand such treatment separates her from other patients and makes her something of a celebrity in the ward. Having survived eight rounds of chemotherapy, she realizes that she will be published in reputable medical journals. But it will be Kelekian and Posner who garner the praise as the authors of these articles, and Vivian admits that she won't even appear in print: "The article will not be about me, it will be about my ovaries" (43). She won't be present at all. She adds, "What we have come to think of as *me* is, in fact, just the specimen jar, just the dust jacket, just the white piece of paper that bears the little black marks" (43). "Published *and* perished," she quips.

Cancer is the plot excuse to bring up a lifetime review. It is the pause, the condition, which allows Vivian Bearing to reflect upon her life. Confronted by circumstances that she cannot control, Bearing reassesses her life and discovers that she is now the victim of her own former practices. Toby Zinman states emphatically, "*Wit* is about the pursuit of knowledge—in medical research and in literature." To risk another metaphor, the boundless pursuit of knowledge is the cancer of the piece. According to Pamela Renner, "[i]f there's a villain in *Wit*, it's not a person or an institution, but a thirst for knowledge regardless of human consequences. Susie's [Vivian's nurse's] honesty is the closest thing to heroism that Edson's drama admits" (36). Medical doctors are definitely not portrayed as heroes and angels of mercy. Excitedly elaborating on his intellectual interest in cancer research to Professor Bearing, Dr. Posner describes the reproductive genius of the diseased cells as "[i]mmortality in culture" (46). Cancer cells, he explains, unlike normal cells, never stop replicating and ultimately kill their host. But unlike viral diseases, such as AIDS, or bacterial diseases, such as TB, the cancer cells cannot spread and transfer to another host. The cancer cells, despite their "immortality," ultimately die along with the host organism. The lack of sociability limits the disease's perfection.

Similarities between Professor Bearing and Dr. Posner strengthen the parallel between the pursuits of literature and science. One is a fifty-year-old English professor, PhD, while the young MD, Bearing's former student, is an ardent cancer researcher. Bearing notes the similarity between them, late in the play, although such recognition brings her no comfort and the doctor could care less. She sees in him the same brilliant mind that she herself possesses and the same lack of empathy for other people. Their own professional "immortality in culture" conducted within their spheres of influence extends to no one else and is destined to die with them as well. Both of them, too, enjoy their respective disciplines because of personal intellectual gratification rather than for any benefit to other students or patients. Bearing, for example, selected Donne as a subject because he was the most difficult, made Shakespeare look like kindergarten, and afforded her the opportunity "to see how good you really are" (18). Posner describes Bearing's class, one of the hardest at the university, as more difficult than biochemistry. Posner chose cancer research because it attracted the best minds, posed as the most challenging intellectual arena, and offered the best grant money. He plans to make a name for himself someday, if he can survive the clinical rounds (dealing with patients), by starting a lab of his own.

For both of them, knowledge is the ego food that sustains their respective professional drives. After all the technical devices in the play allusive of Brecht, a theme pops up mindful of *Galileo*. In that play, the great scientist ultimately recognizes that he served himself instead of humanity. Brecht brilliantly pictures his corpulence in the play and shows how Galileo loves a good idea in the same way that he loves a good cooked duckling. The Pope says of him, "He has more enjoyment in him than any man I ever saw. He loves eating and drinking and thinking. To excess. He indulges in thinking-bouts! He cannot say no to an old wine or a new thought" (109). The intellect, according to Brecht, cannot serve mere appetite but must serve a higher purpose for the common good. While not as politically lofty or motivated as Brecht's, Edson's play nonetheless portrays the exclusive pursuit of knowledge, at the expense of human feeling and emotions and caring for others, as dangerous.

Bearing's literary criticism of the works of John Donne is analogous to Posner's cancer research. She lectures, "In his poems, metaphysical quandaries are addressed, but never resolved. Ingenuity, virtuosity, and a vigorous intellect that jousts with the most exalted concepts: these are the tools of wit" (40). Posner describes Donne's wit as a puzzle which cannot be solved but is intellectually very stimulating: "Fascinating, really. Great training for lab research. Looking at things in increasing levels of complexity" (60). Making the explicit connection between literary and medical research, Posner adds, "When it comes right down to it, research is just trying to quantify the complications of the puzzle" (61). Brushing off Susie's insistence that he helps people with his work, Posner retorts, "Oh, yeah, I save some guy's life, and then the poor slob gets hit by a bus!" (61). Posner denies that what he does actually helps people. In his laboratory, cancer becomes an abstract and rather inhuman problem. Sontag concludes *Illness and Metaphor* by claiming that cancer is the dumping ground for a host of fears about the course of human events: "Our views about cancer, and the metaphors we have imposed on it, are so much a vehicle for the large insufficiencies of this culture: for our shallow attitude toward death, for our anxieties about feeling, for our reckless improvident responses to our real 'problems of growth,' for our inability to construct an advanced industrial society that properly regulates consumption, and for our justified fears of the increasingly violent course of history" (87). Though this was written in 1978, Sontag could well write the same conclusion today. Our aggressive feelings about the disease and our strange behaviors toward those unfortunate enough to have acquired it stem from a sense of helplessness about our ability to control events in the world.

Near the end, Vivian says, "I thought being extremely smart would take care of it. But I see that I have been found out" (55–56). Wit, the play suggests, will take a person only so far. Edson's play reminds an audience that even if human suffering cannot be eliminated, a mandate remains to act kindly toward the dying. Pamela Renner calls Nurse Susie Monahan heroic because she demonstrates caring and compassion toward Vivian as she is dying. Vivian is quick to remark that Susie is not very bright, but when Vivian calls her she comes and provides needed comfort in dire moments. As the play progresses toward the end, small gestures of kindness begin to creep into the action. Prior to the scene in which Susie moisturizes Vivian's hands, the two women, who really have nothing in common except for Vivian's cancer, engage in a quiet and comforting conversation while they eat cold popsicles (which soothe Vivian's digestive tract). In the most touching scene of all, Vivian's mentor, E. M. Ashford, eighty years old, arrives and climbs into the bed for a few moments while tenderly reading Vivian to sleep with a children's story. She offers first to read Donne, but Vivian declines. She doesn't need to hear John Donne work out his metaphysical problems with life, death, and life everlasting. She has gone quite past such mental concerns at this moment and needs now "simplicity" and "kindness" (55). Instead, Ashford reads the book she purchased for her little grandson, *The Runaway Bunny*. The story is "a little allegory of the soul" (63), all about a mother who vows to follow her child wherever she may hide. As Vivian returns to second childhood in the seven ages of Shakespeare, *The Runaway Bunny* trumps John Donne.

The final image of the film dramatically departs from the play. In the film, the Code Blue team arrives in an attempt to revive Vivian, in the course of which they tear away her gown to reveal the actress's bare breasts. The camera frames the shot from the foot of the hospital bed and pulls back as Emma Thompson's voice-over recites Donne's "Death Be Not Proud," an ironic ending given the preceding rough and rude treatment. Accentuating the ravages of the disease and the medical establishment against her, the camera peers at her nude torso, cut off from her head, a final invasion. The dramatic script takes an altogether different tack. Vivian, after dying and enduring the undignified assault from the emergency team, gets up from her bed and moves apart from the crowd to the spotlight downstage. Instead of hearing Donne's poem, her action physically embodies "Death Be Not Proud" as she walks toward a light in an humble search for redemption and grace. As she moves, she removes her cap and bracelet and unties her gowns. The final stage directions read, "The instant she is naked, and beautiful, reaching for the light—Lights out" (66). Initially, Vivian stressed that irony would play a major part of the drama, yet there is nothing ironic in the final stage direction. The nudity, too, reveals the actress playing the part of the cancer victim as healthy and vibrant. The lights go out as soon as she completely disrobes, but the fleeting image of vitality represents a final gift to the audience, as the actress steps out of her role and her costume and shares with the audience the aspiration for spiritual life everlasting. Very simply, very crudely, very effortlessly, her physical actions act out Donne's complex poem. It wasn't so hard after all.

12
Stairway to Heaven

SMUKOV: People, I think, would rather die than change.
UPGOBKIN: Do you really think so?
I believe precisely the opposite.
We would rather change than die.
We have been ordered into motion by History herself, Vashka. When the sun comes out, the sky cracks open, the silent flowers twist and sway . . .

—Tony Kushner, *SLAVS!*

The most cinematic moments of HBO's *Angels in America* happen in the opening credits before the film actually begins. Timed to Thomas Newman's haunting musical score, the viewer swoops and swerves through the clouds on a winged flight across America, dipping below them intermittently to check out monuments of manifest destiny along the way: the Golden Gate Bridge in San Francisco; the Mormon Tabernacle in Salt Lake City; the Gateway Arch in St. Louis; the Hancock tower in Chicago; the Empire State Building in New York. The camera finally perches under the gaze of the angel at the Bethesda Fountain in Central Park, which is also the site to which the action returns in the last scene. As if responding to the proximity of the viewer, the statue groans and averts its head. The Angel has landed.

Even though *Angels in America* has been around for more than a decade, even though it won Tony Awards for best play in 1993 and 1994 (one for each part), Drama Desk Awards, a host of other awards, and the Pulitzer Prize for Drama in 1993, most people now know Tony Kushner's play as a 2003 film by Mike Nichols. *Part One: Millennium Approaches* debuted 7 December 2003, and *Part Two: Perestroika* premiered the following week. In advance of the opening, Alex Abramovich reported in the *New York Times* that the film "will be broadcast and rebroadcast to more than 30 million homes, and the number of people who see it the very first night should easily outnumber those who have seen the play in the several hundred North American stage productions since it opened 10 years ago" (1). The play is still produced today regularly by regional professional theaters, amateur groups, and college and university players, but the number of people who actually see such productions is minuscule compared to the potential television audience. Meryl Streep, one of the stars of the film, made the analogy to Abramovich that " 'It's almost as if HBO had decided that the

Wooster Group [avant-garde theater artists who work in the Performing Garage on Wooster Street in New York City] was going to go straight across America'" (6). Indeed, Nielsen Media Research reported that 4.2 million viewers saw the first installment of the miniseries, making it the most-watched made-for-cable movie of the year. Not to get too carried away, it should not be overlooked that 22.2 million people saw *Survivor,* the reality show on CBS, that same week. Still, an HBO spokeswoman said at the time, "This is only the beginning of what we hope is an enormous audience when this plays out over an aggressive schedule" (Bauder). Trimming the seven-hour play to six hours, HBO broke each of the two parts into three equal chunks of about one hour each and reprised the six individual sections, called chapters, in the days following each premiere episode. It even presented one six-hour marathon of the entire project. All in all, in one thirty-day period it was possible to see at least one chapter of *Angels in America* on any given night.

The pedigree of the film lies beyond reproach. Kushner himself wrote the screenplay, and Nichols, who has earned the respect of both the theater and film communities, directed an all-star cast featuring Al Pacino, Meryl Streep, Emma Thompson, Mary-Louise Parker, Jeffrey Wright (the only actor to have appeared in the original Broadway production), and with cameo appearances by James Cromwell, Michael Gambon, and Simon Callow. Ben Shenkman and Justin Kirk play the roles of Louis Ironson and Prior Walter, the main couple, wonderfully and sympathetically. It's hard to imagine a better cast for any production, and it's easy to understand how the film, digitally processed and preserved, will supplant the play as an introduction to Kushner and his work. The DVD will provide an accessible teaching tool for the increasingly anthologized play. So is anything to be gained by seeing *Angels in America* in the theater for which it was initially conceived?

In his "Playwright's Notes" which precede the play in the published edition of *Millennium Approaches,* Kushner advises the would-be producer that "the play benefits from a pared-down style of presentation, with minimal scenery and scene shifts done rapidly (no blackouts!), employing the cast as well as stagehands—which makes for an actor-driven event, as this must be."[1] He goes on to assert that the "moments of magic [. . .] are to be fully realized, as bits of wonderful *theatrical* illusion—which means it's OK if the wires show" (5). Celebrating the fiction designed to please a theatrical audience, the playwright suggests that it might be all right if the audience is able to see the strings attached to the flying angel (he also says it works better if the angel does fly), which is the most anticipated and stunning image in the play.[2] The stage presentation that shows the illusion honestly gives the audience the freedom to accept or reject it. The simplest methods produce the most powerful results. In his analysis of staging the play, Arnold Aronson says as much when he concludes that the "rough theater" productions that he has seen, some by amateur actors on a bare stage, have often proven more emotionally powerful than fully produced versions (225). Revealingly, and quite surprisingly, he perceives Thornton Wilder's *Our Town* as Kushner's theatrical antecedent.

At one time during the ten-year interim between the drama and its eventual film adaptation, Robert Altman was scheduled to direct the movie. Gordon Davidson, the longtime artistic director of the Mark Taper Forum in Los Angeles, interviewed Altman and Kushner together in the mid-1990s when Altman was still on tap to do the film. About that prospective project, Kushner commented emphatically, "I want the play to have a separate existence. I don't want the film to be in any way sort of a faithful recording" (Davidson 139). Despite that sentiment, Kushner's screenplay and Nichols's film are remarkably similar to the original dramatic texts. The fidelity between film and play exists not simply because Kushner authored both projects, but more importantly because the play uses cinematic elements and techniques for theatrical effects. However many obstacles hindered the film from being made because of its "dangerous" and "lurid" subject matter (homosexuals, disease, Republicans), the greatest hurdle lay in the form of the work itself and its resistance to cinematic adaptation. In his interview with Gordon Davidson, Robert Altman discussed Kushner's dramatic text and the challenge of adapting it to another medium: "There's a big problem with it because he used a lot of film technique in his play, and in the stagecraft, and it's done that way. So when it's translated back to film if I just used that, I think we'd just have an ordinary film" (131). If the entire film had been shot from the perspective of the angels, for example, as in the opening credits, then perhaps something entirely new and dangerous and exciting might have developed. As is, the film rarely approaches the daring and danger of the sprawling historical onstage epic as a harbinger, warning, and prayer for the future of the country and all of humankind.

The time is set in the last three months of 1985 and the first two months of the following year. An epilogue springs the play forward to 1990 and discussions of Gorbachev and reforms and challenges for a new world order. Much of the play looks back to the beginning of the twentieth century (for instance, Ellis Island, Bolshevik Revolution) and even further: Joseph Smith and the founding of the Mormon Church in the nineteenth century; Prior Walter's relatives stitched into the Bayeux Tapestry and later visitations by Prior 1 (thirteenth century) and Prior 2 (seventeenth century); racism and slavery. Above all else, though—and this accounts for the play's particular setting in history—the action condemns the Ronald Reagan presidency (1980–88) and his administration's cold-blooded indifference to the AIDS crisis. The president's refusal to acknowledge that disease and the devastation brought by it, the play argues, waged evil on par with almost any other atrocity, including the Holocaust, of the last century.

With all of history spread before him, particularly American history of the past century, Kushner transposed film techniques to the stage, an aspect not unnoticed by opening-night reviewers. Clive Barnes, reviewing in the *New York Post,* observed that the play's "almost cinematic sense of intercut and intercross is everywhere pervasive" ("Angelically Gay"). In *Newsweek,* Jack Kroll marveled that the play "ranges far and wide in 34 scenes that shift with cinematic speed from sharp-focus emotions to wide-angle ideas" ("Mourning"). What these critics responded to were the multiple scenes, often quite short, that picked up in the middle of things and then switched to another scene, another place, another time before switching back to resume former arguments. Moving easily and rapidly from funeral homes to cemeteries to offices to apartments in Brooklyn and Manhattan to houses in Salt Lake City, to courthouses, to promenades, to Antarctica, to the heavens above and Heaven itself, the play takes place here, there, and everywhere. Scene topples scene as the playwright strings his plot. Suddenly, Prior steps out of a scene to act out what happened previously in a flashback scene with the Angel. The theater normally functions in a narrative and progressive mode, action moving forward in time. The presence in the here and now that so much of drama demands, and that Aristotle requires, Kushner flouts brilliantly. The action takes place wherever he says it takes place. The Antarctica that Harper retreats to as an escape can be nothing more than a bare stage. The film, through a pronounced lighting change and the arrival of police officers, grounds the play in a recognizable place and makes it explicit that Harper's Antarctica is really just Brooklyn's Prospect Park and that her hallucinations have been the product of her desperation, drugs, dehydration, and exposure to the cold.

The plot of the play resists a simple narrative with a single protagonist and, again borrowing from history, presents a kind of Jacobean double plot bound by AIDS and acts of betrayal. Prior Walter discovers that he has the disease, and his lover, Louis, unable to face the ugliness of the situation, abandons him, forcing him to find strength to survive that he didn't know he possessed. Roy Cohn, drawn from the historical figure, also gets word of his deadly diagnosis during the course of the action and ultimately dies in *Part Two,* deserted by his surrogate son and would-be lover, Joe Pitt, the Mormon struggling with sexual identity who finally leaves his wife, Harper; comes out to his mom in Utah; and engages in an affair with Louis, a brief liaison that ties the two plots together. There's also an angel, of course, as well as an imaginary travel agent who directs Harper's tour of Antarctica, and an ex–drag queen male nurse who ministers both to Prior and Roy. One patient lives; the other dies.

After seeing both plays, John Simon concluded in his review, "the final tab-

leau implies full remission or, at any rate, denies us the dramatically necessary impact of his [Prior's] death" ("Angelic Geometry"). Simon reveals his appetite for
nineteenth-century melodrama, à la *Camille,* by his insistence on death to confer
meaning upon the event. Impishly yet strategically, Kushner dries up deathbed
tears by playing a joke and giving the obligatory scene to Cohn in the hospital.
Cohn, on account of all his horrible deeds, can only engender a modicum of
sympathy. But, faced off against his old nemesis, the Ghost of Ethel Rosenberg,
and preparing to get his final comeuppance, Cohn fakes his own death in order
to break Ethel's cold facade, bolts upright in bed to gloat over fooling her, re-
lapses suddenly, curses, and dies abruptly (for real this time!). This treatment of
death, light as it is, wipes away any moral stain about the cause of death and any
smug attitudes about a deserved end. Prior doesn't die at all. In the epilogue, he
voices his surprise that he's still alive but resolves to live as fully as he can with
whatever time he's allowed. The play ends, then, not with a final death, but with
an affirmation for "[m]ore life" as Prior demands (*Perestroika* 133). Such an open
ending agrees with this chronicle of a historical epoch that touches upon all of
history with hope for the years to come.

The dramatic text of *Angels in America* projects its image to an audience in
highly theatrical yet cinematically borrowed ways that set it apart from the eventual film version. A perspicuous moment occurs with the long-awaited arrival of
the Angel at the very end of *Millennium Approaches.* As the lights change colors
eerily, a terrified yet fascinated Prior gasps, "*Very* Steven Spielberg" (118). It's a
funny line. The Angel's impending crash through the roof creates a true theatrical spectacle. (The playwright advises potential producers to allow a week of
technical rehearsal for this singular effect!) Prior's reference to Spielberg calls attention to the fact that what follows will be purely theatrical and made up; but
what could be more honest for a theatrical audience than that admission? The
Hollywood reference also buys permission from the audience for the succeeding
moment to fail. How could the cheap tricks of the poor theater rival the eminence and special effects of such a great film director as Steven Spielberg?[3] This
is another instance in which Kushner allows the wires to show in order for the
audience to relax and enjoy the simple spectacle. Kushner casts Prior's fantastical experience in cinematic terms that an audience can understand and accept.
If the supernatural were to visit, people might well describe that occurrence in
terms of movies they've seen. It's not all that unusual to describe an experience
as if it were in a movie. As David Savran suggests, a reading of the Angel must
be mediated by the technological wonders hatched by Hollywood (19). *E.T.* produced tears, and *Close Encounters of the Third Kind* terrified millions. Films live
in the imagination as waking dreams and ticketed hallucinations. They are in

the world, and they are real. Prior's initial response to the supernatural may exude humorous skepticism, but it also expresses the old theatrical willing suspension of disbelief.

Like Prior, who does later become a prophet, Harper says, "I see more than I want to see" (51). Invoking movie references, too, Harper hears voices and sees visions of men with knives lurking in her apartment that, she claims, mistakenly, was the setting for Roman Polanski's *Rosemary's Baby*. When husband Joe tells her that they can move to Washington and live in Georgetown, she doesn't feel any safer—that's where *The Exorcist* was filmed! Harper, the valium-popping Mormon standing on the "[t]hreshold of revelation" (33), stares into Prior's eyes in a mutual fantasy scene early in the play and says, movingly, "Deep inside you, there's a part of you, the most inner part, entirely free of disease. I can see that" (34). For his part, Prior tells her that she's dreadfully unhappy and that she is married to a homosexual. Both these prophecies turn out to be true. In *Part Two,* together in the diorama room of the Mormon Visitors Center, Harper and Prior watch the tableau of Mormon dummies but see Joe and Louis (who have engaged in an affair) on the stage. She tries to comfort Prior's tears by saying, "You shouldn't do that in here, this isn't a place for real feelings, this is just storytime here, stop" (64). She attempts to assuage Prior's pain by claiming that his visions are "just the magic of theatre or something" (65). But theater is literally "the seeing place," and the appearance of fantastical elements defines for the viewer the real magic of theater—knowingly false, contrived, and made-up events reduce an audience to tears or peals of laughter with hits that touch upon truths on some deep level that can be discovered only through the gratuitousness of theater. Its complete falseness, which is honest, unlocks hidden secrets.

The film version doesn't include the Spielberg reference, and the fantasy element is largely absent from the scene at the Mormon diorama. As reconstructed in the film, Joe, Louis, and Prior don't even appear in that scene. The film doesn't gain any resonance from the metatheatrical elements or self-referencing present in the dramatic script. Indeed, if the Spielberg reference were kept in the film, it would invoke a comparison between Spielberg and Nichols and call attention to the fact that the supernatural aspects in the latter's film are really quite lame. For all his abundant gifts as a director, including especially his talent for depicting nuanced human relationships layered and laced with irony and humor, Nichols has never been known for his skill in the special-effects department. His weakness in that department is noticeable and critical in this film. Whereas the stage production draws strength from its own tired clichés and tawdry imitations, which often further stoke the audience's imagination, the realistic mandate for film (the camera recorded the action somewhere!) and the audience demand for great special effects (how real does it look?)—a standard established by Spielberg and embellished by the Jerry Bruckheimers of the industry—create expectations that the film simply cannot fulfill.

In the film, the giant book on its pillar cracking through the floor is just silly; the destruction of Prior's apartment when the Angel bursts through the ceiling looks like a toy model with Styrofoam fragments of plaster and lath; the Angel (Emma Thompson) is made up to look like a pinup from the 1980s complete with a wind machine to keep her hair in constant brushed-back motion; the thunderbolt she wields looks ridiculous; she levitates Prior, flames peel away their clothes, and they share "plasma orgasmata" in another encounter that is hard to watch without laughing. Humor is part of the display, surely, but the audience should also accept what's happening as honest and truthful. In *Part Two,* when Prior ascends to Heaven, he climbs a ladder with little flames (in the shape of alephs) emanating from each rung. In the theater, the simplicity of this gesture could be executed easily to great effect. A ladder from the stage to the fly space above would be the only thing required to convey the moment. It would be simple, humorous, but deeply affective as well, because the audience assumption about Heaven is that it is some unseen space above. Yet this is another unsuccessful fantasy moment in the film because there is no clear idea about Heaven's location. The ladder looks cheesy with its little flames, and the shot looking up the ladder shows the stars above and the ladder disappearing in a forced perspective at a made-up vanishing point. Yes, the audience intellectually understands that this is Prior's "stairway to heaven," but the amusing gesture does not stir the senses visually or viscerally.

One scene of emotional power in the film steals directly from the theater. Prior 1 and Prior 2, ghosts from Prior's ancestry marvelously played by Michael Gambon and Simon Callow, visit the surviving heir in preparation for the angel's royal incipience. They invite Prior to dance and conjure Louis, Prior's lover, as a spectral partner. As the two dance together, this fantasy moment is staged in purely theatrical terms. The ghosts stand on either side of the framed shot and gesture "upstage" toward Louis, who descends from a curved staircase ringed with rope lights and beckons Prior to join him on the "dance floor" of Prior's living room. The viewer sees this scene through the "proscenium arch" of Prior's adjoining living room. Thus Prior, in his bed, is roughly in the position of a theatrical audience, and he joins Louis for the slow dance on the "stage" as if at the end of an enchanting Stuart masque. The scene would be impossible to stage in a theater, but it draws upon theatrical technique and tradition for a wonderful cinematic effect. It's camp, sure, but it's also fun, moving, and a glimpse of what a better world might be. It was my favorite moment in the film. After watching for several minutes, the ghosts retire, the last (Callow) saying, "The twentieth century. Oh dear, the world has gotten so terribly, terribly old" (114). He leaves, the music abruptly stops, and the film cuts, fantasy over, to find Prior dropping to the floor, alone again, back in reality, in his apartment.

The theatrical principle of things being both completely fake yet deeply affective extends to the realm of characterization as well. Kushner stipulates that eight actors should play all twenty roles in the play, thus requiring doubling and tripling of parts. Seeing an actor play more than one part transfers focus away from the identification of the actor with the role and directs attention instead upon the function of the part. This theatrical technique also celebrates the craft of acting. When the same actor plays Joe as well as one of the ghosts, the audience gains a comparative measure of the actor's skill. The Angel who descends from Heaven seeking Prior's aid also plays the nurse, Emily, who treats Prior's disease. The actor who plays Louis's former lover, Prior, also appears as the man whom Louis picks up in the park, a technique that amplifies Louis's guilt and shame over his betrayal. Doubling, then, works both theatrically and thematically.

The film follows the play's strategy of theatrical and thematic doubling up to a point. Meryl Streep plays Hannah, but she also plays the rabbi in the opening scene and the Ghost of Ethel Rosenberg later (as in the play). Jeffrey Wright, as Belize, also plays the part of Mr. Lies (as in the play). Emma Thompson, too, plays the Angel, Emily, and the woman in the South Bronx as the dramatic text indicates. The doubling ends here, though, with these three stars playing multiple parts. In Kushner's text, the actors playing Hannah and Harper also double in men's parts such as Henry, Cohn's doctor, and Justice Department official Martin Heller. The film drafts additional actors James Cromwell and Brian Markinson to play these roles. Streep is the only character to cross gender as the rabbi in the opening scene, and she is heavily made up to the point that she is unrecognizable. Jeffrey Wright is similarly made up to be undetectable as the same actor in both of his roles. A theatrical audience sees through the role to the actor in a transparent performance, while the movie actor builds an opaque performance in which the audience can't see under the makeup. The film denies the multiple roles as a tribute to bravura acting and thus tamps thematic resonance.

Comparisons between doubled and tripled roles deepen individual characterizations, but such splits are not merely external in this play. Dialectical splits within characters highlight the capacity for change and growth (or decay) over time. Externally, too, in this play that graphically details the outward signs and symptoms of a terrible disease, the conception of character as changeable, not fixed, is one of the things that make the action tolerable. As the action progresses, Prior, who initially seems to be the weakest character in the play, gains strength despite his diseased condition and emerges as the bravest individual by the end. Louis is a good and honest man, yet his cowardice leads him astray to an almost unforgivable betrayal of his lover. Suffering throughout, often quite humorously and always self-consciously, he rediscovers his capacity for goodness at the conclusion. Harper, whom Joe tries to save via marriage, ultimately saves herself by leaving him and escapes, not to a drug-induced hallucination but to the friendly skies on a night flight to San Francisco. She, who has evoked the most devastating images of apocalypse in the play, speaks peacefully and hopefully of salvation aboard her jumbo jet. Hannah, a provincial Mormon from Utah who hangs up on her son when he proclaims his homosexuality and who later says that pity is something she just doesn't have, moves to New York and sticks by her son's ex-lover's lover, Prior, and stiffens his spine. By the epilogue, set five years later, Kushner describes her as looking like a New Yorker (in other words, she holds a copy of the *Times* and sports an expensive and fashionable hairstyle and wardrobe). Roy Cohn, the most hated and hateful character in the play, voices the full dialectical dimensions of Kushner's gay fantasia by brilliantly arguing that homosexuality is only a label used to assign a pecking order of political clout.

The most obvious dramaturgical technique Kushner displays to reflect life's heterogeneity is one he calls "split scenes," in which he divides the stage into more than one playing area to accommodate multiple scenes at the same time. Reviewers recognized this device as a kind of film cut to move easily from action on one part of the stage to another without a scene break in between. The crucial difference, however, is that the stage technique allows for simultaneous presentation whereas a film cut relies upon sequence and the temporal juxtaposition of images. Onstage, the audience sees everything at once. Kushner doesn't specify how to split his scenes: between stage left and stage right (similar to a split screen on film or television); upstage and downstage; down left and up right; down right and up left; above and below. He leaves that challenge to the director to determine according to the function of a particular scene. At the most rudimentary level, the split scenes provide spatial separation that signifies distinct locales. The phone call between Joe in Central Park and his mother, Hannah, in Salt Lake City is an easy example. Joe stands in one area of the stage and Hannah in another, and they talk to each other on the phone. Although the audience sees both of them clearly, it is understood that they can't see each other and that they are far apart. The film, on the other hand, establishes distance by cutting from one locale to the next, and then cutting back and forth between the phone booth in New York and Hannah's home in Utah. This same technique is used in a later scene in which Prior calls the hospital and speaks to Belize at his workstation. The stage audience sees them both at the same time but understands that the characters cannot see each other; the film convention cuts back and forth between speakers to establish complete physical separation.

The various split scenes function in several more complex and interesting ways throughout the play. By having two scenes onstage at one time, the principle of doubling continues and the double plot of the play weaves together. Scenes from both plots run parallel to each other simultaneously. Early in the play, for example, Louis voices his fears to the rabbi that he might abandon his newly sick and diagnosed lover. On another part of the stage, Joe returns to his apartment from one of his many walks to discuss with his wife the possibility of moving to Washington. Placement side by side makes it impossible not to link one scene with the other. It's no surprise, then, when Joe later does leave Harper, and it is no surprise, either, that his new lover is Louis. The audience sees them together in similar situations, though not interacting, long before they actually meet. Similarly, the split scene later in act 1 presents the two couples, Harper and Joe in Brooklyn, Prior and Louis in Manhattan, facing difficult questions. In one, Harper asks her husband whether or not he's gay. In the other, Louis asks whether Prior would hate him forever if he couldn't handle the unpleasantness of Prior's disease. Thus, at the end of the first act, the theme of abandonment is clearly established in both plots, and tracks are laid for the entanglements and heartbreaks that follow. *Part Two* continues to show parallels between the plots as the action begins to resolve. In act 4, scene 1, Louis attempts to ease his guilty conscience and make peace with Prior. On another part of the stage, Joe visits Roy in the hospital and receives a blessing from the older man as his surrogate son. Each scene ends in an argument. Unconvinced by Louis's confession of feeling black and blue on the inside, Prior demands that Louis return only when he has "something to show." Immediately before that exchange, Joe enrages Roy by telling him that he left his wife for a man. Roy gets out of bed and pulls the IV tubing out of his arm, a dramatic gesture that spurts blood profusely about the room and definitely shows a lot.

The split scenes also effectively comment upon each other in a point/counterpoint relationship. Roy schmoozes Joe in the second act of *Millennium Approaches* at an expensive bar with a fatherly heart-to-heart talk about Joe's future. At this point Roy's motives, sexual or otherwise, remain unclear. Only later does he reveal that he needs Joe to take a job in the Justice Department in Washington to save him from disbarment. The scene opposite Roy and Joe in the bar features Louis and his pickup fucking in the Ramble of Central Park, a comment on the relationship between the naive, young, and idealistic Mormon and his manipulative, self-serving mentor. In *Part Two*, Belize refers to Joe as Roy Cohn's "buttboy." He tells Louis, "I don't know whether Mr. Cohn has penetrated more than his spiritual sphincter. All I'm saying is you better hope there's no GOP germ, Louis, 'cause if there is, you got it" (93). The scene in the park shows what's really happening subtextually in the genteel setting of the fancy bar.

An even better example of one scene commenting on another occurs in *Part*

One (act 3, scene 2) when Louis sits in a coffee shop with Belize and rattles on and on about politics and America as a means of hiding his own guilty conscience, while on another part of the stage Prior undergoes a physical exam in which he strips naked for Emily to inventory his sores and deteriorating physical state. In the film, the images focus on the physical examination while most of Louis's speech is heard as voice-over. That's the only way the film can make the two scenes one. The stage, however, presents both scenes at the same time. Similarly, another split scene in *Part Two* presents Hannah and Harper on one side of the stage in the Brooklyn apartment, and Joe and Louis in bed together on the other side in Louis's Lower East Side dwelling. Hannah tries to comfort her daughter-in-law, but Harper actually crosses the boundary between the two scenes and speaks to Joe directly, as if perhaps she wasn't really there but only in his thoughts. In their brief exchange (Louis is sleeping and doesn't notice her), she tells her husband that he can't save Louis, just as he couldn't save her, although that's why he said that he married her. The scene visualizes the psychic connection between them and stages what cannot be seen in an objective presentation of an emotional reality. Not surprisingly, this scene is absent in the film.

Finally, and most excitingly, the split scenes amplify the action in the play. The play reaches a fevered pitch in *Millennium Approaches* (act 2, scene 9) as both couples fight over the reasons for their breakup. It is, as Harper announces at the beginning of the scene, the moment of truth, during which Joe discloses that he has no sexual feelings for his wife and Louis states that he must find a way to save himself (and leave his relationship with Prior). At the end, Harper flees her apartment with Mr. Lies to Antarctica and Louis walks out the door. The film follows the text almost verbatim in a series of abrupt cuts from one scene to the other, the Brooklyn apartment and Prior's hospital room. The film scene works by sequential juxtaposition: first one, and then the other. The play, on the other hand, by presenting both scenes simultaneously, heightens the dramatic effect. As written, the exchanges between one location and the next are short and abrupt and move back and forth very quickly. In performance, the actors must take their cues from the actors playing in the other scene. In the film, the energy is manufactured through editing; the actors probably played each scene in its entirety, and then the film editors and director subsequently made the appropriate splices to promote the escalating emotional tenor of the newly conjoined scenes.

Doubled roles, dialectical characterizations, and split scenes are not merely techniques to dazzle an audience but are the means by which the playwright reaches his audience with a message. Certainly, this epic work roves unrestricted where the author fancies, but Alisa Solomon picks up on a different meaning of "fantasia," that which refers to a specific kind of musical composition "allowing for a number of themes to develop contrapuntally" in a "dramatic structure [which] is itself pleasurably polymorphous" (118). The staging of the play, its physical presence in time and space before an audience, reveals its layered meanings as surely as the words in the text. Thematically, the play progresses dialectically through a series of binary oppositions: freedom and responsibility, movement and stasis, love and justice. In a series of speeches in *Part One* (act 2, scene 7) that are not in the film, Louis articulates the themes of the play and its physical movement:

> Nowadays. No connections. No responsibilities. All of us . . . falling through the cracks that separates what we owe to our selves and . . . and what we owe to love.
> [. . .]
> Land of the free. Home of the brave.
> [. . .]
> [. . .] Maybe we are free. To do whatever.
> Children of the new morning, criminal minds. Selfish and greedy and loveless and blind. Reagan's children.
> You're scared. So am I. Everybody is in the land of the free. God help us all. (71–74)

Amid the chaos of freedom that reigns on Earth, the Angel descends from Heaven to preach cessation and stasis. Human beings, capable of vast change, have acted selfishly and destructively and have shaken Heaven so badly that God has left. "Be still. Toil no more" is the directive from above (*Perestroika* 48). Freedom, movement, human desire branded the bodies of victims in the play with lesions, diarrhea, blood, cramps, fever, delusions, shortness of breath, loss of mobility, severe pain, fatigue, and swollen glands. Such physical ailments are not just talked about in graphic detail but shown on the stage in the treatments and depictions of both Roy and Prior. But, as Roy says, "Pain's . . . nothing, pain's life" (24). Amazingly, then, Prior ultimately refuses the heavenly request to be still. "We can't just stop," he tells the Angels in Heaven. "We're not rocks—progress, migration, motion is . . . modernity. It's *animate,* it's what living things do. We desire. Even if all we desire is stillness, it's still desire *for*" (130). He concludes here, as he will reaffirm at the end: "I want more life" (133). This pursuit of life, the search to fulfill desire is not pretty; it's messy, but not dirty, as Louis quips to Joe about his apartment. Roy puts this quest in more graphic, more physical, even physiological terms: "This is . . . this is gastric juices churning, this is enzymes and acids, this is intestinal is what this is, bowel movement and blood-red meat—this stinks, this is *politics,* Joe, the game of being alive. And you think you're. . . . What? Above that? Above alive is what? Dead! In the clouds! You're on earth, goddammit! Plant a foot, stay a while" (*Millennium* 68).

Such physicalization of human desire plays out beautifully in the theater, not because the theater is a live event but because the human figure, exposed in its entirety, is vulnerable, and the stage, teeming with physical activity, is a play-ground of desire. Nowhere is this more evident than in the seduction scene be-tween Louis and Joe in *Part Two,* which defines an erotic connection in terms that are only possible in a theatrical environment. After an embrace, Louis de-scribes the erotics of smell: "Smelling. Is desiring. We have five senses, but only two that go beyond the boundaries . . . of ourselves. When you look at someone, it's just bouncing light, or when you hear them, it's just sound waves, vibrating air, or touch is just nerve endings tingling. Know what a smell is? [. . .] It's made of the molecules of what you're smelling. Some part of you, where you meet the air, is airborne" (*Perestroika* 30). Like the smell of fresh toast in *True West,* the success of this theatrical moment requires all the participants—actors and audi-ence alike—to share the same space at the same time. It is an interactive moment that demands seeing everything at once simultaneously.

Ultimately, as Belize says over the dead body of Roy Cohn, forgiveness is where love and justice meet, the point at which the personal greets the political. That Louis can say the Kaddish, the prayer for the dead, at Cohn's bedside is a gesture that seeks to resolve all opposites. The final scenes feature consecu-tive reconciliations and partings of the way between characters who have been at odds throughout the entire drama: Harper and Joe, Hannah and Joe, Prior and Louis. It's not a happy ending; they are scarred and they are changed, and none is involved with the same relationship at the end as he or she was at the be-ginning. But the end is hopeful and gives reason to look ahead with optimism. Harper's last lines read, "Nothing's lost forever. In this world, there's a kind of painful progress. Longing for what we've left behind, and dreaming ahead. At least I think that's so" (*Perestroika* 142).

Frank Rich's review of *Millennium Approaches* in 1993 praised the ideas in it but emphasized that the playwright's vision of theater and imaginative use of the stage offered the possible salvation not only of the theater as a cultural insti-tution but of humanity itself: "Mr. Kushner's convictions about power and jus-tice are matched by his conviction that the stage, and perhaps the stage alone, is a space large enough to accommodate everything from precise realism to surrealis-tic hallucination, from black comedy to religious revelation. In *Angels in America,* a true American work in its insistence on embracing all possibilities in art and life, he makes the spectacular case that they can all be brought into fusion in one play" ("Embracing All Possibilities"). Kushner does this not by building a ho-mogenous structure but by creating a form that freely lets opposites play. Despite the presence of Roy Cohn, whom other characters cite as one of the great "evil-doers" of the twentieth century, and despite AIDS, the plague of our time, the only real villains in the play are habits of being and modes of thought that have become too rigid and inflexible.

Kushner's rebuttal to these hardened visions of the world presents a stage filled with characters who undergo changes and develop the willingness to change, who discover parts of themselves that they didn't know existed at the start of the play—all in a landscape in which scenes play against scenes to create a tapestry of all that is humanly possible. Triumphed as an AIDS play, as a gay play, as a political play, Kushner's *Angels in America,* through its methods of presentation, invites an audience, gay or straight, to see itself as part of a diverse and heterogeneous crowd driven by desire: for life, for each other, for whatever. *Angels in America,* with its epic story, loose construction, bold theatrical techniques, outrageous characters (good and bad), angry rhetoric, stunning images, and ultimately hopeful message, celebrates life's (and theater's) abundance.

Conclusion
Revivals Versus Remakes

Belief in the future growth of an artistic, penetrating and emotionally arresting cinema is not antagonistic to an equally firm belief in the future development of the theatre.

—Allardyce Nicoll, *Film and Theatre*

Subsequent performances "revive" old plays, but directors "remake" films, a distinction that underscores the human element of the former mode and the technological/mechanical basis of the latter. I began this book by questioning the valorization of theater as a "live" event over film and television, but notions of revival begin to reintroduce sneakily the significance of "liveness" by implying that the drama needs only to add the actors in order to reconstitute as a dynamic form, as if the text lies in wait and wants to be resuscitated by performance. If only it were that simple.

The revival of a play may bring an old text back to life onstage, but many dead parts remain encrusted upon a proposed new production such as ancient and antiquated dramatic conventions; theater architecture; cultural standards, values, and expectations; technologies; and literature of the time as well as the author's subsequent and total literary output. Theater directors, charged with the responsibility for staging a successful event, interpret, adapt, and cut loose the historical ties upon the text and start a fresh production practically from scratch in order to meet the expectations and demands of a contemporary audience.

Future theatrical productions of dramatic texts will succeed not insofar as they do what the playwright may have originally intended, but to the extent that they champion spectacle and explore the possibilities for simultaneous action within a homogenous space. Screenwriters imagine their films taking place in various locations. All the world is a potential stage for their work. For playwrights, too, although one stage is the entire world of their work, they also write with a specific space in mind. It may be big, it may be small; it might be a traditional proscenium, or an arena, or a thrust; it might be a laboratory, a living room, a hallway; it might be outside, on the street, in the park, on a truck, in the field. Still, playwrights imagine a specific space for their work, just as screenwriters do, and they write for something to happen within that space. A performance in the mind sparks a production that may never be realized on a stage, yet the reality of that unseen space informs and empowers the entire drama.

Mise-en-scène, the discovery and development of spectacle, makes a performance more meaningful and exciting than a private read. The director hosts an event and invites the playwright, designers, actors, technicians, and, finally, the audience to come together at a certain time and a certain space to partake in a performance. Like a good party host, the director mingles among the participants and sparks interactions that would not happen without the presence of someone to bring disparate people and groups together. The theatrical space might not be what the playwright initially envisioned. Circumstances in the world that sparked the creative effort may no longer be accessible. The world of the play may no longer seem as topical to the playwright as it did at the time of composition. Nevertheless, the director determines a context for the play to happen now and projects an imagined work into dimensional space. The director sets the play in color, with movement, bodies in space, lighting, words emanating toward a listening audience. The theater beckons: everything that is to happen will happen on the stage. And then? After? Nothing. The ghost light presides over the empty space.

Long after a production has been wheeled out to the dumpster, after the party wanes, only the memories and the favors (posters, photos, programs) of it remain and it begins to take on a life of its own in the recollections and accounts of the participants and onlookers. Always in the process of dying, theater, that Fabulous Invalid, cannot be revived. It always remains, though, for playwrights, directors, designers, actors, technicians, and a willing audience to remake it.

Notes

Chapter 1: Revaluations of Virtues

1. Critics generally credit D. W. Griffith as the director who first developed the cinema as a unique form. Gilberto Perez summarizes in *The Material Ghost* (1998): "As film historians have often said, [Griffith] made the shot rather than the scene the basic unit of film construction. His basic innovation was the convention of the shot: if the theater asks its audience to take the stage as a whole world, the movies after Griffith have asked their audience to agree, for as long as each shot lasts on the screen, to look at just the piece of the world framed within that shot" (24–25). See also Robert Richardson, *Literature and Film* (1985): "What Griffith had done was to separate film from theatre, for in the beginning, film, like theatre, presented a flowing tableau in a fixed space to a spectator (the camera and, of course, the viewer) who was also set in a fixed place" (37).

2. Chekhov wrote the part of Tuzenbach in *Three Sisters* for Meyerhold, who had left the Moscow Art Theatre for good and never performed the role. He did, however, later send a picture of himself to the playwright with the inscription, "From the pale-faced Meyerhold to his God" (Brietzke 3).

3. In addition to his recent film accomplishments, Sam Mendes (b. 1965) directed Judi Dench on stage in *The Cherry Orchard,* Ralph Fiennes in *Troilus and Cressida,* and Nicole Kidman in *The Blue Room*; and he directed *Cabaret,* which won four Tony Awards, including Best Revival of a Musical.

4. *Four Flicks,* the Rolling Stones' DVD following their World Licks Tour, includes three concerts and more than fifty songs, documentaries, bonus tracks, club songs, and outtakes.

5. In *The Paradox of the Actor* (1773, pub. 1830), Diderot, using David Garrick as a model, concludes that the great actor presents passions by studying the means to produce them objectively. Hence, the paradox: the actor who plays Othello remains quite calm and in control of his body and emotions, even as he strangles Desdemona, laments his actions, and commits suicide. This argument about emotion plays out today in discussions of actor training, whether it be from the outside-in, which emphasizes technical per-

fection and visible aspects of character influencing "interior" choices, or the inside-out, which stresses having an emotional and psychological root for actions and seeing how they manifest themselves organically, physically.

6. Ironically, Plato, who casts all artists from his ideal republic, displays an artist's sensibility in what scholars agree is some of the finest Greek ever written. He voices a stout antitheatrical prejudice, yet the dialogic form in which he excels makes for masterful drama. Unlike Plato, whose vehemence toward his subject belies his attraction to the material, Aristotle takes a dispassionate view of drama and draws upon empirical evidence to back his claims.

7. It's impossible not to relate this narrative theory to male sexual desire and, naturally, then look for an alternative model. Peter Brooks, the Yale professor—not Peter Brook, the English director and author—applied the human desire to get to the end of the story to what he termed "narrative psychology" in *Reading for the Plot: Design and Intention in Narrative* (1984). In this provocative book, he equates narrative desire, the drive to finish the story, with Freud's death wish. Just as only the end of a story, a novel, a play fully reveals its meanings, death confers meaning upon a life. A paradox of reading, of life, and of sex is that the desire for pleasure (and meaning) hastens the end of experience.

8. For a thorough and accessible analysis of this production, see Johan Callens, "'Black Is White, I Yells It out Louder 'n Deir Loudest': Unraveling the Wooster Group's *The Emperor Jones*," *Eugene O'Neill Review* 26 (2004): 43–69.

9. Peter Brook's production of *Marat/Sade* in 1964 is perhaps the most famous example of Artaud's "Theater of Cruelty" in practice. Like Shelley's play, Peter Weiss's text lends itself readily to practice designed to affect an audience physically and psychically.

10. The *Poetics* originally had two books, though one, presumably on comedy, was lost. See Gerald Else's introduction to *Poetics*, 10. Perhaps like Aristophanic lovers, the two books have always been looking for each other as their perfect mates throughout history.

Chapter 2: Dramatic Projections

1. I discovered this firsthand when I was still in college and the theater department moved from a found space, a converted barn, to a two-thousand-seat performing arts center. The former theater, with its twenty-foot proscenium opening, required very little technical skill from an actor in order to be seen and heard. After the move up the hill, however, the lavish new facility required a different kind of actor, one with enough training to handle the chasm of an enormous orchestra pit which put the audience more than fifteen feet away from the front of the stage and a proscenium opening of more than twenty yards. Not only did the new space require a different kind of actor, it necessitated a different kind of play, one that could "breathe to the perimeters of the theater."

2. Ned Beatty criticized his fellow actors and movie stars Jason Patric and Ashley Judd for not having the necessary theatrical chops to play Brick and Maggie, respectively, in the 2003–2004 production of *Cat on a Hot Tin Roof* on Broadway at the Music Box

Theatre. Later, Judd hurt herself during a performance and withdrew from the production during the last weeks of the run.

3. I recall years ago chatting in the greenroom with an actor who loved to act in plays but who wished to direct films. For him, it was simply a matter of control. He felt, and he would find vast agreement I think, that in the theater the stage director does not have as much control as the actors. Because they perform the play in front of an audience, the actors have the ultimate power to alter a performance as they see fit. Certainly, there are many myths about the power of the stage director, but more times than not, it's a battle of trust and diplomacy with actors. The film director, on the other hand, is often perceived as an all-powerful tyrant who makes the final decisions concerning a performance. Film actors agree that they can't tell how a film will turn out as it's being shot. Editing largely determines whether a film will be good or bad. This accounts, no doubt, for many actors turning to directing as their careers advance. The credits often begin with "A film by . . ." and end with, lest you forgot the name, "Directed by . . ." The director of a film is often in an analogous position to the author of a play.

4. Any shot of the World Trade Center reminds the audience of the morning of 11 September 2001. The twin towers will always date any film to the last three decades of the twentieth century. More emphatically, any shot of the towers will stir feelings in the audience that are undoubtedly unintended by the filmmaker.

5. In classical plays the actors stand up. In modern, realistic plays characters sit down, and the scenery (for example, chairs) thus encroaches upon the acting scene. The difference in performance requirements for acting while standing as opposed to sitting is enormous.

6. See Bert O. States, *Great Reckonings in Little Rooms: On the Phenomenology of Theater* (Berkeley: University of California Press, 1985), 32–36.

7. See epigraph by Ron Vawter (from David Savran's *Breaking the Rules: The Wooster Group*) to Paula Vogel's book *The Baltimore Waltz and Other Plays* (New York: Theatre Communications Group, 1996): "I always saw myself as a surrogate who, in the absence of anyone else, would stand in for him. And even now, when I'm in front of an audience and I feel good, I hearken back to that feeling, that I'm standing in for them" (Vogel 3).

Chapter 3: A Vicious Cycle at Sea

1. The ephemeral nature of theater leaves no physical trace and allows memories to create and perpetuate experience. O'Neill expresses concern that the presence of a film will overshadow the memory of the great production in his mind.

2. See O'Neill's letter to Barrett Clark in *Selected Letters* (87). The emphasis on suspenseful plotting makes *In the Zone* a very effective melodrama. The lack of plot and the evocation of mood and atmosphere in *The Moon of the Caribbees* point drama in a new direction.

3. See note 2 for this chapter. The lack of action in *Moon* gives it an expository feel that made it a logical choice to go first in Ford's movie.

4. See Richard Hayes, "'The Scope of the Movies': Three Films and Their Influence on Eugene O'Neill," *Eugene O'Neill Review* 25 (2001): 37–53. Hayes pays particular attention to *Bound East for Cardiff* and says that a theatrical audience can't possibly see what O'Neill describes in his stage directions concerning Yank's dying condition in his bunk. He argues that O'Neill "clearly thought about the character in terms that were cinematic" (40).

5. While the sea represents a kind of malevolent fate in *"Anna Christie,"* the sea as freedom and escape is voiced in all periods of O'Neill's playwriting, from Paddy in *The Hairy Ape* (1921), to *Mourning Becomes Electra* (1931), to Edmund in *Long Day's Journey into Night* (1941).

6. See Arthur Gelb and Barbara Gelb, *O'Neill* (New York: Harper and Row, 1962); Louis Sheaffer, *O'Neill: Son and Playwright* (Boston: Little, Brown, 1968) and *O'Neill: Son and Artist* (Boston: Little, Brown, 1973); and Stephen A. Black, *Eugene O'Neill: Beyond Mourning and Tragedy* (New Haven: Yale University Press, 1999).

7. O'Neill left the Provincetown Players for good after the success of *The Hairy Ape* in March 1922. In search of better, more professional productions, as well as cutting-edge techniques, he formed The Experimental Theatre, Inc. (also known as the Triumvirate) with Kenneth Macgowan, Robert Edmond Jones, and himself.

8. Until the recent conflicts in the Middle East, the Navy used to recruit on television by advertising, "See the world. . ."

9. George Cram (Jig) Cook, Susan Glaspell's husband and the leader of the Provincetown Players, is credited as director for the original production.

Chapter 4: There's Something about Mary

1. With so much talk, talk, talk, the play *The Children's Hour* contains all the typical, often deemed essential, elements: exposition (there's something about Mary), inciting moment (Mary's punishment), conflict (young teachers versus Mrs. Tilford), rising action (Mrs. Tilford electing to call her friends at the end of act 2), falling action (start of third act), climax (Martha's suicide), denouement (Mrs. Tilford's final visit to Karen).

2. See Cavell 50–53, in which he claims that *These Three* is "psychologically deeper and more adult" than Wyler's later remake (51).

3. Although not the tragic heroine of the play, Mrs. Tilford is the character that makes the fateful decision to remove Mary from the school and, worse, to call all her friends to do the same. Mrs. Tilford, too, is the one who suffers at the end of the play. Who would want to spend life on Earth with Mary? Mrs. Tilford does represent the normative values of society, and therefore her fall from grace can prove instructive for an audience.

4. Mary's overt lies and general awfulness divert attention away from the main problem: the impending marriage of Joe and Karen. At the end of the play, after Joe and Karen decide to part, Martha says, seemingly convincingly, that she wanted them to marry. Mary's shenanigans interrupt the solution of that problem and take the power of choice away from Karen, who never has to pick between Martha and Joe.

Chapter 5: Bedroom Ballet in the Delta

1. While I do consider *Cat* a more hopeful play than either *Streetcar* or *Menagerie,* the ambiguity and ambivalence in the former play make it also more interesting.

2. Richard Brooks (1912–92) was nominated for an Academy Award as best director for *Cat on a Hot Tin Roof* in 1958. Some of his other notable credits include *Elmer Gantry* (1960), *The Professionals* (1966), *In Cold Blood* (1967), and *Looking for Mr. Goodbar* (1977).

3. Waiting on the sidelines but never out of view, the character whom all others constantly watch and beg for attention is Brick. With a physical beauty that is almost godlike, Brick represents a kind of Achilles figure (weeping for Patroclos), whose delayed entry into the game of life (if it ever happens) will permanently alter the playing field.

4. See John S. Bak, " 'sneakin' and spyin' ': From Broadway to the Beltway: Cold War Masculinity, Brick, and Homosexual Existentialism," *Theatre Journal* 56.2 (May 2004): 225–49. Bak's article examines Brick's alleged homosexuality from a number of angles—social, cultural, historical, political, philosophical. His conclusion supports my contention: "Questions surrounding Brick's homosexuality are not, and perhaps should never be, conclusively affirmed or denied, for such certitude would surely depoliticize the play's intent of turning that suspicion back upon the audience's desire to know, implicating its own sexual epistemology as being at the core of the play's final tragic ambiguity" (249).

Chapter 6: Jungled Dreams

1. *Death of a Salesman* (Columbia Pictures, 1951), directed by László Benedek, starring Fredric March, was not successful. For a description and analysis of the big-screen version of the play, see Brenda Murphy, *Miller: Death of a Salesman* (New York: Cambridge University Press, 1995), 127–39. Murphy's book, part of the "Plays in Production" series, provides an excellent gloss to Broadway, international, and media productions of Miller's most famous play.

2. The portrayal of business in 1949 pales in comparison to the cutthroat economy of today's business circles in such plays as Mamet's *Glengarry Glen Ross.* I recall the revival on Broadway in 1999, when Arthur Miller commented that his play was as relevant today as it was when it opened. He did add, however, that he had perceived one distinct change. Audiences no longer could understand Willy's surprise that his loyalty to Howard's company over many years didn't count for anything. Contemporary audiences did not understand how Willy could consider loyalty an issue whatsoever regarding employment considerations.

3. My wife, Carol, brought this to my attention after we attended the 1999 production on Broadway with Brian Dennehy. I've never read anything that suggests Willy is actually right in his estimation that Biff throws his life away out of spite. In any event, the play's reliance upon the discovery of the affair as the moment of crisis is a bit superficial and disingenuous. Biff clearly can't deal with the realization of his father's profound

flaws; his lack of development after that is a sign that he refuses to surpass his formerly beloved (and still beloved) father. He's not a "bum," but he is still a boy.

Chapter 7: Getting the Guests

1. See *The Taming of the Shrew* (4.5.2–7):

PETRUCHIO: Good Lord, how bright and goodly shines the moon!
KATE: The Moon! the sun—it is not moonlight now.
PETRUCHIO: I say it is the moon that shines so bright.
KATE: I know it is the sun that shines so bright.
PETRUCHIO: Now by my mother's son, and that's myself,
It shall be moon, or star, or what I list, . . .

2. As a further sign of blandness, Albee at one time considered calling Nick simply "Dear." The visiting couple was, then, "Honey" and "Dear."

3. Playwright Albee evidently does not ascribe the same importance to the "bit" as I do. He cut it from the recent Broadway production (2005) directed by Anthony Page and starring Kathleen Turner and Bill Irwin and did not include it in the subsequent published edition of the play. I am grateful to my students in Twentieth-Century American Drama at Columbia, particularly Samuel Reisman, for bringing the textual changes in the new edition to my attention.

4. Once again, the playwright thinks he knows more than the critic! Albee cut Honey's return to the stage and the dialogue that fosters George's revenge plot in the 2005 production. In this revised version, the audience no longer gets to see George in the process of discovery as he lights upon a fresh idea. Instead, director Anthony Page punctuated the end of the second act with George throwing his book against the chimes.

Chapter 8: Lamebrains across Texas

1. Like Shakespeare, Shepard's prose offers rich imagery. To make a film of *True West,* a director would have to substitute visual images of neighborhoods and freeways for Shepard's evocative language. A film treatment of Shepard's play, for example, might follow Lee on his little tour of the neighborhood and might later trace Austin's night-of-crime spree that resulted in the accumulation of many toasters. In this way, a film could create an original experience.

Chapter 9: Cadillacs Are for Closers

1. The Empire State Building in the background of the New York City skyline provides a recognizable landmark for the audience to gauge the real estate salesmen's distance from and desperation for success.

2. Plays with music, of course, offer many of the dramatic qualities of a good score

behind a film. *The Grapes of Wrath* comes immediately to mind, along with plays that explicitly or implicitly deal with rock music such as Shepard's *The Tooth of Crime* or Václav Havel's *Temptation*. On the whole, though, integrated music is rare in the theater. How effective might a production of *Three Sisters* be if Andrei were actually to play the violin onstage? Or, in the wake of John Cage, what if all sound were treated as music, such as the foghorn in *Long Day's Journey into Night* and Mary's footfalls upstairs in the final act of that play? While it would not be appropriate to the theatrical medium to play a score under the dialogue as in film—in which often the music creates the emotional tone of the scene instead of the actors—sound and music can nonetheless highlight, emphasize, amplify, or contradict the visible action and spoken dialogue to create potent meanings and images.

3. Chebutykin's speech in act 3 of *Three Sisters* is a shining example of this principle. He delivers a monologue and imparts important information about the past and the woman he operated on in the hospital that could not come out in dialogic form. His drunkenness provides an excuse and an outlet for him to talk within the conventional boundaries of realism.

4. One of the novel things about Mamet's play is that there is no traditional exposition at all. The first three scenes play as if they are occurring simultaneously. The action, such as it is, doesn't ignite until Roma's curtain line for act 1.

5. Mamet studied acting in New York at Sanford Meisner's Neighborhood Playhouse. See interview with Mamet in Henry I. Schvey, "Celebrating the Capacity for Self-Knowledge," *David Mamet in Conversation,* ed. Leslie Kane (Ann Arbor: University of Michigan Press, 2001), 60–72. Asked about his training, Mamet replied, "I studied at the bookstore. But the Neighborhood Playhouse was founded on the teachings of Stanislavski, who was very influenced by Aristotle: most of the Stanislavski system is a practical aesthetic for the actor based on the Aristotelian idea of unity" (60).

6. In our modern age today, we're conditioned not to think of ourselves as what we do. We're inclined to keep our identity separate from our employment status. A person is apt to say, "I do this for a living, but that's not who I am." The United Way commercials in 2003 for the National Football League featured a series of players who each proclaimed, "I am a player in the NFL, but that's not who I am." The campaign, of course, promoted the idea that players are also active husbands, fathers, and participants in the communities in which they live.

7. The second act of the play "opens up" the action analogous to the way that films are alleged to "open up" the action of plays. After relegating the action in the Chinese restaurant to a series of three dialogues, each confined to one part of the stage, the real estate office encompasses the entire playing area of act 2 and all the characters are present. The 2005 Broadway production at the Bernard Jacobs Theatre, directed by Joe Mantello with performances by Alan Alda and Liev Schreiber, used the front curtain to make the change explicit. The second act, spread over the entire stage, seemed almost like a different play.

8. Visually, the office where the interrogation takes place is upstage. The door to the office is filmed upstage in most shots as well. As I maintained earlier, plot is an excuse for

something to happen. Here, that something plays out downstage in the wide-open office area, while the machinations of the plot, the criminal investigation, whirl offstage and mostly out of sight.

Chapter 10: Making Oneself Big

1. See August Wilson, "I Want a Black Director," *New York Times* (26 Sept. 1990), sec. I, 15 (OP-ED). I'm not convinced that one has to be black in order to direct the plays or, even more radically, to act in them. Currently, when relatively few good roles are available to black actors, it would be poor taste in the least for white actors to play such roles. The same is true for directors. But when the hard-fought battle for equal opportunity and access to all parts is won, then it will be interesting to see the racial breakdown in productions of Wilson's plays. Interestingly, while Wilson has been criticized for his insistence upon blacks performing and directing his plays, no similar charge has been levied against any number of white playwrights and the white folks who usually do their plays.

Chapter 11: Cancer and the Classroom

1. Lehman added "Let's go to the roadhouse!" The roadhouse scene, recall, was the only one not in the play (although the dialogue still comes from the play). Almost all the words in the film are Albee's.

2. The distinction between presenting/representing is a Brechtian one. In the former mode, the actor narrates a performance in the third person: "Then, she did this . . ." The audience is aware of the actor and the character at the same time. In the example from the play, the mature actress plays the part of herself as a little girl as well, which promotes a storytelling aspect. In a representational mode, identified with the style of realism, the actress "becomes" the character, such that a little girl is required to play the part of a "little girl."

Chapter 12: Stairway to Heaven

1. Kushner's note, reminiscent of director and adapter Frank Galati's note in *The Grapes of Wrath,* indicates some anxiety that technology and spectacle will overshadow the acting and, inferentially, the dramatic text. While both these plays may well be "actor-driven," the right kind of spectacle helps them to achieve "epic" status.

2. The influence of Brecht upon Kushner cannot be overstated. Kushner studied directing at New York University with Carl Weber, a former protégé of Brecht's and a member of the Berliner Ensemble, to whom Kushner dedicated his first play, *A Bright Room Called Day.*

3. My friend and colleague from the Eugene O'Neill Society, Daniel Larner of Western Washington University, alerted me to the significance of the Spielberg reference via his comments on the American Theatre and Drama Society (ATDS) Listserv in 2003.

Works Cited

Abramovich, Alex. "Hurricane Kushner Hits the Heartland." *New York Times* 30 Nov. 2003, sec. 2: 1+.

Albee, Edward. *A Delicate Balance.* 1966. New York: Plume–Dutton Signet, 1997.

———. *Who's Afraid of Virginia Woolf?* 1962. New York: Signet–New American Library, 1983.

Angels in America. By Tony Kushner. Dir. Mike Nichols. Perf. Al Pacino, Meryl Streep. HBO Films. Premiere 7 Dec. 2003.

"*Anna Christie.*" Dir. John Griffith Wray. Perf. Blanche Sweet. Ince Studios, 1923.

———. Dir. Clarence Brown. Perf. Greta Garbo. MGM, 1930.

Appia, Adolphe. *Actor—Space—Light.* Trans. Burton Melnick. Rev. ed. New York: River Run Press, 1982.

Aristotle. *Poetics.* Trans. Gerald F. Else. 1967. Ann Arbor: Ann Arbor Paperbacks–University of Michigan Press, 1986.

Arnheim, Rudolf. *Art and Visual Perception: A Psychology of the Creative Eye.* 1954. Rev. ed. Berkeley: University of California Press, 1974.

———. *Film as Art.* 1957. Berkeley: University of California Press, 1984.

———. *Visual Thinking.* 1969. Berkeley: University of California Press, 1997.

Aronson, Arnold. "Design for *Angels in America:* Envisioning the Millennium." Geis and Kruger 213–26.

Artaud, Antonin. *The Theater and Its Double.* Trans. Mary Caroline Richards. 1958. New York: Grove Press, 1979.

Auslander, Philip. *Liveness: Performance in a Mediatized Culture.* New York: Routledge, 1999.

Barnes, Clive. "Angelically Gay about Our Decay." Rev. of *Angels in America.* By Tony Kushner. Dir. George C. Wolfe. Perf. Ron Liebman, Joe Mantello, Stephen Spinella, Kathleen Chalfant, Ellen McLaughlin. Walter Kerr Theatre, New York, 1993. *New York Post* 5 May 1993. *New York Theatre Critics' Reviews* 54 (1993): 210.

———. Rev. of *True West.* Perf. Peter Boyle, Tommy Lee Jones. The Public Theatre, New York. *New York Post* 24 Dec. 1980. *New York Theatre Critics' Reviews* 42 (1981): 369–70.

———. "Theater Must Do What Theater Does Best: Wow Us with Wonderment." *New York Post* 8 July 2001, 32.

Barr, Tony. *Acting for the Camera.* 1982. New York: Perennial Library–Harper and Row, 1986.

Barranger, Milly S. *Theatre: A Way of Seeing.* 5th ed. New York: Wadsworth, 2002.

Bauder, David. "HBO's *Angels in America* Seen by 4.2M." *Miami Herald.Com* 9 Dec. 2003. 9 Dec. 2003 <http://www.miami.com/mld/miamiherald/entertainment/7452323.htm>.

Bazin, André. *What Is Cinema?* Trans. Hugh Gray. Vol. 1. Berkeley: University of California Press, 1967.

Benjamin, Walter. "The Work of Art in the Age of Mechanical Reproduction." *Illuminations: Essays and Reflections.* Ed. Hannah Arendt. Trans. Harry Zohn. New York: Harcourt, Brace and World, 1968. 219–53.

Bentley, Eric. "Lillian Hellman's Indiscretion." *The Dramatic Event: An American Chronicle.* Boston: Beacon Press, 1954. 74–77.

———. "Tennessee Williams' New Play." *New Republic* 11 Apr. 1955: 28–29.

Bigsby, C. W. E. *David Mamet.* London: Methuen, 1985.

Black, David. *The Magic of Theater: Behind the Scenes with Today's Leading Actors.* New York: Macmillan, 1993.

Bone, David W. "Sea across the Footlights." *New York Times* 15 Jan. 1922, sec. 3: 3.

Bottoms, Stephen J. *Albee: Who's Afraid of Virginia Woolf?* New York: Cambridge University Press, 2000.

———. *The Theatre of Sam Shepard: States of Crisis.* New York: Cambridge University Press, 1998.

Brantley, Ben. "Finding out What It's Like to Really Be Your Brother." Rev. of *True West.* Perf. Philip Seymour Hoffman, John C. Reilly. Circle in the Square Theatre, New York. *New York Times* 10 Mar. 2000, sec. E: 1+.

Braudy, Leo. "Acting: Stage vs. Screen." Mast, Cohen, and Braudy 387–94.

Brecht, Bertolt. *Brecht on Theatre: The Development of an Aesthetic.* Ed. and trans. John Willett. New York: Hill and Wang, 1964.

———. *Galileo.* English version by Charles Laughton. Ed. Eric Bentley. New York: Black Cat–Grove Press, 1966.

Brewster, Ben, and Lea Jacobs. *Theatre to Cinema: Stage Pictorialism and the Early Feature Film.* New York: Oxford University Press, 1997.

Brietzke, Alexander K. "Nothing Is but What Is Not: Chekhovian Drama and the Crisis of Representation." Diss., Stanford University, 1992.

Brook, Peter. *The Empty Space.* 1968. New York: Atheneum, 1982.

———. *The Open Door: Thoughts on Acting and Theatre.* New York: Pantheon–Random House, 1993.

Caine, Michael. *Acting in Film: An Actor's Take on Movie Making.* New York: Applause, 1997.

Cargill, Oscar, N. Bryllion Fagin, William J. Fisher, eds. *O'Neill and His Plays: Four Decades of Criticism.* New York: New York University Press, 1961.

Cat on a Hot Tin Roof. Dir. Richard Brooks. Perf. Elizabeth Taylor, Paul Newman, Burl Ives. 1958. DVD. Warner Home Video, 1999.

———. By Tennessee Williams. Dir. Anthony Page. Perf. Ned Beatty, Ashley Judd, Jason Patric. Music Box Theatre, New York. 6 Mar. 2004.

Cavell, Stanley. *The World Viewed: Reflections on the Ontology of Film.* New York: Viking Press, 1971.

Chaikin, Joseph. *The Presence of the Actor.* 1972. New York: Theatre Communications Group, 1991.

Chekhov, Anton. *Major Plays.* Trans. Ann Dunnigan. 1964. New York: Signet Classic–Penguin, 1982.

The Children's Hour. Dir. William Wyler. Perf. Audrey Hepburn, Shirley MacLaine, and James Garner. 1961. DVD. MGM, 2002.

Chubb, Kenneth, and the editors of *Theatre Quarterly.* "Metaphors, Mad Dogs and Old Time Cowboys: Interview with Sam Shepard." Marranca 187–209.

Clum, John M. *Acting Gay: Male Homosexuality in Modern Drama.* New York: Columbia University Press, 1992.

Clurman, Harold. *The Fervent Years: The Group Theatre and the Thirties.* Intro. Stella Adler. 1945. New York: Da Capo, 1983.

Coe, Robert. "Saga of Sam Shepard." *New York Times Magazine* 23 Nov. 1980: 56+.

Dance of Death. By August Strindberg. New version by Richard Greenberg. Dir. Sean Mathias. Perf. Ian McKellen, Helen Mirren, David Strathairn. Broadhurst Theatre, New York. Dec. 2001.

Davidson, Gordon. "A Conversation with Tony Kushner and Robert Altman." *Tony Kushner in Conversation.* Ed. Robert Vorlicky. Ann Arbor: University of Michigan Press, 1998. 128–47.

Death of a Salesman. By Arthur Miller. Dir. Elia Kazan. Des. Jo Mielziner. Perf. Lee J. Cobb, Mildred Dunnock. Morosco Theatre, New York. 1949.

———. Dir. Michael Rudman. Perf. Dustin Hoffman, Kate Reid, Stephen Lang, John Malkovich. Broadhurst Theatre, New York. 1984.

———. Dir. Robert Falls. Perf. Brian Dennehy, Elizabeth Franz. Eugene O'Neill Theater, New York. 1999.

———. By Arthur Miller. Dir. Alex Segal. Perf. Lee J. Cobb, Mildred Dunnock, James Farentino, George Segal. 1966. DVD. Kultur, 2002.

———. By Arthur Miller. Dir. Volker Schlöndorff. Perf. Dustin Hoffman, Kate Reid, Stephen Lang, John Malkovich. 1985. DVD. Image, 2003.

De La Fuente, Patricia. "Edward Albee: An Interview." 1980. *Conversations with Edward Albee.* Ed. Philip C. Kolin. Jackson: University Press of Mississippi, 1988. 143–54.

Dinner with Friends. Adapted from play by Donald Margulies. Dir. Norman Jewison. Perf. Dennis Quaid, Andie MacDowell, Toni Colette, Greg Kinnear. HBO Films, 2001.

Dolan, Jill. "'Lesbian' Subjectivity in Realism: Dragging at the Margins of Structure and Ideology." *Performing Feminisms: Feminist Critical Theory and Theatre.* Ed. Sue-Ellen Case. Baltimore: Johns Hopkins University Press, 1990. 40–53.

Eco, Umberto. *The Name of the Rose*. Trans. William Weaver. 1980. New York: Harcourt Brace Jovanovich, 1983.

———. *The Open Work*. Trans. Anna Cancogni. Cambridge, MA: Harvard University Press, 1989.

Edson, Margaret. Interview with Jim Lehrer. *NewsHour*. PBS. 14 Apr. 1999.

———. *Wit*. New York: Dramatists Play Service, 1999.

Eisen, Kurt. "O'Neill on Screen." *The Cambridge Companion to Eugene O'Neill*. Ed. Michael Manheim. New York: Cambridge University Press, 1998. 116–34.

Elam, Harry J., Jr. "The Dialectics of August Wilson's *The Piano Lesson*." *Theatre Journal* 52.3 (Oct. 2000): 361–79.

Else, Gerald F. Introduction. *Poetics*. By Aristotle. 1967. Ann Arbor: Ann Arbor Paperbacks–University of Michigan Press, 1986. 1–14.

The Emperor Jones. By Eugene O'Neill. The Wooster Group. Dir. Elizabeth LeCompte. Perf. Kate Valk, Willem Dafoe. The Performing Garage, New York. 1998.

Esslin, Martin. *An Anatomy of Drama*. New York: Hill and Wang, 1976.

Falk, Doris. *Lillian Hellman*. New York: Frederick Ungar, 1978.

Fornes, Maria Irene. *The Conduct of Life*. *Plays*. New York: PAJ Publications, 1986.

Galati, Frank. *John Steinbeck's* The Grapes of Wrath. New York: Dramatists Play Service, 1991.

Gates, Anita. "Inhabiting One Brother, Honoring Another." *New York Times* 11 Aug. 2002, sec. 13 (Television): 4–5.

Geis, Deborah R., and Steven F. Kruger, eds. *Approaching the Millennium: Essays on Angels in America*. Ann Arbor: University of Michigan Press, 1997.

Glaspell, Susan. *The Road to the Temple*. London: Ernest Benn, 1926.

———. *Trifles*. *Plays by Susan Glaspell*. Ed. C. W. E. Bigsby. 1920, 1987. New York: Cambridge University Press, 2002.

Glengarry Glen Ross. Screenplay by David Mamet. Dir. James Foley. Perf. Jack Lemmon, Al Pacino, Ed Harris, Alan Arkin, Kevin Spacey, Jonathan Pryce, Alec Baldwin. 1992. DVD. Artisan, 2002.

———. By David Mamet. Dir. Joe Mantello. Perf. Liev Schreiber, Alan Alda. Bernard B. Jacobs Theatre, New York. 2005.

Godfather, The. Screenplay by Mario Puzo. Dir. Francis Ford Coppola. Perf. Marlon Brando, Al Pacino, Robert Duvall, Abe Vigoda. 1972. DVD. Paramount, 2001.

Gottfried, Martin. *Arthur Miller: His Life and Work*. Cambridge, MA: Da Capo–Perseus, 2003.

The Grapes of Wrath. Based on the novel by John Steinbeck. Screenplay by Nunnally Johnson. Dir. John Ford. Perf. Henry Fonda. Twentieth Century-Fox, 1940.

Gurney, A. R. *The Dining Room*. 1982. *Collected Plays 1974–1983*. Vol. 2. Lyme, NH: Smith and Kraus, 1997.

———. *Sylvia*. 1996. *Collected Plays 1992–1999*. Vol. 4. Hanover, NH: Smith and Kraus, 2000.

Gussow, Mel. *Edward Albee: A Singular Journey*. New York: Simon and Schuster, 1999.

The Hairy Ape. Based on the play by Eugene O'Neill. Screenplay by Robert D. Andrews and Decla Dunning. Dir. Alfred Santell. Perf. William Bendix. United Artists, 1944.

Hauser, Arnold. *The Social History of Art.* Vol. 4. Trans. Stanley Godman. 1958. New York: Vintage, 1985.

Hellman, Lillian. *Six Plays* [*The Children's Hour, Days to Come, The Little Foxes, March on the Rhine, Another Part of the Forest, The Autumn Garden*]. 1960. New York: Vintage–Random House, 1979.

Hirschberg, Lynn. "Just-High-Enough Art." *New York Times Magazine* 7 July 2002: 16–21.

Holmin, Lorena Ross. *The Dramatic Works of Lillian Hellman.* Diss, Uppala University, 1973.

Howe, Tina. *The Art of Dining.* 1978. *Coastal Disturbances: Four Plays* 55–126.

———. *Birth and After Birth.* 1973. *Approaching Zanzibar and Other Plays.* New York: Theatre Communications Group, 1995. 79–142.

———. *Coastal Disturbances.* 1986. *Coastal Disturbances: Four Plays* 185–250.

———. *Coastal Disturbances: Four Plays.* New York: Theatre Communications Group, 1989.

———. *Museum.* 1975. *Coastal Disturbances: Four Plays* 1–54.

Jennings, C. Robert. *Playboy* Interview with Tennessee Williams. 1973. *Conversations with Tennessee Williams.* Ed. Albert J. Devlin. Jackson, MS: University Press of Mississippi, 1986. 224–50.

Jones, Robert Edmond. *The Dramatic Imagination: Reflections and Speculations on the Art of the Theatre.* New York: Duell, Sloan and Pearce, 1941.

Kauffmann, Stanley. "What Price Freedom?" Marranca 104–107.

Kaufman, George S., and Moss Hart. *You Can't Take It with You. Six Plays by Kaufman and Hart.* New York: Modern Library–Random House, 1942. 229–324.

Kenton, Edna. *The Provincetown Players and the Playwrights' Theatre, 1915–1922.* Ed. Travis Bogard and Jackson R. Bryer. Jefferson, NC: McFarland, 2004.

Knopf, Robert, ed. *Theater and Film: A Comparative Anthology.* New Haven: Yale University Press, 2005.

Kroll, Jack. "Mourning Becomes Electrifying." Rev. of *Angels in America.* By Tony Kushner. Dir. George C. Wolfe. Perf. Ron Liebman, Joe Mantello, Stephen Spinella, Kathleen Chalfant, Ellen McLaughlin. Walter Kerr Theatre, New York, 1993. *Newsweek* 17 May 1993. *New York Theatre Critics' Reviews* 54 (1993): 213.

———. "Wild Wild West." Rev. of *True West.* Perf. Philip Seymour Hoffman, John C. Reilly. Circle in the Square Theatre, New York. *Newsweek* 20 Mar. 2000: 70.

Kushner, Tony. *Angels in America, Part One: Millennium Approaches.* New York: Theatre Communications Group, 1993.

———. *Angels in America, Part Two: Perestroika.* Rev. ed. New York: Theatre Communications Group, 1996.

———. *SLAVS! Thinking about the Longstanding Problems of Virtue and Happiness.* New York: Broadway Play Publishing, 1996.

Lahr, John. "The Vicious Campfire: Talking Trash with Shepard and Mamet." Rev. of *True West*. Perf. Philip Seymour Hoffman, John C. Reilly. Circle in the Square Theatre, New York. *New Yorker* 27 Mar. 2000: 120–22.

Lawrence, Jerome, and Robert E. Lee. *Inherit the Wind*. New York: Random House, 1955.

Lessing, Gotthold Ephraim. *Laocoön*. Trans. William A. Steel. New York: E.P. Dutton and Co., 1930.

Linney, Romulus. *Childe Byron*. 1977. *Six Plays* New York: Theatre Communications Group, 1993.

———. "O'Neill." *Southern Review* 38.4 (Autumn 2002): 842–48.

Lonely Are the Brave. Dir. David Miller. Perf. Kirk Douglas. Universal, 1962.

The Long Voyage Home. Dir. John Ford. Prod. Walter Wanger. Photo. Gregg Toland. Writ. Dudley Nichols. Perf. John Wayne, Thomas Mitchell, Barry Fitzgerald, Ian Hunter, John Qualen, Mildred Natwick. United Artists, 1940.

Mamet, David. *American Buffalo*. 1976. New York: Grove Press, 1996.

———. *Glengarry Glen Ross*. New York: Grove Press, 1984.

———. *On Directing Film*. New York: Viking-Penguin, 1991.

Manvell, Roger. *Theater and Film: A Comparative Study of the Two Forms of Dramatic Art, and of the Problems of Adaptation of Stage Plays into Films*. Rutherford, NJ: Fairleigh Dickinson University Press, 1979.

Margulies, Donald. *Dinner with Friends*. New York: Dramatists Play Service, 2000.

———. *Sight Unseen and Other Plays* [incl. *What's Wrong with this Picture?* (1988)]. New York: Theatre Communications Group, 1995.

Marks, Peter. "*Wit*." Rev. of *Wit*. By Margaret Edson. Dir. Derek Anson Jones. Perf. Kathleen Chalfant. MCC Theatre, New York. 1998. *New York Times* 18 Sept. 1998, sec. E: 3.

Marranca, Bonnie, ed. *American Dreams: The Imagination of Sam Shepard*. 1981. New York: Performing Arts Journal Publications, 1993.

Mast, Gerald, Marshall Cohen, and Leo Braudy, eds. *Film Theory and Criticism*. 4th ed. 1974. New York: Oxford University Press, 1992.

McBride, Stewart. "Sam Shepard: Listener and Playwright." *Christian Science Monitor* 23 Dec. 1980: B1–B3.

McCabe, Terry. *Mis-directing the Play: An Argument against Contemporary Theatre*. Chicago: Ivan R. Dee, 2001.

McKevitt, Karen. "Theater Audiences: Live Is Still Better." Letter to the editor. *New York Times* 2 Sept. 2001, Late ed., sec 2: 2.

Mellen, Joan. *Women and Their Sexuality in the New Film*. New York: Horizon Press, 1973.

Millennia Music and Media Systems. Press release. "Rolling Stones HBO Live Concert Uses 80+ Channels of Millennia HV-3 Preamplifiers." 27 Jan. 2003. 26 Jan. 2004 <http://www.mil-media.com/pdf/pressrelease-stones.pdf>.

Miller, Arthur. *All My Sons*. 1947. New York: Penguin, 2000.

———. *Death of a Salesman*. 1949. New York: Penguin, 1998.

Moody, Richard. *Lillian Hellman: Playwright.* New York: Pegasus–Bobbs-Merrill Company, 1972.

Mourning Becomes Electra. Dir. Dudley Nichols. Perf. Rosalind Russell, Raymond Massey. RKO, 1947.

Murphy, Brenda. *Tennessee Williams and Elia Kazan: A Collaboration in the Theatre.* New York: Cambridge University Press, 1992.

Naremore, James, ed. *Film Adaptation.* New Brunswick, NJ: Rutgers University Press, 2000.

Nelson, Richard. *Two Shakespearean Actors.* Boston: Faber and Faber, 1990.

Nicoll, Allardyce. *Film and Theatre.* 1936. New York: Arno Press and The New York Times, 1972.

Norman, Marsha. *'night Mother.* New York: Hill and Wang, 1983.

Odets, Clifford. *Waiting for Lefty.* 1935. *Six Plays of Clifford Odets.* New York: Modern Library–Random House, 1939.

Of Mice and Men. Screenplay by Eugene Solow. Dir. Lewis Milestone. Perf. Burgess Meredith, Lon Chaney Jr., Betty Field. 1939. DVD. Image, 1998.

———. Screenplay by Eugene Solow. Dir. Reza Badiyi. Perf. Robert Blake, Randy Quaid, Cassie Yates. 1981.

———. Screenplay by Horton Foote. Dir. Gary Sinise. Perf. John Malkovich, Gary Sinise, Sherilyn Fenn. 1992. DVD. MGM/UA, 2003.

O'Neill, Eugene. *Complete Plays.* Ed. Travis Bogard. 3 vols. New York: Library of America, 1988.

———. *Selected Letters of Eugene O'Neill.* Ed. Travis Bogard and Jackson R. Bryer. New York: Limelight, 1994.

Orlandello, John. *O'Neill on Film.* Rutherford, NJ: Fairleigh Dickinson University Press, 1982.

Panofsky, Erwin. "Style and Medium in the Motion Pictures." Mast, Cohen, and Braudy 233–48.

Parks, Suzan-Lori. *The America Play and Other Works.* New York: Theatre Communications Group, 1995.

———. *Topdog/Underdog.* New York: Theatre Communications Group, 2001.

Perez, Gilberto. *The Material Ghost: Films and Their Medium.* Baltimore: Johns Hopkins University Press, 1998.

Phelan, Peggy. *Unmarked: The Politics of Performance.* 1993. New York: Routledge, 1996.

Phillips, Gene D. *The Films of Tennessee Williams.* East Brunswick, NJ: Associated University Presses, 1980.

The Piano Lesson. Teleplay by August Wilson. Dir. Lloyd Richards. Perf. Charles S. Dutton, Alfre Woodard. 1995. VHS. Hallmark Home Entertainment, 1998.

Pinter, Harold. "Writing for the Theatre." 1962. *Complete Works: One.* New York: Grove Press, 1976.

Private Conversations. Dir. Christian Blackwood. 1985. *Death of a Salesman.* DVD. Image, 2003.

Reds. Dir. Warren Beatty. Perf. Warren Beatty, Diane Keaton, Jack Nicholson. Paramount, 1981.

Renner, Pamela. "Science and Sensibility." *American Theatre* 16.4 (Apr. 1999): 34–36.

Rich, Frank. "Embracing All Possibilities in Art and Life." Rev. of *Angels in America, Part One.* By Tony Kushner. Dir. George C. Wolfe. Perf. Ron Liebman, Joe Mantello, Stephen Spinella, Kathleen Chalfant, Ellen McLaughlin. Walter Kerr Theatre, New York, 1993. *New York Times* 5 May 1993. *New York Theatre Critics' Reviews* 54 (1993): 214.

———. "Shepard's *True West.*" Rev. of *True West.* Perf. Peter Boyle, Tommy Lee Jones. The Public Theatre, New York. *New York Times* 24 Dec. 1980. *New York Theatre Critics' Reviews* 42 (1981): 366.

Richardson, Robert. *Literature and Film.* New York: Garland Publishing, 1985.

Rodenburg, Patsy. *The Actor Speaks: Voice and the Performer.* New York: St. Martin's Press, 2000.

———. *The Right to Speak: Working with the Voice.* New York: Routledge, 1992.

Roudané, Matthew C. "*Death of a Salesman* and the Poetics of Arthur Miller." *The Cambridge Companion to Arthur Miller.* Ed. Christopher Bigsby. New York: Cambridge University Press, 1997. 60–85.

Savran, David. "Ambivalence, Utopia, and a Queer Sort of Materialism: How *Angels in America* Reconstructs the Nation." Geis and Kruger 13–39.

Schechner, Richard. "A New Paradigm for Theatre in the Academy." *The Drama Review: The Journal of Performance Studies* 36.4 (1992): 7–10.

Shawn, Wallace. *The Designated Mourner.* 1996. New York: Noonday Press–Farrar, Straus, and Giroux, 1997.

Shepard, Sam. *Fool for Love and Other Plays* [*Angel City, Geography of a Horse Dreamer, Action, Cowboy Mouth, Melodrama Play, Seduced, Suicide in B-flat*]. 1984. New York: Bantam–Bantam Doubleday Dell, 1988.

———. *The Late Henry Moss; Eyes for Consuela; When the World Was Green: Three Plays.* New York: Vintage–Random House, 2002.

———. *A Lie of the Mind.* New York: New American Library, 1987.

———. *Seven Plays* [*Buried Child, Curse of the Starving Class, The Tooth of Crime, La Turista, Tongues, Savage Love, True West*]. 1981. New York: Bantam–Bantam Doubleday Dell, 1984.

———. *Simpatico.* New York: Vintage–Random House, 1996.

———. *States of Shock; Far North; Silent Tongue.* 1992. New York: Vintage–Random House, 1993.

———. "Time." Marranca 210–11.

———. *The Unseen Hand and Other Plays* [*Chicago, Icarus's Mother, Operation Sidewinder,* and eleven others]. 1972. New York: Vintage–Random House, 1996.

Simon, John. "Angelic Geometry." Rev. of *Angels in America, Part Two: Perestroika.* By Tony Kushner. Dir. George C. Wolfe. Perf. Ron Liebman, Joe Mantello, Stephen Spinella, Kathleen Chalfant, Ellen McLaughlin. Walter Kerr Theatre, New York, 1993. *New York Theatre Critics' Reviews* 54 (1993): 385.

———. "Switch-hitters." Rev. of *True West*. By Sam Shepard. Dir. Matthew Warchus. Perf. Philip Seymour Hoffman, John C. Reilly. Circle in the Square Theatre, New York. *New York* 27 Mar. 2000: 103.

Solomon, Alisa. "Wrestling with *Angels:* A Jewish Fantasia." Geis and Kruger 118–33.

Sontag, Susan. *Illness as Metaphor; and AIDS and Its Metaphors.* New York: Picador–St. Martin's Press, 1990.

———. "Theatre and Film." *Styles of Radical Will.* 1969. New York: Farrar, Straus and Giroux, 1987.

Steinbeck, John. *The Grapes of Wrath.* 1939. New York: Penguin, 1992.

———. *Of Mice and Men.* 1937. New York: Penguin, 2002.

———. *Of Mice and Men* [acting edition]. 1937. New York: Dramatists Play Service, 1964.

Strange Interlude. Adapted from play by Eugene O'Neill. Dialogue continuity Bess Meredyth. Dir. Robert Z. Leonard. Perf. Norma Shearer, Clark Gable. MGM, 1932.

These Three. Dir. William Wyler. Perf. Merle Oberon, Miriam Hopkins, Joel McCrea. Samuel Goldwyn, 1936.

Three Days of the Condor. Dir. Sydney Pollack. Perf. Robert Redford, Faye Dunaway. Paramount, 1975.

True West. By Sam Shepard. Dir. Robert Woodruff. Magic Theatre, San Francisco. 1980.

———. Perf. Peter Boyle, Tommy Lee Jones. The Public Theatre, New York. 1980.

———. Dir. Gary Sinise. Perf. John Malkovich, Jeff Perry. Steppenwolf Theatre, Chicago. 1982.

———. Dir. Gary Sinise. Perf. John Malkovich, Gary Sinise. Cherry Lane Theatre, New York. 1982.

———. Dir. Alan A. Goldstein. Perf. John Malkovich, Gary Sinise. VHS. Academy Home Entertainment, 1983.

———. Dir. Matthew Warchus. Perf. Philip Seymour Hoffman, John C. Reilly. Circle in the Square Theatre, New York. 2000.

———. Dir. Gary Halverson. Perf. Bruce Willis. Showtime, 2002.

Tucker, Patrick. *Secrets of Screen Acting.* New York: Routledge, 1994.

Vardac, A. Nicholas. *Stage to Screen: Theatrical Method from Garrick to Griffith.* 1949. New York: Benjamin Blom, 1968.

Vogel, Paula. *The Baltimore Waltz.* 1992. *The Baltimore Waltz and Other Plays.* New York: Theatre Communications Group, 1996.

Watt, Douglass. Rev. of *True West*. Perf. Peter Boyle, Tommy Lee Jones. The Public Theatre, New York. *New York Daily News* 24 Dec. 1980. *New York Theatre Critics' Reviews* 42 (1981): 366–67.

Watt, Stephen. *Postmodern/Drama: Reading the Contemporary Stage.* Ann Arbor: University of Michigan Press, 1998.

Westbrook, Brett Elizabeth. "The Lesbian Vanishes: Lillian Hellman's Adaptation of *The Children's Hour,* 1936." *Bright Lights Film Journal* 29 May 2003 <http: www.brightlightsfilm.com/28/thesethree1.html>.

Who's Afraid of Virginia Woolf? Dir. Mike Nichols. Prod. Ernest Lehman. Perf. Elizabeth Taylor, Richard Burton, George Segal, Sandy Dennis. 1966. DVD. Warner Brothers, 1997.

———. Dir. Anthony Page. Perf. Kathleen Turner, Bill Irwin. Longacre Theater, New York. 2005.

Wilder, Thornton. *Three Plays.* 1957. New York: Perennial Classics–HarperCollins, 1998.

Williams, Tennessee. *Cat on a Hot Tin Roof.* New York: New Directions, 1975.

———. *Plays 1937–1955.* Ed. Mel Gussow and Kenneth Holdich. Vol. 1. New York: Library of America, 2000.

———. "Three Players of a Summer Game." 1952. *Collected Stories.* 1985. New York: New Directions, 1994.

———. "The Timeless World of a Play." Preface to *The Rose Tattoo.* Williams, *Plays 1937–1955* 1:647–51.

Wilson, August. *Fences.* New York: Plume–Dutton Signet, 1986.

———. *Jitney.* New York: Overlook Press, 2003.

———. *Joe Turner's Come and Gone.* New York: Plume–Dutton Signet, 1988.

———. *Ma Rainey's Black Bottom.* New York: Plume–New American Library, 1985.

———. "A Note from the Playwright." 1995. *Seven Guitars.* New York: Plume–Dutton Signet, 1997.

———. *The Piano Lesson.* New York: Plume–Dutton Signet, 1990.

———. *Seven Guitars.* 1996. New York: Plume–Dutton Signet, 1997.

———. *Two Trains Running.* 1992. New York: Plume–Dutton Signet, 1993.

Wilson, Edwin. *The Theater Experience.* 1976. 7th ed. New York: McGraw-Hill, 1998.

Wit. Adapted from play by Margaret Edson. Screenplay by Mike Nichols and Emma Thompson. Dir. Mike Nichols. Perf. Emma Thompson. HBO Films. Premiere 24 Mar. 2001.

Worthen, W. B. "Drama, Performativity, and Performance." *PMLA* 113.5 (Oct. 1998): 1093–1107.

Zinman, Toby. "Illness as Metaphor." *American Theatre* 16.8 (Oct. 1999): 25.

Index

American Theatre, 146

America Play, The, 29

Angel City, 106, 109, 110, 112

Angels in America, 132, 145, 156–69; adherence of film to dramatic antecedent, xiv; cinematic credits of film, 156; contrapuntal dramatic structure resists stasis, 166–168; dialectical splits within characters, 163–64; doubling roles in theater and film, 163–64; dramatic and visual challenge, xvii; film borrows techniques from theater, 162–63; HBO audience dwarfs theatrical counterpart, 156–57; imaginative use of stage celebrates life's abundance, 168–69; impressive artistic pedigree of film, 157; plot resists simple narrative, 159–60; realistic mandate of film, 161–62; split scenes as dramaturgical technique, 164–66; stage as playground of desire, 168; theatricality, 157–58, 160–61; themes of reconciliation and forgiveness, 168; use of cinematic elements and techniques for theatrical effects, 158–59

Anna Christie, 36–37, 44

Another Part of the Forest, 53

Appia, Adolphe, 32

Arabesque patterns of plot, 7

Archer, William, 11

Aristotle, 12–17, 107, 130, 159; dramatic structure, 127; on character as habitual action, 125; on comedy, 17, 174n10; six elements of drama, 12. *See also* spectacle

Arkin, Alan, 117

Arnheim, Rudolf, 2, 30, 33

Aronson, Arnold, 158

Art and Visual Perception, 33

Artaud, Antonin, 5, 11, 12, 14, 15, 23, 28, 174n9. *See also* spectacle, mise-en-scène

Art of Dining, The, 26

As Is, 145

Association for Theatre in Higher Education (ATHE), 6

Astor Place Riot, 25–26

Aura, 7

Auslander, Philip, xix, 7, 9, 12

Autumn Garden, The, 53

Back Bog Beast Bait, 108

Baldwin, Alec, 117, 118, 122, 124

Baltimore Waltz, The, 32, 145, 175n7

Barnes, Clive, 10, 105, 159

Barr, Tony, 20

Barranger, Milly S., 11

Bazin, André, 28

Beatty, Ned, 174n2

Beatty, Warren, 49–50

Benjamin, Walter, xix, 7, 21, 27
Bentley, Eric, 52–53, 63, 73, 74
Beyond the Horizon, 44
Bible, The, 17
Bigsby, C. W. E., 127–28
Birth and After Birth, 31
Black, David, 11, 30
"Blue Skies," 121, 123
Bogdanovich, Peter, 40
Bone, David, 44
Bottoms, Stephen J., 97, 101, 109
Bound East for Cardiff, xviii, 37, 38, 40, 41–42, 47, 49; first O'Neill play performed, 37, 46. *See also* Glencairn Cycle
Boyle, Peter, 103
Brecht, Bertolt, xvi, xviii, 10, 12, 14, 23, 153–54; "Epic Theater," 15–16
Brewster, Ben 5
Broadway Theatre Archive, 80
Brook, Peter, 14, 23, 27–28
Brooks, Peter, 174n7
Brooks, Richard, xiii, 65, 66, 177n2
Bruckheimer, Jerry, 162
Bryan, William Jennings, 17
Bryant, Louise, 49–50
Buried Child, 105, 112–13
Burton, Richard, xv, 94

Caine, Michael, 19, 20
Callow, Simon, 157, 162
Camille (La Dame aux camélias), 145, 160
Camus, Albert, 49
Catharsis, 7, 28
Cat on a Hot Tin Roof, 64–77, 90, 174–75n2; bed and console cabinet visualize themes of life, death, and fear of intimacy, 67; bed as central, fixed image and meaning of play, 64–65, 67, 69, 70, 71; Brick as passive object of desire, 75–76, 177n3; Brick's unbending puritanical code, 76–77; compromised union at conclusion affirms life and living, 77; drama capitalizes upon familiar unities, 67; dramatic and visual challenge, xvii; feminization of Brick similar to playwright's Southern heroines, 72; film downplays sex, 64; happy ending of Hollywood film, 65; influence of Hays Code on film version, xiii; Kazan's decision to "open play out," 67; Maggie as titular character and protagonist, 71–72; Maggie personifies redemptive life force, 72–75; Maggie steals sexual energy normally reserved for Williams's male heroes, 72, 77; mendacity as means of survival, 69–70; pervasive theme of death, 68–69; pivotal confrontation scene moves throughout house in film, 66–67; questions of homosexuality, 73–74, 177n4; scenic expansiveness of film dilutes purity of play, 64–67; sexual desire as antidote to fear of death, 70–71; stage setting as cage, 67–69; Williams didn't like film version, 65
Cavell, Stanley, 53
Cenci, The, 15
Chaikin, Joseph, 15
Chaney Jr., Lon, xvi
Chekhov, Anton, xviii, 4–5, 10, 45–46, 47, 56
Cherry Lane Theatre, 103, 115
Cherry Orchard, The, 5, 10
Chicago, 105–6
Childe Byron, 32
Children of the Sea, 47
Children's Hour, The, 51–63; contrived ending, 56; drama promotes desire to see what can't be seen, xvii, 51, 53, 57–64; elegant living room as seat of power, 53–55; explicitness of films, 53, 57; film versions compared to play,

51–53, 55–57, 60, 61; influence of Hays Code on film versions, xiii, 51–52; Karen and Martha as victims, 55–56; Mary incites action, 55; Mrs. Tilford as audience's tragic surrogate, 55–60, 176n3; problem of Karen's impending marriage unexplored, 61–62, 176n4; quality of mercy, 62–63; temptations of power, 58–60; typical play structure, 176n1; voyeuristic performance dynamic, 57–58

Chris Christophersen, 44

Christian Science Monitor, 109

Cinema. *See* film

Cirque du Soleil, 14

Close Encounters of the Third Kind, 160

Close-up, 19, 20, 23, 95, 96, 118, 148–50

Clum, John, 73

Clurman, Harold, xi

Coastal Disturbances, 26, 32

Cobb, Lee J., 80

Coe, Robert, 107, 108

Conduct of Life, The, 32

Cook, George Cram (Jig), 46, 176n9

Coppola, Francis Ford, 130

Copy, 7–8. *See also* film

Cowboy Mouth, 109, 112

Cowboys and *Cowboys #2,* 105, 108

Cromwell, James, 157, 163

Cukor, George, 145

Curse of the Starving Class, 105, 106, 112–13

Dale, Jim, 30

Dance of Death, 30

Darrow, Clarence, 17

Darwin, Charles, 17

Davidson, Gordon, 158

Days to Come, 53

"Death Be Not Proud," 146, 155

Death of a Salesman, 78–90, 121, 129–30, 132; Biff as shining son and bright fu-

ture, 89; Biff's self-revelation validates experience of common man, 89; building up and casting off, 87–88; buried secret comes to light, 79; condensed stage picture of 1966 TV version, 80–82; creative adaption of play to television medium in 1985, 82–86; dramatic and visual challenge, xvii; dramatic use of color in film, 84; dynamic lighting in film, 83–84; early provisional titles, 78; expressionistic use of red in film, 84–85; gaps between walls, xv, 83, 86; faithfulness of television adaptation to play, xiii–xvi, 177n1; intimacy of film, 85; looming apartments block sun, 88–89; ostensible departure from well-made play formula, 79; refusal to grow up as major theme, 90; static resonance of central image, 78–79, 86; tragedy of man who cannot walk away, 79–80, 86, 87

Dennehy, Brian, 177n3

Designated Mourner, The, 32

Desire Under the Elms, 26

Diderot, Denis, 11, 173n5

Dining Room, The, 25

Dinner with Friends, 22

Dionysius in 69, 6

Directing, 32–34, 170–71

Dolan, Jill, 58

Donne, John, 145, 146, 147, 151–55

"Do Not Go Gentle into That Good Night," 75

Douglas, Kirk, 111

Drama Desk Awards, 156

Dumas *fils,* Alexandre, 145

Dunnock, Mildred, 80

Duvall, Robert, 130

Drama: "hereness," 24–25; linguistic roots, 13; relationship to theater, xviii; projectionable, 18, 19; split scenes, 25–26. *See also* theater

Drama Review, The, 6
Dynamo, 26

Eco, Umberto, 17
Editing, 22
Edson, Margaret, defined *Wit,* 152. *See also Wit*
Edward Albee: A Singular Journey, 94
Eisen, Kurt, 37
Eisenstein, 3
Elam, Harry, 135
Ellington, Duke, 121
Emperor Jones, The, 14
Empty Space, The, 14, 23, 27–28
E.T., 160
Exorcist, The, 161

Falk, Doris, 52
Farce, 25, 26
Fences, 136, 137, 141
Fervent Years, The, xi
Field, Betty, xvi
Film: advantage of materiality, xiii; audience sees what director sees, 24; brevity of shot, 23; common language and experience, xii, 1–2, 7; complementary with theater, xvi–xviii; flexibility of editing, 21–23; narrative art, 3, 7; obviates need for realism in theater, 27; "opening up" a play, 80; realistic imperative, 30–31; scale of performance, 20–21; segments human body, 30; "then" and "there," 27, 28–29; world is contingent, 3, 16; worldly medium, 10, 11, 21, 26–27. *See also* projection; sequence
Film Adaptation, xviii
Film as Art, 2
Foley, James, xiv, 117, 119, 121. *See also Glengarry Glen Ross*
Fool for Love, 106, 109
Ford, John, xiii, xvi. *See also The Long Voyage Home* (film)

Foreman, Richard, 14
Fornes, Maria Irene, 32
Fourteen Hundred Thousand, 106
Free and Clear, 78
French scenes, 23
Freud, 29

Galati, Frank, xvi, 180n1
Galileo, 153–54
Gambon, Michael, 157, 162
Garbo, Greta, 36–37, 145
Garrick, David, 173n5
Gem of the Ocean, 137
Gest (also gesture), 11, 14–17, 32, 83, 111. *See also* Brecht, "Epic Theater"
Gilman, Rebecca, 9
Glaspell, Susan, 24, 46
Glass Menagerie, The, 65
Glencairn Cycle, 35–50; descriptions of individual plays, 37–38, 175n2; endless sea voyage as existential fate, 45–48; functions as line drawings for later masterpieces, 35, 48–49; musical score of distinct voices, 41; named as such, 38; similarity to *The Iceman Cometh,* 48; stage balances intimacy and alienation, 41–43; stage directions appeal to reading public, 40, 176n4; synergistic relationship between film and theater, 35; theatrical gift of sacrifice, 49–50, 175n7; works directly upon emotions, 49; written for proscenium theater, 39
Glengarry Glen Ross, 117–31, 132; business world offers cruel metaphors for human interaction, 130–31; character as pure action, 124–26; comparison of musical score in film to use of music in plays, 178–79n2; context on stage created improvisationally, spontaneously, 126; deviations of film adaptation from dramatic text, xiv–xv; dramatic and visual challenge, xvii; editing capability gives film flexibility,

122–23; film borrows inciting moment from traditional dramatic structure, 122; film places action in specific, realistic context, 120–22, 130; human interaction reduced to sales pitch, 124–26, 129–30; intimacy of film version tugs at heartstrings, 117–19; ironic theme of brotherhood, 129; objective stage view presents salesmen as caged lab rats, 119–20; play abstracts human behavior by removing it from realistic context, 130; play contains no exposition, 123–24; play within play heightens theatricality, 129; plot an excuse for something to happen, 127–28; sales transaction as performance provides drama's high point, 128; second half of film follows closely act 2 of play, 123; selling swampland as cruel, ironic commentary on tragic action, 130–31; survival of fittest presents subjects simultaneously in homogenous space, 127

Godfather, The, 130
Grapes of Wrath, The, xvi, 45
Great God Brown, The, 35
Greenwich Village, 103, 105
Griffith, D. W., 173n1
Grotowski, Jerzy, 23
Group Theatre, xi
Gurney, A. R., 25, 31
Gussow, Mel, 94–95

Hairy Ape, The, 36, 43–44, 84–85
Hallmark Hall of Fame, 132, 139–41
Hamburg Dramaturgy, 2
Harris, Ed, 117
Hart, Moss, 25
Hauser, Arnold, xix, 22
Hays Code: censorship grip, xiii, 51–52
HBO, xiv, 8, 9, 22, 31, 144, 156–57
Hedda Gabler, 56
Helbrun, Theresa, 36

Hellman, Lillian. *See also The Children's Hour*
Henry V, 24
Hepburn, Audrey, xiii, 52
Histrionic, 31
Hoffman, Dustin, xiv, 82, 84
Hoffman, Philip Seymour, 104
"Holy Theatre," 14, 28
Homogenous space, xii, 3, 22, 24, 127
Hopkins, Miriam, 51
House Un-American Activities Committee, 52
Howe, Tina, 26, 31, 32
Hurt, William, 11

Ibsen, Henrik, 79, 98
Icarus's Mother, 106
Iceman Cometh, The, xviii, 35, 48–49
Ile, 44
Illness as Metaphor, 145, 154
Immediacy, 11, 23
Inherit the Wind, 17
Inside of His Head, The, 78
In the Zone, 37, 38, 40, 42. *See also* Glencairn Cycle
Intimacy, 1, 18, 20, 85, 144, 146, 149
Ionesco, 26
Irwin, Bill, 178n3

Jacobs, Lea, 5
Jagger, Mick, 8
Jewison, Norman, 22
Jitney, 136–39, 141
Joe Turner's Come and Gone, 136, 137, 139, 143
Jones, Robert Edmond, 33, 86
Jones, Tommy Lee, 103
Judd, Ashley, 174–75n2

Kauffmann, Stanley, 106, 107
Kaufman, George S., xvi, 25
Kazan, Elia, 67–68, 71–72, 78
Keaton, Diane, 49–50

King Hedley II, 137
King Lear, 18–19, 57
Kirk, Justin, 157
Knopf, Robert, xvii
Kroll, Jack, 103, 104, 159
Kushner, Tony: advises pared-down style of presentation, 157; influence of Brecht, 180n2; separate existence of his play apart from film adaptation, 158. *See also Angels in America*

Lady of Larkspur Lotion, 72
Lahr, John, 104
Lang, Stephen, xiv
Laocoön, 2–3; *coexistence* of things, 3; *consecutiveness* of speech, 3. *See also* sequence; simultaneity
La Turista, 106, 112
Late Henry Moss, The, 107
Lawrence, Jerome, 17
Lee, Robert Edwin, 17
Lehman, Ernest, 144, 180n1
Lehrer, Jim, 152
Lemmon, Jack, xv, 117–18, 130
Les Misérables, 8–9
Lessing, Gotthod Ephraim. *See Laocoön*
Lie of the Mind, A, 26, 106–7, 109
Light, James, 38
Linney, Romulus, 32, 49
Little Foxes, The, 53
Liveness, 1, 7, 11, 12, 31, 170
Liveness: Performance in a Mediatized Culture, 7
Lloyd, Christopher, 147, 149
Lonely Are the Brave, 111
Long Day's Journey into Night, 44, 49, 96–97
Long Voyage Home, The (film), 35–41, 44–45, 48; creates sense of claustrophobia, 40–41; defies "opening up" drama, 35, 40–41; departs from source material, 38–41; dramatic and visual challenge, xvii; intimacy of close-ups, 39–40, 42; makes social statement, 44–45; shows sailors in action performing work, 38–39; unifies O'Neill's one-acts, xiii, 37
Long Voyage Home, The, (one-act play), 37, 38, 42–43, 47–48, 49. *See also* Glencairn Cycle

Ma Rainey's Black Bottom, 136, 137, 139, 143
Mabou Mines, 14
McBride, Stewart, 109
McCabe, Terry, 33
McCarthy, Joseph, 52
McCrea, Joel, 51
McKellen, Ian, 30
MacLaine, Shirley, xiii, 52
Mad Dog Blues, The, 108
Magic of theater, 1, 10–11, 21, 161
Magic of Theatre: Behind the Scenes with Today's Leading Actors, 11
Malkovich, John, xiv, 103, 115
Mamet, David, 95; on character, 125; on his Aristotelian training as an actor, 179n5; writes few details in stage directions, 120. *See also Glengarry Glen Ross*
Mantello, Joe, 179n7
Manvell, Roger, 19
Marat/Sade, 174n9
Margulies, Donald, 22, 32
Markinson, Brian, 163
Marks, Peter, 144, 146, 151
Mellen, Joan, 52
Mendes, Sam 5, 173n3
Merchant of Venice, The, 62–63
Meredith, Burgess, xvi
Metatheatricality, 57, 150–51, 161
Meyerhold, 4–5, 173n2
Mielziner, Jo, 78, 86
Milestone, Lewis, xvi

Millennia Music and Media Systems, 8

Miller, Arthur, 121, 130; comparison of *Salesman* to *Glengarry Glen Ross*, 177n2; original idea for scene design, 86. *See also Death of a Salesman*

Mirren, Helen, 30

Mis-directing the play, 33

Mise-en-scène. *See* spectacle

Molière, xviii, 32

Montage, 3, 22

Moody, Richard, 51, 53

Moon of the Caribbees, The, 38, 43, 47; elements of modern drama, 37; stages cross section of ship, 39. *See also* Glencairn Cycle

Motion Picture Production Code. *See* Hays Code

Mourning Becomes Electra, 35, 36, 44

Moscow Art Theatre, 4

Murphy, Brenda, 67–68

Museum, 26

Name of the Rose, The, 17

Naremore, James, xviii

Narrative. *See* film

Nelson, Richard, 25

New Critics, 49

Newman, Paul, 65

Newman, Thomas, 156

Nichols, Dudley, 35–38

Nichols, Mike, 132; film cannot duplicate stage dynamics, 94–95; transposing plays into films, xiii–xvi; weak special effects, 161–62. *See also Angels in America; Who's Afraid of Virginia Woolf?; Wit*

Nicholson, Jack, 49–50

'night, Mother, 24–25

"No More Masterpieces," 11

Normal Heart, The, 145

Norman, Marsha, 24

North, Alex, 84

"Note from the Playwright, A" (Wilson), 138

"Note of Explanation" (Williams), 71–72

Nuryev, 13

Oberon, Merle, 51

Odets, Clifford, 26

Off-Broadway, 105–6

Of Mice and Men, xvi

On Directing Film, 125

O'Neill, Eugene, 14, 26, 84–85, 96–97; anti-theatrical prejudice, 35–37; as an actor, 46, 50; experimental plays, 49; lifetime dates, 36; portrayed in *Reds,* 49–50; recurring patterns in plays, 43–50; revolt from amateur theater, 46. *See also* Glencairn Cycle

O'Neill, Oona, 37

O'Neill on Film, 40

Open Door, The, 28

Open Work, The, 17

Operation Sidewinder, 106

Original, 7–8. *See also* performance; theater

Origin of Species, The, 17

Orlandello, John, 36, 40

Our Town, 29, 158

Pacino, Al, 117, 130, 157

Page, Anthony, 178n3–4

Panofsky, Erwin, 16

Papp, Joseph, 103

Parker, Mary-Louise, 157

Parker, Sarah Jessica, 31

Parks, Suzan-Lori, 28–29

Parodox of the Actor, The, 173n5

Patric, Jason, 174–5n2

Perez, Gilberto, 21, 24

Performance, 11–12, 19–20

Performance Group, The, 6

Period of Grace, 78

Phelan, Peggy, 11–12

Phillips, Gene D., 66

Piano Lesson, The, 132–43; celebrates capitalism and American way of life, 141–42; communal singing and power of simultaneous action and images, 142–43; drama of enslavement, 138–39; dramatic and visual challenge, xvii; fable of play, 132–35; making oneself "big" as metaphysical conceit running in all Wilson's plays, 136–38; playwright's teleplay deviates from dramatic text, xiv–xv; TV version compared to other adaptations, 132; TV version verifies passivity of dramatic action, 139–41; video vs. stage treatment of family history, 142

Pinter, Harold, 18, 147

Plato, 12, 27, 53, 75, 174n6

"Playwright's Notes" (Kushner), 157

Plot, 12–17, 151; an excuse for something interesting to happen, 128; arabesque patterns, catharsis, recognitions, and reversals, 13

Poetics, 12

Polanski, Roman, 161

Potter, Beatrix, 146

Presence of the Actor, The, 15

Presentational techniques, 68, 150, 151, 180n2

"Principle of Coexpressibility," 16

Private Conversations, 82

Progressive action, 22, 123

Projection: on stage and in film, 18–21. *See also* directing

Provincetown, MA, 46, 49–50

Provincetown Players, 46

Provincetown Playhouse, 37–38

Pryce, Jonathan, 117

Pudovkin, 3

Pulitzer Prize, 144, 156

Radio Golf, 137

Rashomon, 22

Reading for the Plot: Design and Intention in Narrative, 174n7

Realism, 20, 27–31, 57, 58, 81, 108

Recognitions (in plot), 7, 127

Red Cross, 106

Reed, John, 49–50

Reid, Kate, xiv

Reilly, John C., 104

Remakes, 170–71

Renner, Pamela, 153, 154

Representational techniques, 68, 180n2

Reversals (in plot), 7, 127

Revivals, 170–71

Rich, Frank, 104, 168

Road to the Temple, The, 46

Rodenburg, Patsy, 18

Rolling Stones, The, 8

Romeo and Juliet, 13

Rosemary's Baby, 161

Rose Tattoo, The, 67

Roudané, Matthew C., 79

Russian formalists, 28

Sartre, Jean-Paul, 49

Savran, David, 160

Schechner, Richard, 6, 7, 10

Schlondörff, Volker, xiv, 82, 85

Schreiber, Liev, 179n7

Scopes Monkey Trial, 17

Seagull, The, 4–5, 10

Segal, Alex, 81

"Selective realism," 78

Sequence, 3–4, 142–43

Seven Guitars, 136, 137, 138

Sex and the City, 9, 31

Shakespeare, xviii, 7, 21, 57, 62, 94–95, 116, 145, 153

Shawn, Wallace, 32

Shearer, Norma, 36

Shelley, 15

Shenkman, Ben, 157

Shepard, Sam, 26; against stylization, 108; on double nature of brothers,

108; scraping writing down to the bone. *See also True West*

Sight Unseen, 22

Simon, John, 104, 159–60

Simpatico, 107

Simultaneity, 3–4, 12, 16, 24, 25, 26, 41–43, 100, 115, 119, 127, 143, 150; baseball analogy, 4; three-ring circus analogy, 4

Sinise, Gary, 103, 115

Smith College (Northampton, MA), 93

Solomon, Alisa, 166–67

Sontag, Susan, 145, 154; plays can't be made from movies, xi; relation of one shot to another, 22–23

Sopranos, The, 9

South Coast Repertory Theatre, 144

Spacey, Kevin, 117, 118

Spectacle, xii, 4–6, 12, 14, 17, 97–98, 160, 170–71, 180n1; Aristotle's disregard of, 13; mise-en-scène, 4, 14–15, 26, 65, 171; most important element, 12. *See also* Brecht, "Epic Theater"

Spielberg, Steven, 160–62, 180n3

S.S. Glencairn, 38. *See also* Glencairn Cycle

Stage to Screen: Theatrical Method from Garrick to Griffith, 5

Stanislavsky, Konstantin, 4, 23, 125

States, Bert, 31, 175n6

States of Shock, 106

Steinbeck, John, xvi

Steppenwolf Theatre Company, xvi, 103

Stoppard, Tom, xix

Strange Interlude, 35, 36

Strathairn, David, 30

Streep, Meryl, 156–57, 163

Streetcar Named Desire, A, 65, 69, 72–73

Style, 33

Suicide in B-flat, 109

Survivor, 157

Sweet, Blanche, 37

Sylvia, 31

Taming of the Shrew, The, 94

Taylor, Elizabeth, xv, 64, 65–66, 94

Tennessee Williams and Elia Kazan: A Collaboration in the Theatre, 67–68

Theater: artificiality, 26, 28; as spatial art, 3; audience sees for itself, 23–24; bigger than life, 31–32; can't compete with film's realism, 28; complementary with film, xvi–xviii, 10–11; death of, 1, 6–11; director as party host, 32–34; dynamic casting beyond type or even species, 30–31; empathy, 73–74; entrances and exits determine basic units of action, 23; ephemeral nature, xiii; exploits limitations, 23–34; formal qualities and intrinsic values, xii; failure of realism, 29–30; "here" and "now," 28–29; historical move toward realism, 27; human figure as primary focus, 27–29; need to reclaim cinematic techniques, 5–6; ontological distinction, 12; relationship to drama, xviii, 13; scale of performance compared to film, 20–21; suggestiveness of medium, 11; traditional virtues reconsidered, 1–2; "uninterrupted continuity" and "irreversible direction," 21–23; whole-bodied performances on full display, 30, 31–32, 143, 168. *See also* drama; homogenous space; magic of theater; performance; projection; simultaneity; spectacle

Theater and Film, xvii

Theater and Its Double, The, 14

Theater Experience, The, 10–11

"Theater of Cruelty," 174n9

"Theater of Images," 14

Theatre: A Way of Seeing, 11

Theatre Guild, 36

Theatre of Sam Shepard: States of Crisis, The, 109

Theatre to Cinema: Stage Pictorialism and the Early Feature Film, 5

Theatricality, 24, 129

These Three, xiii, 51, 53, 57, 61; viable lesbian couple in heterosexual love triangle, 55–56

Thirst, 49–50

Thomas, Dylan, 75

Thompson, Emma, 132, 144, 147, 148, 155, 157, 162, 163

Three Days of the Condor, 26–27

"Three Players of a Summer Game," 71

Three Sisters, 5, 173n2

"Timeless World of a Play, The" (Williams), 67

Toland, Gregg, 38–41, 56

Tone, Franchot, xi

Tooth of Crime, The, 106, 108, 109

Topdog/Underdog, 29

Trifles, 24

True West, 103–15, 132, 168; dramatic and visual challenge, xvii; metaphors of play need open space to breathe, 116; production history, 103–4; search for salvation, 112–13; short shrift given to televised productions, xiii–xiv, 104, 115–16, 178n1; simultaneity of layered images on stage, 114–15; straightforward action resembles musical score, 107–11; stress points in text reveal enduring theatricality, 103, 111; watershed mark in playwriting career, 103–7

Tucker, Patrick, 19–20

Turner, Kathleen, 178n3

Twelfth Night, 34

Two Shakespearean Actors, 25–26

Two Trains Running, 137, 138

Uncle Vanya, 5, 56

Unmarked, 11–12

Unseen Hand and Other Plays, The, 105

Vardac, Nicholas, 5

Vawter, Ron, 175n7

Vigoda, Abe, 130

Vogel, Paula, 32

Waiting for Lefty, 26

Walton, Tony, 82–83

Watch on the Rhine, 53

Watt, Douglass, 104

Watt, Stephen, 7

Westbrook, Brett Elizabeth, 57

Wharf Theatre, 46, 50

What's Wrong with This Picture?, 32

Who's Afraid of Virginia Woolf?, 91–102, 144; dramatic and visual challenge, xvii; editing and close-ups of film emphasize emotional heart of play, 94–97; faithfulness of cinematic adaptation to play, xiii–xvi; film opens up stage play, 92–94; Nick and Honey as surrogates for theatrical audience, 98–101; primitive stage drama counters suspense-thriller dazzle of film, 91–92; Shakespearean dynamics of play impossible to achieve in film, 94–95; subject of play is performance or spectacle, 97–102; subverts well-made play formula, 101–2

Wilder, Thornton, 28–29, 158

Williams, Tennessee. *See also Cat on a Hot Tin Roof*

Willis, Bruce, 115

Wilson, August, argues for a black theater, 180n1; artistic credo, 138. *See also The Piano Lesson*

Wilson, Edwin, 10–11

Wilson, Robert, 14

Wit, 132, 144–55; adherence of film to dramatic antecedent, xiv; cancer not inherently theatrical subject, 144–45; cancer patient (Professor Bearing) as text of study (research), 152; caution against pursuit of knowledge at expense of feelings for others, 152–54; declines intimacy, 146; direct address and narration in theater, 150–52; Donne's poetry more suitable for library than theater, 145–46; dramatic and visual challenge, xvii; filmic techniques project physical deterioration and suffering over time, 146–48; film more intimate than play, 144; invasiveness of camera in film version, 148–50; lecture-hall presentation as stylistic conceit, 144; limits of wit, 154–55

Wood, Ron, 8
Woodruff, Robert, 103
Wooster Group, The, 14, 157
World Trade Center, 26–27
Worthen, W. B., 6–7
Wright, Jeffrey, 157, 163
Wyler, William, xiii, 51–52

You Can't Take It with You, 25

Zinman, Toby, 146, 152–53